Date Due

NOV 7 1979		DEC - 7 1989	
DEC 19 1979	AUG 21 1992	FEB 25 1992	
APR 15 1983	OCT 19 1992		
DEC 1 1983			
JUN 21 1984	NOV -9 1992	MAR 17 1994	
	DEC -1 1992	APR -7 1994	
AUG 13 1984	FEB -9 1993		
JAN 30 1985	OCT 21 1993	OCT 21 1994	
OCT 21 1991		NOV 13 1994	
MAR 27 1992	NOV 15 1993	DEC 1 1994	
		DEC 1 1994	

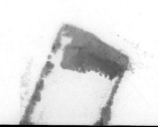

ATTACHMENT BEHAVIOR

ADVANCES IN THE STUDY OF
COMMUNICATION AND AFFECT

Volume 1 ● NONVERBAL COMMUNICATION
   Edited by Lester Krames, Patricia Pliner, and Thomas Alloway

Volume 2 ● NONVERBAL COMMUNICATION OF AGGRESSION
   Edited by Patricia Pliner, Lester Krames, and Thomas Alloway

Volume 3 ● ATTACHMENT BEHAVIOR
   Edited by Thomas Alloway, Patricia Pliner, and Lester Krames

A Continuation Order Plan is available for this series. A continuation order will bring delivery of each new volume immediately upon publication. Volumes are billed only upon actual shipment. For further information please contact the publisher.

ADVANCES IN THE STUDY OF COMMUNICATION AND AFFECT

Volume 3

ATTACHMENT BEHAVIOR

Edited by

Thomas Alloway, Patricia Pliner, and Lester Krames

Erindale College
University of Toronto
Mississauga, Ontario
Canada

PLENUM PRESS · NEW YORK AND LONDON

Library of Congress Cataloging in Publication Data

Symposium on Communication and Affect, 5th, Erindale College, 1975.
  Attachment behavior.

  (Advances in the study of communication and affect; v. 3)
  Includes bibliographies and index.
  1. Parent and child. 2. Infant Psychology. 3. Interpersonal relations. I. Alloway,
Thomas. II. Pliner, Patricia. III. Krames, Lester. IV. Title.
BF723.P25S95 1975   155.4'18   76-45647
ISBN 0-306-35903-0

Proceedings of the Fifth Annual Symposium on Communication and Affect
held at Erindale College, University of Toronto, March, 1975

© 1977 Plenum Press, New York
A Division of Plenum Publishing Corporation
227 West 17th Street, New York, N.Y. 10011

Printed in the United States of America

Contributors

ELIZABETH F. BOYD
National Institute of Mental Health and University of Maryland, Baltimore County, Maryland

ROBERT B. CAIRNS
Department of Psychology, University of North Carolina at Chapel Hill, Chapel Hill, North Carolina

CARL M. CORTER
Department of Psychology, Erindale College, University of Toronto, Mississauga, Ontario, Canada

JACOB L. GEWIRTZ
National Institute of Mental Health and University of Maryland, Baltimore County, Maryland

BARBARA DAVIS GOLDMAN
Department of Psychology, University of Waterloo, Waterloo, Ontario, Canada

MICHAEL LEON
Department of Psychology, McMaster University, Hamilton, Ontario, Canada

ROBERT S. MARVIN
Department of Psychology, University of Virginia, Charlottesville, Virginia

HILDY S. ROSS
Department of Psychology, University of Waterloo, Waterloo, Ontario, Canada

PAUL F. SIMONDS
Department of Anthropology, University of Oregon, Eugene, Oregon

STEPHEN J. SUOMI
Department of Psychology, University of Wisconsin, Madison, Wisconsin

Contents

CHAPTER 1

Beyond Social Attachment: The Dynamics of Interactional Development 1

ROBERT B. CAIRNS

Attachment and the Establishment of Interactions 1
Isolation and Adaptation 4
    Immediate Effects 4
    Intermediate Effects 6
    Long-Term Effects 7
Isolation → Adaptation: A New Perspective 9
The Formation of New Relationships 10
Long-Term Isolation Effects and Changes 11
On Social Development in Children 14
    Isolation in Infants 15
    New Relationship Formation 16
    Toward Principles of Interactional Development 18
Concluding Comments 20
References 21

CHAPTER 2

An Ethological–Cognitive Model for the Attenuation of Mother–Child Attachment Behavior 25

ROBERT S. MARVIN

Attenuation of Attachment Behavior in Nonhuman Primates 26
Post-Infancy Changes in Mother–Child Attachment Behavior 29
    The Cookie Test 32
    The Strange Situation 33
Further Changes in Mother–Child Attachment Behavior 37
    The Early Development of Perspective Taking 40

Observations of Further Changes in Mother–Child
   Attachment Behavior 42
Summary and Conclusions 49
References 59

CHAPTER 3
Establishing New Social Relations in Infancy 61
HILDY S. ROSS AND BARBARA DAVIS GOLDMAN

Stranger–Infant Study 62
Peer Study 68
Discussion 74
References 78

CHAPTER 4
*Brief Separation and Communication between
Infant and Mother* 81
CARL M. CORTER

The Nature of Infant–Mother Separation 81
Attachment and Responses to Brief Separation 84
   Research Strategy 87
The Role of Nonsocial Stimuli 88
   Study 1 88
   Study 2 90
The Role of Social Stimuli 90
   Study 3 90
The Role of Mother's Departure and Absence 92
   Study 4 92
   Study 5 96
Sex Differences in Response to Separation 97
Maternal Response to Separation 99
   Study 6 99
Conclusions 105
References 106

CHAPTER 5
*Experiments on Mother–Infant Interaction Underlying Mutual
Attachment Acquisition: The Infant Conditions the Mother* 109
JACOB L. GEWIRTZ AND ELIZABETH F. BOYD

Introduction 109
   The Conceptual Context 110

Attachment: Metaphor and Process 111
Researches on Directions of Influence in
    Mother–Infant Interchange 113
A Program of Research on the Directions of Influence in
Mother–Infant Interchange 116
Experiment 1 117
   Method 117
   Results 121
Experiment 2 125
   Method 125
   Results 129
Discussion 134
Summary and Conclusion 139
References 141

CHAPTER 6
*Peers, Parents, and Primates: The Developing Network
of Attachments* 145
PAUL E. SIMONDS

Network Analysis 147
Bonnet Macaques 150
   Grooming 150
   Play 151
   Mounting 152
Interspecific Comparisons 158
Baboons 159
   Savannah Baboons 160
   Hamadryas Baboons 162
   Forest Baboons 164
Langurs 166
Orangutans 168
Conclusions 169
References 175

CHAPTER 7
Pheromonal Mediation of Maternal Behavior 177
MICHAEL LEON

The Synchrony of the Mother–Litter Interaction 177
The Properties of Maternal Pheromone 178
The Developmental Course of the Pheromonal Bond 180

The Role of Pup Stimulation in the Control of
   Maternal Pheromone 182
Hormonal Mediation of Pup Stimulation 184
The Site of Maternal Pheromone Emission 185
The Site of Maternal Pheromone Synthesis 187
Maternal Pheromone Synthesis 188
The Mechanism for Maternal Pheromone Emission 189
Control of the Increase in Food Intake in Lactating
   Female Rats 190
How Do Pups Come to Approach the Odor of Their Mother? 193
The Function of the Pheromonal Bond in the
   Mother–Litter Interaction 194
References 195

CHAPTER 8
Development of Attachment and Other Social Behaviors in
Rhesus Monkeys 197

STEPHEN J. SUOMI

Unlearned Response Systems in Monkeys 199
Interactions Between Maturation and Social Environments 202
Mechanisms Underlying the Development of Specific Social
   Attachment Behaviors 212
Summary and Perspectives 222
References 223

Index 225

CHAPTER 1

Beyond Social Attachment:
The Dynamics of Interactional Development

Robert B. Cairns

Department of Psychology
University of North Carolina at Chapel Hill
Chapel Hill, North Carolina

In social development, second in occurrence is not necessarily second in importance. For most social behaviors, events that occur after infancy have the greatest priority for understanding contemporary social adaptation.[1] Accordingly, this essay is addressed to what happens ''beyond attachment,'' or, more generally, to how interactions are maintained and changed in ontogeny. In the course of development, the individual necessarily relates to others—in playing, in fighting, in working, in mating, in caring for the young. These interchanges are as critical for the survival of the species as the mother-infant relationship is for the survival of the young. Consideration of how they are linked to the initial social attachment and to each other brings us immediately to the nuclear issues of social fixedness, continuity of relationships, and social adaptation; in short, to the dynamics of interactional development.

Attachment and the Establishment of Interactions

Before going beyond social attachment, it seems worthwhile to consider briefly how the interchanges of attachment themselves arise. Systematic efforts

---

[1]Adaptation is a slippery concept that requires definition at the onset. In this chapter I do *not* use it as synonymous with health, normality, happiness, or contentment. Rather, it is used in its accepted biological meaning, which is ''adjustment to environmental conditions; specifically modification of an animal or plant (or its parts or organs) fitting it more perfectly for existence under the conditions of its environment.'' Social adaptation to some environments requires the development of activities that may depart markedly from the norm of the species.

to account for the mother-infant social bond have been underway for just over two decades, following the pioneering contributions of J. P. Scott, H. F. Harlow, T. C. Schneirla, and J. S. Rosenblatt in animal behavior, and J. Bowlby, J. Gewirtz, M. S. Ainsworth, R. Schaffer, and H. L. Rheingold in human infants. These investigators approached the problem from different theoretical perspectives, and on the surface it would appear initially that their single common bond was the conviction that traditional learning accounts were full of holes. After some early confusion, due partly to semantics and partly to differences in methodology, more substantial agreement was achieved. The consensus in its present form includes two major points: (a) the importance of psychobiological events in the attachment formation process and (b) the need to employ dyadic procedures in its analysis.

This common ground is reflected in the recent chapters in *Attachment and Dependency* (Gewirtz, 1972), a multiauthored volume whose writers attacked the concepts on four different fronts: social-learning, psychobiological, ethological-psychoanalytic, and clinical-developmental. The concepts barely survived. In each view, the postnatal formation of interchanges is seen to be a normal outgrowth of behavioral-biological synchronization of the mother and child. The process is described by different theories at various levels, with the most specific being the psychobiological view, which implicates the placentophagic activity of the mother (consuming the placenta and the afterbirth), the rooting-suckling reflexes of the offspring, the maternal licking and stimulation of the infant, and the ectothermic "clumping" of the neonate as providing an optimal setting for survival and early response synchrony. The initial actions of the mammalian mother and her offspring are thus mutually supportive and, to a significant extent, reciprocal. But some gaps remain in psychobiological and sociobiological accounts, regardless of the perspective. Children, in particular, constitute a special problem for biological models, in that human infants develop strong social bonds without the benefit of placentophagia and other correlated biological activities. Such acts may facilitate, but not be necessary for, the establishment of bonds. More generally, appeals to the evolutionary functions of human infant-parent relationships, no matter how eloquently expressed in terms of phyletic adaptations, cannot substitute for proximal accounts of what happens during development, and why.

The second common emphasis follows from the first, in that it requires the researcher to take into account simultaneously information from both members of the relationship and the context in which it occurs. The dyad has become the preferred unit of analysis, not the responses of the individuals taken separately. Even when dyadic language is not employed, writers today are sensitive to mutual contingencies within relationships. Biological events are but one basis for synchronizing mother-infant behaviors: mutual expectations, joint actions, and social norms can also support the consolidation of relationships, particularly in humans. Notwithstanding its virtues, the dyadic methodology also has been embarrassed by certain shortcomings. Because there are few standard procedures for data collection and analysis, the picture obtained from the employment of inter-actional procedures has not always been in focus. For many applications of rela-tional analysis, standard group statistical methods are not only awkward, they are also irrelevant. Recent efforts to produce more powerful techniques for the dyadic design and analysis have just begun to come to the fore (see, for instance, Patterson, 1974; Castellan, 1977; and the chapter by Ross & Goldman, this volume).

The upshot of these empirical and theoretical advances has been to view the first attachment relationship to be necessary for survival and one for which both the mother and infant are prepared. The bond thus arises from the intermeshing of their needs and actions. Observational analyses of children and experimental studies of nonhuman mammals indicate that species-typical preconditions facili-tate, but are not necessary for, the establishment of mutual dependencies and the social preferences.

Neither of these emphases was dominant just 10 years ago. In 1966, psychobiological factors were hardly acknowledged by social learning accounts, and, although implicated, they were rarely spelled out in ethological-instinctual models. Nor were the essential ideas of interactional analyses grasped, although the theoretical foundations had been laid some quarter of a century ago for developmental psychology by R. R. Sears (1951). These advances constitute genuine breakthroughs in our understanding of the establishment processes, gains that provided for a revised view of the essential conditions for attachment establishment.

Much of the recent work on attachment has been concerned with plotting the structure of the bond, or the anatomy of the relationships that occur between mother and offspring. One achievement of this work has been to show that the infant does indeed serve to control the mother, with its cries, glances, vocaliza-tions, and expressions. These demonstrations of infant control serve as a healthy antidote to the earlier views that the young are shaped simply by environmental contingencies. Submerged but not entirely lost in this reversal of directionality has been the fact that the mother (or other caretakers) nonetheless determines what kinds of initiations the child can make, and how often, by arranging the circumstances in which he is placed. The relationship may be a two-way street, but the parents determine which lanes are used, and how the traffic is controlled. That is to say, parents are not only exceedingly more competent (i.e., flexible and capable of multiple responses) than their offspring, they also determine the range of conditions and experiences to which the young are exposed.

An account of the properties of the parent-child bond, important as it is in its own right, seems unlikely to settle the issues of continuity and change for a couple of reasons. First, the relationship between the mother and offspring does not remain static; it is changed over time. In the normal course of events, the shifts in this filial interchange are drastic, even among those species whose young tend to remain in the vicinity of the mother. How do these changes arise? Second, new relationships are promoted and modified over time. Even in relatively solitary species the young must adapt to a range of other individuals to meet basic societal and survival demands; in the social mammals, the new relationships are legion.

Hence, the key to understanding the varied social interchanges of the individual is not likely to be found in an exclusive focus on the anatomy of the first attachment relationship. Rather, direct analysis must be made of the principles of change: the ways that the young adapt to new social environments and relationships and modify the old. To determine the linkage between the attachment relationship and those that follow, it seems reasonable to analyze what happens just beyond attachment, when the infant is removed from the parents and is placed alone or with strangers—unfamiliar peers or adults. Our limited goal here will be to outline some relevant phenomena as they have been studied in nonhuman mammals, then to explore certain implications for understanding development of interactions in children.

Investigations of the effects of separation and new relationship formation have typically focused on only one of the three phases of adaptation. These correspond roughly to (a) the *immediate* effects produced by change, (b) the *intermediate* effects (which can extend over hours, days, and months), and (c) the *long-term* effects observed at early maturity. An additional distinction can be made with regard to the context in which the individual is observed: whether the effects are observed in the context of the new environment (the one in which the individual has been placed) or in the old environment (the one from which he was removed). No little confusion has been generated in discussions of social adaptation and change by the failure to distinguish among the effects observed at different phases of adaptation, and among the effects observed in different contexts. For instance, an individual that is well adapted to isolation may be ill prepared for a normal social environment, and vice versa. These distinctions on the relativity of adaptation phase and context are of basic importance in forming an adequate picture of the primary features of interactional development.

Isolation and Adaptation

Immediate Effects

One of the primitive features of the early social relations of the young mammal is produced when the infant is isolated from other individuals and placed entirely alone. For most young mammals, but not all, forced separation from the mother is a traumatic and disorganizing experience. A relaxed, contented infant can be abruptly transformed into a restless, vocalizing, extremely agitated organism. Jensen and Tolman (1962) provide a graphic description of what happens in rhesus monkeys:

> Separation of mother and infant monkeys is an extremely stressful event for both mother and infant as well as for the attendants and for all other monkeys within sight or earshot of the experience. The mother becomes ferocious towards attendants and extremely protective of her infant. The infant's screams can be heard over almost the entire building. The mother struggles and attacks the separators. The baby clings tightly to the mother and to any object which it can grasp to avoid being held or removed by the attendant. With the baby gone, the mother paces the cage almost constantly, charges the cage occasionally, bites at it, and makes continual attempts to escape. She also lets out occasional mooing-like sounds. The infant emits high pitched shrill screams intermittently and almost continuously for the period of separation.

The effect is not limited to primates; we find the phenomenon even more striking in sheep, a species that is presumably less cognitive but more gregarious than primates (Cairns, 1966a; Cairns & Johnson, 1965; Cairns & Scholz, 1969). If one were not aware of the immediately preceding event (separation from the mother), he would conclude that an isolated lamb was in great pain or physical duress. When removed from other sheep, two-month-old lambs become extremely agitated and active, running full speed around the isolation chamber. On occasion, the circling pattern gives way to a line drive directed at the steel door or the wall. At the last instant, some lambs leap upward and others run headfirst directly into the ceramic tile wall of the laboratory. After recovering, the animals repeat the running and butting, an activity accompanied by distressful, plaintive, high-pitched "baa's."

Studies of short-term isolation in other mammals confirm that the separation-disruption response is a general one. Descriptions of the behavior of young puppies when they are first removed from their mothers parallel the accounts of lamb and primate behavior. In young dogs, the most prominent feature of the animals' responsiveness is its vocalization (Elliot & Scott, 1961; Ross, Scott, Cherner & Denenberg, 1960; Cairns & Werboff, 1967). Rates of yelping in some breeds are astounding, ranging up to 200 instances per minute. Because pups 3 to 4 weeks of age are unable to move about as readily as young lambs the same age, there is less locomotion and jumping. Rodents 12 to 14 days of age and younger show an increment in activity following removal of the mother (Hofer, 1975). However, in contrast to the foregoing observations, the effects are not immediate. Differences from normal levels do not appear until some 4–8 hours following separation, and are associated with cyclic changes in weight and, presumably, hunger (but see Hofer, 1975, for a discussion of the modulating role of maternal odor).

While the research focus has been on the young during isolation, observations of the mother indicate that she undergoes considerable disruption as well. Recall from the Jensen and Tolman (1962) account that the rhesus monkey mother grimaces, screams, and shows a general pattern of emotional duress. A similar pattern is observed in adult ewes (unpublished). Maternal rats become not only immediately distressed but also sometimes aggressive upon being separated from their litters (Scholz, 1974). The general point seems to be that both infants and their mothers are influenced by the separation; even though the manner of expression may differ, states of emotional distress are observed in both.

Overall, such findings have been interpreted as an index of the attachment bond between the infant and the mother, and as the association of fear and anxiety with the basic relationship. It is in the latter perspective that we read John Bowlby's recent warning that

> the effects of separation from mother can be likened to the effects of smoking and radiation. Although the effects of small doses appear negligible, they are cumulative. The safest dose is a zero dose. (Bowlby, 1973, pp. 72–73)

But before linking the occurrence of separation-induced disruption to long-term psychopathology, it seems reasonable to take a longer look at the processes that govern the response of the young to separation. Isolation effects have been typically assessed in brief ten-minute experimental tests in nonhumans, and even shorter intervals in human infants. The adoption of such brief time intervals may be justified on ethical grounds in that it minimizes the amount of stress for the young. Unfortunately, it also has been responsible for perpetuating a distorted picture of the adaptative competencies of the young organism. To plot the course of the adaptative process, parametric information is required. One must be willing to wait out the extreme discomfort of the infant and mother to observe the next stage.

Intermediate Effects

From the perspective of continuity and social adaptation, the events that occur immediately following the heightened arousal are as dramatic as the immediate agitation itself. The point can be illustrated in observations that we made some years ago on young puppies which had been placed in isolation (i.e., removed from the mother and littermates and placed alone) at four weeks of age (Cairns, 1967). These animals were observed for a continuous 30-minute period immediately on separation, then at successive intervals (after 1, 2, 4, 8, 12, 16, and 24 hours, then daily over the next 8 weeks). In the first 30 minutes, the usual pattern of heightened arousal was observed, coupled with heightened activity, hyperventilation, and heart rate increases, replicating the 10-minute tests of Elliot and Scott (1961), and Ross et al. (1960). However, the animals became calmed relatively soon, by the end of the eighth hour.

Are the animals becoming pathologically depressed, fatigued, or adapted to events in the new environment? It has been commonly accepted that the attachment disruption process proceeds, successively, from heightened anxiety and fear to depression, withdrawal, and "mourning" or a wasting away (Bowlby, 1973). However, direct observations of puppies provide little support for a picture of either fear or depression in the intermediate stage. Rather, what occurs following the extravagant disruption is an increase in normal maintenance activities, including eating, grooming, gnawing, and sleeping. Displacing the intense, high-arousal behaviors are actions of a normal, species-typical form. By the end of the second day, the shift to normative levels of eating and sleeping was virtually complete: the puppies had seemingly adapted to the companionless environment.

These outcomes were not unexpected. Parallel results had been obtained in an earlier study of young sheep that had been isolated from their long-term companions (Cairns, 1966b; Cairns & Scholz, unpublished observations). The pattern of heightened activity—quieting—normal, maintenance responses was obtained. The most significant changes occurred in the hours immediately following the isolation, with adaptation to the new setting—as reflected in the resumption of normal eating and feeding patterns and a cessation of heightened activity—virtually complete by the end of 2 to 4 days in the new setting. Recurrent introduction, and removal, at different intervals following the first separation indicated that the young had become accustomed to the absence of their companions.

Long-Term Effects

Follow-up observations of both pups and lambs some weeks and months later, while they were still in isolation, provided a picture of continued adaptation to the setting. In terms of the gross indices of health — appearance, weight, activity level, vigor — they were quite like the same-age animals that had not been socially isolated. Nor were there differences in susceptibility to disease or mortality. We were initially puzzled by these animals' seeming to get along so well, in the light of the ill effects that had been reported following isolation in nonhuman primates. Rather than a picture of depression, the young sheep and dogs appeared to grow at a normal rate, if adequate space for movement, exercise, and exploration was made available.

On the surface, these results would appear to be in conflict with those obtained in studies of various primates (e.g., Kaufman & Rosenblum, 1967; Preston, Baker, & Seay, 1970; Rosenblum & Kaufman, 1968; Schottman & Seay, 1972). In point of fact, there are compelling reasons to believe that the primate and nonprimate results share considerably more similarities than differences. The problem has been that primate investigations focused initially on what the young animal was deprived of but gave little attention to what he was exposed to and the conditions where he was placed. These conditions, both interpersonal and environmental, have now been shown to be of basic importance in determining the course of adaptation and whether or not depression or adjustment is observed.

In the first place, even among primate species there is considerable variation in reaction to maternal separation. Rosenblum and Kaufman (1968) point out that the young bonnet macaque infants do not show severe disturbance following removal from the mother. The diminished reactivity to separation is correlated with the acceptance of the infant by other, nonmaternal females in the isolation setting. Similar differences in maternal care, including reaction to separation, have been observed in the java monkey and patas monkey (Seay, Schottman, & Gandolfo, 1972). Second, the importance of the physical conditions of isolation was underscored by Mason (1963, 1967), who found that a simple shift in the conditions of isolation—the installation of a pendulum swing—significantly ameliorated the initial arousal associated with maternal and social deprivation. The inclusion of a rag for puppies or a pacifier for babies has similar calming effects in the immediate reactive phase (Scott & Bronson, 1964; Wolff, 1969). More generally, the effects of isolation have usually been confounded with the effects of restriction, where isolation has involved placement in highly con-strained, deficit conditions. Third, and perhaps most important, the nature of the social setting into which the deprived infant has been placed was typically uncontrolled. As we will discuss later, the reactions of others prove to be criti-cally important for the rapidity of the adjustment of the young to separation (Mason & Kenney, 1974; Schottman & Seay, 1972) and to the nature of the effects produced in reunion.

In overview of the nonhuman primate results, it seems clear that the typical pattern observed in most other mammals is found in this group as well: height-ened activity, quieting, and resumption of maintenance activities. The essential questions have concerned the third phase, and whether it is depressed below the levels required for normal physical adjustment, i.e., "wasting away." The avail-able data now indicate that the relative activity of the young in isolation is sufficient to maintain normal growth processes. Whether the activity is above or below that found in nonisolated animals appears to depend on the availability of events—both social and nonsocial—that can elicit and maintain activity in isolation.

One final comment should be made on whether these results regarding the course of adaptation are found only in very young animals. Surprisingly, few adults of any species have been placed in isolation and their reactions systemati-cally plotted. The meager information available suggests that the outcomes are parallel to those obtained in young animals. The conclusion on this matter must be only tentative, however. In the one attempt that we made to explore the time course of adult adaptation, mature Basenji dogs were placed in total isolation. The activity diminished after approximately three hours, and the animals showed the same adaptation process as the very young. What has been viewed as a phenomenon found only in the young may well apply with equal force to older animals.

Isolation → Adaptation: A New Perspective

The observations on the parametric course of the behavior changes of young mammals in isolation pose serious questions for views that would focus principally on the pathological features of the phenomenon. Attention to the dramatic initial responses of the young to isolation—the first 10 minutes—has preempted consideration of the more mundane settling down adaptation to the new living conditions. The course of dynamic changes in behavior seems not unlike that described by Cannon (1929) in his account of the physiological responses to emergency situations. In brief, the change in social context serves to produce a state of heightened preparedness for action, with accompanying sympathetic arousal. The young become primed, in effect, to perform vigorous responses—flight or freezing, escape or crying, retreating or clinging—as these are determined by the circumstances and species-typical propensities. When these vigorous actions are ineffective or unnecessary, the arousal gives way to cyclic homeostatic processes and the emergence of tonic levels of activity, including the maintenance responses of eating and sleeping. Adaptation—both physiological and social—to the new circumstances occurs within a reasonably short period. While the physiological evidence on the matter is meager, it seems unlikely that young mammals could sustain a prolonged arousal state, and happily so, since they would effectively retard social adaptation and survival. The contingencies in the new setting, then, would seem to determine the nature of the adaptation as well as its course.

Accordingly, the transient emotionality promotes a range of vigorous activities, of which vocalization and crying are but one component. Depending on the age of species, there is a sharp increase in intense responses (jumping, scratching, running, orientation) and inhibition of grooming and resting. The diminution of the most vigorous actions is associated with the onset of cyclic internal states, including hunger and fatigue. Thereafter, both the social and nonsocial activities of the young organism are reorganized and fitted to both internal requirements and the demands of the new environment. Viewed from the perspective of adaptational and survival requirements, the sheer rapidity of the habituation to the changed but benign circumstance becomes less puzzling: prolonged activation and arousal would be as hazardous to survival as no activation at all.

One further comment seems called for on what some might consider a virtue of this conceptual reorientation, and others a handicap. The revised view considers the events that occur during the following mother-infant separation to be a particular case of a more general biological-behavioral process, one consistent with the framework outlined by Cannon (1929) and Schneirla (1965). Drastic shifts in environmental circumstances, occasioned by maternal separation and placement in isolation, call into play processes which prepare the young for a full range of adaptive responses. For some systems, particularly those having to do with the physiology of the organism, the extent of the long-term reorganization would be relatively modest. For more labile systems, including those that involve social actions, the reorganization may be drastic in order to prepare the young for the minimal social demands of isolation. But if the young are reintroduced to a context where new social interchanges are required, still further social reorganization may be required, an issue that brings us to a consideration of how new relationships are formed, and old ones are transformed.

The Formation of New Relationships

Up to now we have restricted the discussion to instances in which the young organism has been removed from the parents and littermates, then placed alone (i.e., isolated). What happens if he is not left alone, but placed with unfamiliar individuals? When one shifts focus from what the infant is deprived of to what he is exposed to, the events and individuals present in the new setting become of the greatest importance. In particular, the others and their reactions to the infant might be expected to have a considerable impact on the course of adaptation, and the nature of the adaptation that occurs. Furthermore, understanding of these social adaptation processes should provide a key to clarifying how new relationships are established, and how they are linked to old ones.

Insofar as we have information on the transplantation of nonhuman mammals from one individual or social group to another, the outcomes reflect the joint operation of biological, interactional, and social organizational variables. Without attempting to do justice to the details, accounts of the course of adoption of infant primates (and to a lesser extent, puppies, lambs, and mice) indicate the following:

1. Regardless of setting, a change in the circumstances is associated with an increase in activity and arousal levels in both the transplanted infants and the individuals with which the infants are placed. In lambs, the arousal induced in the host is intense enough to elicit severe rejection (Hersher, Richmond, & Moore, 1963), or in mice, mutilation (MacCombie & Cairns, 1975). The point is that the reactions elicited in both the host and the infant during the introduction phase may retard or preclude further interchanges.

2. Under benign conditions of transplantation, involving even species that are foreign to the infant, the young rapidly form preferences for the new species, preferences that rival or surpass those for conspecifics (Kummer, 1968; Kuo, 1930; Mason & Kenney, 1974). Ordinarily these conditions are arranged so that the essential needs of the infant are met, and the social competencies of the young are not inconsistent with the interactional demands of the context in which they are placed.

3. The reactions of the host or adopting animals determine, in part, the course, nature, and outcomes of the transplanted animal's activities and preferences. Rejection by the new or host animals can serve to effectively prevent the formation of a new social preference, an outcome that is routinely observed when attempts are made to foster young lambs or goats into a new flock (Hersher, Richmond, & Moore, 1958). Similarly, Rosenblum and Kaufman (1968) have demonstrated that the bonnet and pigtail monkeys differ markedly in their treatment of the adopted infant.

4. Maturation-produced changes in the young and the host during the course of development serve to realign the relationship so that initial acceptance can be translated into rejection, or the young can develop to a point that its actions overwhelm the host (e.g., Cairns & Werboff, 1967).

The functional analysis of the formation of relationships thus indicates that social plasticity is controlled by the joint characteristics of the young and the individuals with whom they are placed. From the foregoing, the following variables appear to be of importance: (a) initial arousal and the intensity of introduction in both the transplanted infant and the host; (b) infant interactional competencies and psychobiological status (as determined by its age, species, and prior experience); (c) host interactional competencies and status (as determined by the same factors as infant competency and status, but including the social organization of the group); and (d) mutual ontogenetic accommodation (i.e., the extent to which the actions of the host are synchronized with maturation-paced changes in the infant, and vice versa).

In short, the problem is not simply whether or not the infant is in a critical period. The success or failure of social adaptation depends at least in equal measure on whether the individuals with whom the infant is placed are themselves capable of change, and the extent to which the activities of each can be modified to permit synchronous actions. While this description may appear to be much ado about the obvious, the empirical consideration of interactional properties has been infrequent. Rather, work has been preempted by emphasis on the presumed flexibility of infants and whether they were still in the critical period or susceptible to change. Interactional analysis assumes, on the contrary, that continuities in social behavior reflect the operation of processes which permit plasticity in both the young and old; a point that seems important enough to examine in some detail.

Long-Term Isolation Effects and Changes

Despite meager evidence on its behalf, the view that early social experiences are foundational and relatively irreversible has occupied an honored status in developmental theory (see, for instance, White, 1975). Empirical findings or theoretical statements to the contrary have been commonly ignored or considered anomalous. As a case in point, 10 years ago I offered a proposal that was out-of-step with the dominant views of the time on this matter (Cairns, 1966b). One of the major implications of the statement was that social preferences and interchange were susceptible to change—indeed, quite rapid change—throughout development. The argument was that the young organism's social interactions were organized around and integrated with the behaviors of others in his social environment, and that social preferences or attachment were by-products of that integration. Hence, the theory permitted interchanges to undergo shifts, becoming integrated differently in different social contexts, and being paced by developmental changes. In retrospect, the argument seems adventuresome in the light of the slender evidence then available.

Over the past decade, sufficient new information has been gathered over several species to reopen the essential questions. With the introduction of appropriate developmental designs—involving systematic crossover of conditions of rearing at different stages in ontogeny—it became recognized that most birds and mammals were capable of considerably more social adaptation than they had been given credit for in initial accounts of "deprivation." On the basis of recent studies, it is now clear that the effects of imprinting are reversible or extendible (Klinghammer, 1967; Salzen & Meyer, 1968; Einsiedel, 1973), that many of the effects of isolation can be wiped out or significantly modified (Suomi & Harlow, 1972; Cairns & Nakelski, 1971; Cairns & Werboff, 1967); and that sexual deficits can be ameliorated (Drori & Folman, 1967; Gerall, Ward, & Gerall, 1967). Now, as Kagan and Klein (1973) have recently argued, the stage has been set for a major reconsideration of the issue of developmental fixedness.[2]

Adaptation is not inevitable, however. While the recognition that social behavior can be modified past infancy and early childhood is a step forward, the essential problem is not "whether" but "how." A box score of the studies of social plasticity reveals that some behaviors are more readily influenced than others, and that serious discrepancies exist in the outcomes reported by investigators who are concerned with the same phenomena. Some investigators find successful rehabilitation, and others find failures, in much the same way that investigators of infants find stranger-fear and others, stranger-attraction.

---

[2]There is a mild irony in what kinds of demonstrations were required to produce acceptance of social plasticity. Even 10 years ago, there was ample evidence from studies of birds and various mammalian species, including monkeys, to indicate that there is considerable social adaptability beyond infancy and into maturity (see, for instance, the excellent reviews of imprinting by Bateson, 1966, and Klinghammer, 1967; and the effects of isolation and reversal by Meier, 1965; Cairns & Johnson, 1965; and Cairns, 1966b). The erroneous empirical generalizations on fixedness and social irreversibility were due, in large measure, to incomplete crossover research designs in attempts to modify the effects of isolation in rhesus monkeys and imprinting in precocial birds. When more careful assessments were made of the conditions of change in these phenomena, rehabilitation was discovered.

Not surprisingly, the same variables that influence transplantation success, or the transfer of the infant from one social environment or individual to another, seem to be implicated in social rehabilitation as well. These include the competencies and reactivity of the isolate and the characteristics of the individual or group to which he is introduced. In addition, long-term isolation has positive properties of its own, inducing changes in the psychobiological structure and functioning of the individual. Hence, long-term isolation is associated with not only maturation-paced biophysical changes but with neurohormonal-based shifts in reactivity to stimulation and habituation (e.g., Welch & Welch, 1969). There is some evidence, in addition, that changes take place in the peripheral structures associated with different social-sexual interchanges (e.g., Drori & Folman, 1967). Such isolation-induced psychobiological events, when expressed in a social relationship, can immediately bias its course and outcome (Cairns, 1973). In the course of development, then, the animal becomes biologically fitted for the quiet, asocial conditions of isolation. These changes can produce disastrous consequences if the animal is abruptly shifted back to a social world.

Such psychobiological modifications make even more important the interactive feedback produced when the isolate is placed into a new social circumstance. Isolated monkeys, for instance, have been influenced to behave more normally by a variety of creatures, including baby female monkeys and adult sheepdogs. It seems entirely likely that they would also be rehabilitated by a kindly human experimenter, or a nonthreatening adult male or female monkey. The essential problem, from a functional analysis of interchanges, would be to create interactions that would permit the isolate to react in a way that would be acceptable to the partner, and hence develop a pattern of mutual interchanges. The partner's capabilities and response biases, determined by species-membership, biological and developmental status, and prior social experiences, would of course restrict the range of interchanges that could be promoted.

The conflicting results obtained with respect to the therapy of previously isolated monkeys illustrate the importance of interactional feedback. When previously isolated adult male rhesus monkeys are placed with another adult male, the interactions rapidly escalate to hyperresponsiveness, mutual fighting, and mayhem (Mason, 1961). But when isolated males are placed with infant female monkeys, the relationship rapidly takes on a benign character (Novak & Harlow, 1975; Suomi & Harlow, 1972). What is the difference? According to Suomi and Harlow, the young animals tended to elicit reciprocal play, and, generally, low-intensity patterns of mutual interchange. They proposed that the key was the nature of the reciprocal feedback, precisely what one would expect on the basis of a dyadic analysis (Cairns, 1972).

One other property of rehabilitation experiments requires comment. It is that previously isolated animals can, if the reactions of their partners permit, adapt very rapidly to the postisolation circumstances, even if these are unique for the species. The observations of Mason and Kenney (1974), where isolated monkeys were placed with tamed mongrel dogs, seem especially relevant. These authors write:

> Initially, most monkeys reacted to the dogs with fear, expressed in grimaces, distress vocalizations, crouching, and withdrawal. These behaviors usually disappeared quickly, however. All but one of the eight subjects approached within 2 hours (5 within 30 minutes), and all approached within 6 hours. (Mason & Kenney, 1974, p. 1210)

Again, the processes of interpersonal adaptation can be timed in minutes and hours as opposed to days and weeks.

From the present perspective, the reunion of the infant and its parents can be seen as a special case of the rehabilitation process. In that both the young and mother have undergone biological and interactional changes during the period of separation, there are good reasons to expect that the reunion relationship will have properties of its own, not necessarily duplicating the preceding interchange or taking up where it left off. Indeed, the data on the rhesus and java monkey indicate that postseparation infants cling to the mother more than nonseparated ones (Hinde & Spencer-Booth, 1967, 1971; Schottman & Seay, 1972). The effects of brief separations can be traced in the infant's social behavior some months later (see, for example, Hinde & Spencer-Booth, 1971). But since both the mother and infant have undergone the separation experience, the shift in the relationship may be due to the infant or the mother. For example, during a 5-week separation, maternal dogs quit lactating and, on reunion with their offspring, nip the pups and reject their attempts to approach and suckle (Cairns, 1972). Whether separation-induced shifts in the relationship prejudice the infant's subsequent, nonmaternal social adjustments seem to depend on the social context into which the individual is thrust and is subsequently maintained. At this juncture, the critical questions remain unanswered.

On Social Development in Children

From the foregoing, there seem adequate grounds to challenge the assumption that the quality and character of subsequent social interchanges are irreversibly fixed for young mammals by the attachment relationship. As an alternative, a developmental analysis would emphasize the continuing adaptive capabilities of the young and those with whom they interact. From the developmental perspective, subsequent social behaviors are not simply the residues of some earlier interactions; they must be considered as well in the light of contemporaneous interchange and survival requirements. As young organisms grow older, they become more, not less, adaptable to the multiple social and survival demands of the environment. A developmental emphasis would not deny the carryover effects of prior relationships; it underscores that prior experiences are being continuously melded into contemporaneous requirements. The focus is thereby shifted to the problem of how prior experiences are mediated from one relationship to another, and from one setting to another.

How do these comments apply to children? Clearly the dynamics of interchange modification—including the ways that children fit into new relationships, acquire new patterns of interchanges, and develop unique strategies of social control—lie at the heart of the developmental perspective. But in dealing with these matters in children, especially verbally competent ones, it would be gratuitous to rely on animal behavior data for more than general guidelines. Organisms clearly differ in their ability to adapt to new circumstances, with primates, in general, and humans, in particular, showing high levels of nonsocial and social plasticity (see Cairns, 1976). Hence, the details of social adaptation in children are appropriately abstracted from the direct study of children's interchanges. After a hiatus of 40 years—due in part to unquestioned faith in the primacy of earliest experiences and in part to methodological limitations—the direct examination of these processes in children is now coming to the fore.

Isolation in Infants

The immediate effects of separation in human infants have been discussed at length in recent treatments of attachment (e.g., see Gewirtz, 1972). The phenomena in children bear striking resemblances to those in related mammalian young. Beginning in the second half of the first year, many babies, but not all, cry under some conditions of separation. The variables that affect the probability and intensity of immediate distress are similar to those that affect the distress of the nonhuman species, e.g., the context in which the child is left, prior experiences of having been left alone, age, and, possibly, the differential handling of the child by its parents. The cross-specific differences observed are in degree, not kind. For instance, one impressionistic observation is that children, in general, are less reliably and less intensely distressed by separation than are young puppies, lambs, and infant monkeys. A second difference is less intuitive. Once human babies become upset by being separated, they tend to remain upset, even if the mother returns (see, e.g., Fleener & Cairns, 1970). Young lambs, on the other hand, become calmed almost immediately by the return of the mother. These comparative differences are nonetheless modest when weighted against similarities, suggesting that the distress induced by separation may indeed be a homology across related mammalian forms.

The consideration of how human infants adapt to isolation, in the short term and the long term, is more puzzlesome, controversial, and important. The problem is that documented observations of long-term isolation-rearing in children are virtually nonexistent. Studies of institution-reared children or mistreated ones, while relevant, do not qualify as instances of isolation. These children have been given particular forms of social stimulation, either from other children in that setting or from adults. The reasons for the paucity of systematic data on the effects of isolation *qua* isolation are obvious; it would be unacceptable to leave children alone, even for short-term periods, in experimental treatments. While a variety of clinical reports indicates that children do indeed adapt to the conditions of separation (e.g., Williams, 1959), others indicate gross failures (e.g., Bowlby, 1973).

In any case, a reasonable argument can be made that the meager and conflicting information on how children adapt to isolation, while serious, is not an overwhelming handicap. The essential problem for social development is to explain how children adapt to strange, social circumstances, as opposed to strange, nonsocial ones (i.e., isolation). Happily, our information is somewhat more adequate on the first issue than to the second. Historically the problem of the formation of new relationships has been linked to the analysis of the fear of strangers.

New Relationship Formation

It has taken a reorientation of the field to recognize that children do indeed rapidly form new relationships. When strangers or unfamiliar persons were initially introduced into the laboratory, they served primarily a diagnostic function, that of identifying when the child becomes fearful of unfamiliar adults. This usage of persons to assess stranger-fear was parallel to the use of isolation to assess attachment strength. Typically, the exposure to the stranger was of quite short duration (i.e., 15 seconds to 3 minutes), just long enough to determine whether or not the child would become upset by his mere presence.

One of the puzzling outcomes of the stranger-fear diagnoses has been the finding that different groups of investigators report different degrees of fearfulness in their infants. While the infants in Bronson's Berkeley laboratory tend to be most fearful, those in Rheingold and Eckerman's (1973) Chapel Hill laboratory show little fear whatsoever. Conflicts in such an elementary phenomenon are bound to produce sides in an argument about who is right or wrong; are infants really not fearful of strangers?

Comparisons of the studies where stranger-fear has been reported (e.g., Bronson, 1972; Tennes & Lampl, 1964) with those where the fear has been negligible or transient (Monahan, 1975; Rheingold & Eckerman, 1973) indicate that methodological differences are paramount, especially differences in how the stranger is introduced and how she interacts. A principal determinant of the child's fear or acceptance seems to be the nature of the reactions of the stranger, and whether they are compatible with the child's behaviors and expectations. A nonresponsive, foreboding stranger can effectively trigger apprehension and withdrawal; so can an overfriendly, possessive one. On the other hand, unfamiliar persons who are sensitive to the reactions of the child, and act in ways that the child can respond to, produce minimal disruption or upset. Even in these instances of stranger-acceptance it is not clear that the child is not, initially, in a state of heightened or mild arousal. On the basis of the foregoing analysis of the effects of interactional change, it would be entirely consistent to expect that any drastic shift in interactional circumstances, including an introduction of new persons, would elicit changes in momentary states of arousal. But whether this heightened activity level is to be translated into disorganized emotional expression, into exploratory acts of looking and smiling, or into reciprocal acts seems to be greatly dependent on the nature of the acts directed toward the child and the "strangeness" of the stranger (Bronson, 1972; Eckerman & Whatley, 1975; Rheingold & Eckerman, 1973).

Curiously lost in the theoretical debate about stranger-anxiety and whence it came is the commonplace observation that in the normal course of living, children of all ages are continually exposed to strangers. These strangers may be babysitters and parental friends, or they may be playmates, nursery school teachers, or persons the child meets in the bus and post office. Some relationships are fleeting; others are durable and intense. A major problem for social development is to determine how a stranger becomes an acquaintance or an attachment object, how new relationships are formed and old ones are changed. Once again, focus on the unique and pathological has diverted attention away from the ubiquitous and normal processes.

The transformation of stranger-fear to "stranger-attachment" has been nicely illustrated in two studies of the course of adaptation to new persons. D. E. Fleener (1973) reported that 10- to 14-month-old infants very rapidly adapt to the characteristics of surrogate mothers. In Fleener's work, the children were left in the care of one of two women for 3 consecutive days, for a total of approximately 7 hours. Even though the children's real mothers were not present during these sessions, the children showed few signs of disruption on being separated from them. At the end of the 3-day series, standard measures of social attachment (i.e., child's response to being separated from the caretaker, preference for the caretaker versus the noncaretaker) were used to assess whether the interchanges had provided the basis for the establishment of a new attachment. The data clearly indicate that the children strongly preferred their caretaker, and that they become disrupted when separated from her.

Rather similar results were obtained as a result of interaction between the stranger and infants in their homes by Monahan (1975). In this work, a precise account was made of the conditional relationships between the actions of the stranger and initiations and reactions of infants. Monahan's stranger, like that in the Fleener (1973) work, was quite active and sensitive to the reactions of the infants. Under these conditions, Monahan found that a new relationship can be established quite rapidly. Moreover, comparisons of the reciprocal interchanges between the infant and the stranger with those between the infant and its mother revealed precious few differences in contingencies. Indeed, because the stranger was somewhat more active than the mother, the child smiled more and showed higher levels of mutual interchange. The rule seemed to be that the more like the mother the stranger behaved, the less stressful was the initial stage of interchange and the more rapid was the adaptation to the new person.

Studies of the social interchanges of the very young fall into a rather significant pattern, one which is consistent with the view of the child as having the capability to effect modest adjustment to the demands of the social context in which he has been placed. What has been viewed as a potentially psychopathological reaction may be just the opposite: namely, evidence on how the restructuring of the child's behavior and relationships gets under way. An initial withdrawal tends to preserve the old relationships by producing either counteraversion or avoidance. Visual exploration of the stranger and smiling (Eckerman & Whatley, 1975) simultaneously provide the occasion for restructuring both the child's and the other's reactions to the demands of a new relationship. The closer the fit between mutual reactions, in terms of providing mutual response synchronization, the more rapid the settling down in the new relationship. In this regard, the results are quite parallel to those observed in nonhuman infants, except that human strangers seem capable of adapting to a considerable range of infant reactions.

Toward Principles of Interactional Development

On the basis of the work that has been completed in the study of children and nonhumans, we are in a position to begin to specify the conditions for relational formation and change. To move beyond attachment, it is necessary to develop concepts that are closer to the actual phenomena of social interchanges than the traditional ideas of social learning theory permit (e.g., social reinforcement, modeling). An account of interactional development, from whatever orientation it may spring, must take into account certain features of interchanges; namely, that children develop multiple interchange patterns, that they are characterized by mutual reciprocity and escalation, and that they tend to be recurrent, consolidated, and generalized. Some comments on each of these features of interchanges seem in order.

First, it is clear that children, even quite young ones, are capable of multiple-interchange patterns. That is, children in the second year of life and older can relate differentially as a function of the different setting and different persons (Holmberg, 1976; Ross & Goldman, this volume; Eckerman, Whatley, & Kutz, 1975). Eighteen-month-old children can play a variety of interpersonal roles, depending on the feedback provided by other persons and the circumstances of interaction. With increasing age, these interactional patterns become more elaborate, and tuned to nuances in the setting and the reactions of others (Sherman, 1975).

Second, underlying these multiple relationships are certain interchange propensities which seem to apply to infants and older children alike. Two of the basic interchange properties are *mutual synchrony* and *escalation*. Mutual synchrony refers to the propensity of children to produce similar, though not identical, responses to those of other children. Mutual synchrony can be distinguished from imitation in that the acts or verbal statements are rarely exact duplications of those of the other child. Rather, they contribute to the theme or organization of the interchange, with each child providing individual notes within a melody. Even in quite young children, some activities become organized around common themes. Such reciprocity permits the interchange to persist, with each child exercising an impact on the subsequent acts of the other in a fluid, sometimes discontinuous fashion. Over time, this primitive response disposition leads to the establishment of complementary acts and similarities in behavior (see Sherman, 1975; Hall, 1973). *Escalation* refers to a particular property of interchanges whereby reciprocated responses increase in intensity. Escalation is commonly triggered by the occurrence of hurtful acts, intended or not, which trigger counterresponses of the same form. The concept has been useful in describing the course of aggressive interchanges in children (e.g., Hall, 1973; Patterson & Cobb, 1971) and various nonhuman species (Cairns, 1973).

Third, interchange patterns are learnable, in that the occurrence of a particular interchange pattern increases the likelihood of its recurrence. The recurrence principle is rather important, in that it describes an essential process whereby specific relational patterns become characteristic of particular dyads and become predictable in the child and those with whom he interacts. Further, repeated interchanges become *consolidated* over persons and settings, in that fewer events are required to call forth the previously integrated social patterns. Recurrence and consolidation suggest how interactional patterns become generalized across settings and relationships. Initially, the speed with which the individual fits a new social context should be associated with the extent to which there is a match between interactional conditions that prevail in the new setting and those of the old.

Generalizations across situations and time would not be automatic but would reflect both the initial perceived similarity of the situations and the demands in the settings (Mischel, 1973). In this regard, the rapidity of children in fitting into a new nursery school would be readily understood: the conditions for adaptation presumably were similar to those to which the children had been accustomed (Schwarz & Wynn, 1971). Fleener's (1973) and Monahan's (1975) results on the rapid adaptation of infants to strangers are seen in the same light. Further, reciprocity should ensure that children exercise a strong effect on each other, in the nursery, in school, and elsewhere. Hence, one effective way to control the behavior of the child is to modify the behaviors of those with whom he interacts (e.g., Hall, 1973; Quilty, 1973).

It is beyond the scope of this chapter to consider the basic psychobiological sources of continuity and change. Clearly, the child's age–sex status elicits reactions from others that are seemingly appropriate and, via reciprocity, expectations can become self-fulfilling. As the child's structures and capabilities change, so do reciprocal behaviors and attitudes. The point to be emphasized is that continuity and change have more substantial roots than only prior learning and cognitive experiences. Developmental pacemakers help to account both for general variations among age and sex groups and for idiographic differences between persons in style and temperament.

Concluding Comments

The thrust of this essay has been that interactions at each stage of social development are critical in their own way. If the attachment process is critical for the infant, it is equally important for the parents, in setting the stage for their affectional patterns and responses toward the child. Insofar as dyadic learning and control processes continue to be active, the child's relations with peers and adults away from home are critical for social adaptation at school and at play. While this essay was not concerned with adjustment at adolescence, the evidence indicates that influences operative at this developmental epoch are also critical for understanding sexual and social behavior at maturity (e.g., Kagan & Moss, 1962). To control and predict social actions at each stage, precise information is required on how contemporaneous biological, environmental, and cognitive constraints support social interchanges. The carryover of preceding relationships—particularly immediately preceding ones—seems great. Insofar as interchanges become consolidated in particular settings, social behavior patterns become increasingly predictable in those contexts. On the other hand, significant shifts in supporting events (in the context, internally, or in social feedback) should set the stage for concomitant social adaptations by the individual, whether young or old.

What issues, then, lie beyond social attachment? From the foregoing, one answer seems clear: research should be concerned with the direct naturalistic and experimental analysis of interchange patterns at the several stages of development. The analysis should be concerned not only with the anatomy of interchanges but also with their dynamics: namely, how interchanges are changed and tailored to new settings, relationships, and demands. It is with regard to the problem of the dynamics of change and transition that the field is most deficient. To obtain this essential information, innovative experimental procedures are required, employed in both naturalistic and laboratory settings. With respect to the active contribution of developmental events, research with children should be focused on how psychobiological events in children, and in those about them, trigger modifications in interaction styles and patterns.

Does an interactional-experimental strategy pay off? Recent animal behavior investigations indicate that it surely does, if prediction and control are the criteria. By manipulating the interactional conditions of rearing, young animals can be reliably produced that are either aggressive or passive, sexually virile or impotent, gregarious or alienated, altruistic or independent. Further, once established, these interchange propensities are sometimes open to drastic modification at maturity. Granted that the recent achievements of developmental sociobiology have been spectacular, what about children? The carefree extrapolation to children is no longer justified, because a firm data base is beginning to emerge on how interchanges are mediated in human social development. The gains have not been rapid, nor have they been easily won. Some 40 years ago Gordon Allport (1937) correctly emphasized that the interchanges of persons are idiographic and unique but that the mechanisms by which they come about are general. An essential problem in his treatment stemmed from an unfortunate choice for a general mechanism—functional autonomy. The concept served to describe developmental continuity but did not account for how it came about, or why changes in interchanges and preferences occurred. Further progress on this matter seems dependent on precise, longitudinal analyses of how interchanges are in fact mediated and transformed in the lives of individual children.

References

Allport, G. *Personality: A psychological interpretation*. New York: Holt, 1937.

Bateson, P. P. G. The characteristics and context of imprinting. *Biological Reviews*, 1966, **41**, 177–220.

Bowlby, J. *Attachment and loss*. Vol. 2. *Separation*. New York: Basic Books, 1973.

Bronson, G. W. Infants' reactions to unfamiliar persons and novel objects. *Monographs of the Society for Research in Child Development*, 1972, **37** (3, 1948).

Cairns, R. B. Development, maintenance, and extinction of social attachment of behavior in sheep. *Journal of Comparative and Physiological Psychology*, 1966, **62**, 298–306. (*a*)

Cairns, R. B. Attachment behavior of mammals. *Psychological Review*, 1966, **72**, 409–426. (*b*)

Cairns, R. Development of social behavior in dogs: An interspecific analysis. Paper read at the Biennial Meeting of the Society for Research in Child Development, New York, April 1967.

Cairns, R. B. Attachment and dependency: A synthesis. In J. L. Gewirtz (Ed.), *Attachment and dependency*. Washington, D.C.: V. H. Winston, 1972.

Cairns, R. B. Fighting and punishment from a developmental perspective. *Nebraska symposium on motivation*, 1972. Lincoln: University of Nebraska Press, 1973.

Cairns, R. B. The ontogeny and phylogeny of social interactions. In M. Hahn & E. C. Simmel (Eds.), *Evolution of communicative behaviors*. New York: Academic Press, 1976.

Cairns, R. B., & Johnson, D. L. The development of interspecies social preferences. *Psychonomic Science*, 1965, **2**, 337–338.

Cairns, R. B., & Nakelski, J. S. On fighting in mice: Ontogenetic and experiential determinants. *Journal of Comparative and Physiological Psychology*, 1971, **71**, 354–364.

Cairns, R. B., & Scholz, S. D. Adaptation to isolation in young sheep. Indiana University, 1969.

Cairns, R. B., & Scholz, S. D. On fighting in mice: Dyadic escalation and what is learned. *Journal of Comparative and Physiological Psychology*, 1973, **85**, 540–550.

Cairns, R. B., & Werboff, J. Behavior development in the dog: An interspecific analysis. *Science*, 1967, **158**, 1070–1072.

Cannon, W. B. *Bodily changes in pain, hunger, fear and rage*. (2nd ed.) New York: Appleton, 1929.

Castellan, N. J. The analysis of behavior sequences. In R. B. Cairns (Ed.), *Social interaction: Methods, analysis, and illustrations* (in preparation, 1977).

Drori, D., & Folman, Y. The sexual behavior of male rats unmated to 16 months of age. *Animal Behaviour*, 1967, **15**, 11–19.

Eckerman, C. O., & Whatley, J. L. Infants' reactions to unfamiliar adults varying in novelty. *Developmental Psychology*, 1975, **11**, 563–566.

Eckerman, C. O., Whatley, J. L., & Kutz, S. L. Growth of social play with peers during the second year of life. *Developmental Psychology*, 1975, **11**, 42–49.

Einseidel, A. E. *The development and modification of object preferences in domestic White Leghorn chicks (Gallus gallus)*. Unpublished doctoral dissertation, Indiana University, 1973.

Elliot, O., & Scott, J. P. The development of emotional distress reactions to separation in puppies. *Journal of Genetic Psychology*, 1961, **99**, 3–22.

Fleener, D. E. Attachment formation in human infants. Paper read at the American Psychological Association, Montreal, September 1973.

Fleener, D. E., & Cairns, R. B. Attachment behaviors in human infants: Discriminative vocalization upon maternal separation. *Developmental Psychology*, 1970, **2**, 215–223.

Gerall, H. E., Ward, I. L., & Gerall, A. A. Disruption of the male rat's sexual behaviour induced by social isolation. *Animal Behaviour*, 1967, **15**, 54–58.

Gewirtz, J. L. (Ed.), *Attachment and dependency*. New York: V. H. Winston, 1972.

Hall, W. M. *Observational and interactive determinants of aggressive behavior in boys*. Unpublished doctoral dissertation, Indiana University, 1973.

Hersher, L., Richmond, J. B., & Moore, A. U. Effect of post partum separation of mother and kid on maternal care in the domestic goat. *Science*, 1958, **128**, 1342–1343.

Hersher, L., Richmond, J. B., & Moore, A. U. Maternal behavior in sheep and goats. In H. L. Rheingold (Ed.), *Maternal behavior in mammals*. New York: Wiley, 1963.

Hinde, R. A., & Spencer-Booth, Y. The behavior of social living rhesus monkeys and their first two and a half years. *Animal Behaviour*, 1967, **15**, 169–196.

Hinde, R. A., & Spencer-Booth, Y. Effects of brief separation from mother on rhesus monkeys. *Science*, 1971, **173**, 111–118.

Hofer, M. A. Studies of how early maternal separation produces behavioral change in young rats. *Psychosomatic Medicine*, 1975, **37**, 245–264.

Holmberg, M. C. Social interchanges in the second and third year: The impact of daycare rearing. Paper read at the Biennial Meeting of the Southeastern Conference on Human Development, April 1976.

Jensen, G. D., & Tolman, C. W. Activity level of the mother monkey, *Macaca nemestrina*, as affected by various conditions of sensory access to the infant following separation. *Animal Behaviour*, 1962, **10**, 228–230.

Kagan, J., & Klein, R. E. Cross-cultural perspectives on early development. *American Psychologist*, 1973, **11**, 974–961.

Kagan, J., & Moss, H. *Birth to maturity: A study in psychological development*. New York: Wiley, 1962.

Kaufman, I. C., & Rosenblum, L. A. Depression in infant monkeys separated from their mothers. *Science*, 1967, **155**, 1030–1031.

Klinghammer, E. Factors influencing choice of mate in altricial birds. In H. W. Stevenson, E. H. Hess, & H. L. Rheingold (Eds.), *Early behavior: Comparative and developmental approaches*. New York: Wiley, 1967.

Kummer, H. *Social organization in the hamadryus baboon*. Chicago: University of Chicago Press, 1968.

Kuo, Z. Y. The genesis of the cat's responses to the rat. *Journal of Comparative Psychology*, 1930, **11**, 1–35.

MacCombie, D. M., & Cairns, R. B. Early experience and social plasticity: Reducing aggression in isolation-reared mice. Paper read at the Annual Meeting of the American Psychological Association, Chicago, September 1975.

Mason, W. A. The effects of social restriction on the behavior of rhesus monkeys. II. Tests of gregariousness. *Journal of Comparative and Physiological Psychology*, 1961, **54**, 287–290.

Mason, W. A. Social development of rhesus monkeys with restricted social experience. *Perceptual and Motor Skills*, 1963, **16**, 263–270.

Mason, W. A. Motivational aspects of social responsiveness in young chimpanzees. In H. W. Stevenson, E. Hess, & H. L. Rheingold (Eds.), *Early behavior: Comparative and developmental approaches*. New York: Wiley, 1967.

Mason, W. A., & Kenny, M. D. Redirection of filial attachments in rhesus monkeys: Dogs as mother surrogates. *Science*, 1974, **183**, 1209–1211.

Meier, G. W. Other data on the effects of social isolation during rearing upon adult reproductive behaviour in the rhesus monkey *(Macaca mulatta)*. *Animal Behaviour*, 1965, **13**, 228–231.

Mischel, W. Toward a cognitive social learning reconceptualization of personality. *Psychological Review*, 1973, **80**, 284–302.

Monahan, L. C. *Mother–infant and stranger–infant interaction: An ethological analysis*. Unpublished doctoral dissertation, Department of Psychology, Indiana University, 1975.

Novak, M. A., & Harlow, H. F. Social recovery of monkeys isolated for the first year of life. 1. Rehabilitation and therapy. *Developmental Psychology*, 1975, **11**, 453–465.

Patterson, G. A basis for identifying stimuli which control behaviors in natural settings. *Child Development*, 1974, **45**, 900–911.

Patterson, G. R., & Cobb, J. A. A dyadic analysis of "aggressive" behaviors. In J. P. Hill (Ed.), *Minnesota symposia on child psychology*. Vol. 5. Minneapolis: University of Minnesota Press, 1971.

Preston, D. G., Baker, R. P., & Seay, B. Mother–infant separation in the patas monkey. *Developmental Psychology*, 1970, **3**, 298–306.

Quilty, R. F. *Modeling as a dyadic/strategy*. Unpublished doctoral dissertation, Indiana University, 1973.

Rheingold, H. L., & Eckerman, C. O. Fear of the stranger: A critical examination. In H. W. Reese (Ed.), *Advances in child development and behavior*. New York: Academic Press, 1973.

Rosenblum, L. A., & Kaufman, I. C. Variations in infant development and response to maternal loss in monkeys. *American Journal of Orthopsychiatry*, 1968, **38**, 418–426.

Ross, H. S., & Goldman, B. D. Establishing new social relations in infancy. Paper presented at the Erindale Symposium on Communications and Affect, Toronto, March 1975.

Ross, S., Scott, J. P., Cherner, M., & Denenberg, V. H. Effects of restraint and isolation on yelping in puppies. *Animal Behaviour*, 1960, **8**, 1–5.

Salzen, E. A., & Meyer, C. C. Reversibility of imprinting. *Journal of Comparative and Physiological Psychology*, 1968, **66**, 269–275.

Schneirla, T. C. Aspects of stimulation and organization in approach/withdrawal processes underlying vertebrate behavioral development. In D. S. Lehrman, R. Hinde, & E. Shaw (Eds.), *Advances in the study of behavior*. Vol. 1. New York: Academic Press, 1965.

Scholz, S. D. *The effects of brief separations upon maternal behavior and infant development in rattus norvegicus*. Unpublished doctoral dissertation, Indiana University, 1974.

Schottman, R. S., & Seay, B. Mother–infant separation in the java monkey. *Journal of Comparative and Physiological Psychology*, 1972, **79**, 334–340.

Scott, J. P., & Bronson, F. H. Experimental exploration of the et-epimeletic or care-soliciting behavioral system. In P. H. Leiderman & D. Shapiro (Eds.), *Psychobiological approaches to social behavior*. Stanford: Stanford University Press, 1964.

Schwarz, J. C., & Wynn, R. The effects of mothers' presence and previsits on children's emotional reaction to starting nursery school. *Child Development*, 1971, **42**, 871–882.

Sears, R. R. A theoretical framework for personality and social behavior. *American Psychologist*, 1951, **6**, 476–483.

Seay, B., Schottman, R. S., & Gandolfo, R. Early social interaction in two monkey species. *Journal of General Psychology*, 1972, **87**, 37–43.

Sherman, S. J. *Social interchanges in children: Formation, stability, and contextual constraints.* Unpublished doctoral dissertation, University of North Carolina, 1975.

Suomi, S. J., & Harlow, H. F. Social rehabilitation of isolate-reared monkeys. *Developmental Psychology*, 1972, **6**, 487–496.

Tennes, K. H., & Lampl, E. E. Stranger and separation anxiety in infancy. *Journal of Nervous and Mental Diseases*, 1964, **139**, 247–254.

Welch, B. L., & Welch, A. S. Aggression and biogenic amine neurohumors. In S. Garattini & E. G. Sigg (Eds.), *Aggressive behavior: Proceedings of the symposium on the biology of aggressive behavior.* Amsterdam: Excerpta Medica, 1969.

White, B. *The first three years.* Englewood Cliffs, N.J.: Prentice-Hall, 1975.

Williams, C. D. The elimination of tantrum behavior by extinction procedures. *Journal of Abnormal and Social Psychology*, 1959, **59**, 269.

Wolff, P. H. The natural history of crying and vocalization in early in fancy. In B. M. Foss (Ed.), *Determinants of infant behaviour IV*. London: Methuen (New York: Wiley), 1969.

An Ethological–Cognitive Model for the Attenuation of Mother–Child Attachment Behavior

Robert S. Marvin

Department of Psychology
University of Virginia
Charlottesville, Virginia

During the past two decades there has been an explosive increase in our knowledge of mother–infant attachment during the first year of life.[1] This increase refers not only to the content of mother–infant interaction and its development but also to the many innovative observational and analytic tools for the study of behavioral development which have evolved in the course of this research. Three of the most important innovations are the following: (a) the construction of behavior catalogues—precisely defined lists of behavior that serve as the data base for naturalistic and standardized observations (e.g., Blurton Jones, 1972; Brannigan & Humphries, 1972); (b) data reduction techniques such as those of Hinde (Hinde & Atkinson, 1970; Hinde, 1974), which allow precise descriptive statements concerning not only the behavior of the individuals, but also of relationships; and (c) comparative studies of nonhuman primates, which have given us many of our basic ideas concerning the infant's development, and the development of his relationship with his mother. From these have developed the basis for a comprehensive theory of mother–infant attachment specifically, and of infant behavioral development in general (e.g., Bowlby, 1969, 1973; Ainsworth, 1969). This theory provides us with an integration of a number of perspectives, including those of both phylogeny and ontogeny (e.g.,

---

[1]Throughout this paper the term *mother* is used for convenience in referring to the child's relationship with any of his attachment figures.

Bowlby, 1969; Ainsworth, 1969), of behavior and cognition (e.g., Bell, 1970), and of anthropology and ecology (e.g., Ainsworth, 1967; Marvin, VanDevender, Iwanaga, LeVine, & LeVine, in press).

In view of these advances, it is curious that we know very little about this crucial interpersonal relationship beyond the first year or 18 months of life. What we do know, from naturalistic and experimental studies, can be summarized as follows from the work of Anderson (1972), Blurton Jones and Leach (1972), Clarke-Stewart (1973), Lee, Wright, and Herbert (1972), Maccoby and Feldman (1972), Marvin (1972), and Shirley and Poyntz (1941).

Two-year-olds tend to maintain as much, or more, proximity to mother as 1-year-olds. When undergoing a separation from the mother which is not of their own initiative, 2-year-old children protest less than do 1-year-olds, but are generally not willing to be left with a friendly stranger. They also make more use of looking and verbal communication in relating to the mother than do 1-year-old children. Although 3-year-olds also tend to be upset by brief separations which are not of their own initiative, they are less so than 2-year-olds, and they are more willing than younger children to be left for brief periods in the company of friendly strangers. Finally, there is some evidence that a major change takes place in preschool children's reactions to separation sometime around 4 years of age.

One qualification should be made concerning these apparent age-changes. While there are age-differences in the intensity and frequency of children's attachment behavior in separation situations, it appears that the organization of attachment behavior—the way in which this system is structured—remains basically the same from one to three years of age (see Bowlby, 1969).

Attenuation of Attachment Behavior in Nonhuman Primates

As was mentioned earlier, comparative studies of nonhuman primates have supplied us with many of our basic ideas and methods for the study of the infant and its relationship with its mother. Recent naturalistic field studies of nonhuman primates have been particularly useful in that they have focused on a wide range of variables in the infants' behavioral development, his relationship with his mother, and his relationship with the troop in general. A holistic picture has emerged of the primate infant's development, and of the multiplex relationships within which that development takes place. In fact, it was largely from these studies that Bowlby developed his theory of human infant–mother attachment. As the following summary suggests, the same appears to be the case for developing a framework within which to conceptualize further changes in this relationship past infancy. The summary is taken primarily from the work of Carpenter (1964), Lawick-Goodall (1968), Hall and DeVore (1965), Hinde (1974), Jay

(1965), and Shaller (1963), and is presented elsewhere in expanded form (Marvin, 1972).

First, without exception these observers conclude, either explicitly or implicitly that the close relationship between mother and infant appears to be designed to protect the infant from various sources of danger (e.g., from predators, from physical hazards, or from potentially harmful interaction with conspecifics). Their observations suggest that at each point in the infant's development, the organization of this attachment behavior, and of his relationship with his mother generally, is organized in relation to a number of other developing physical and behavioral systems, and that developmental changes in attachment behavior are functionally related to changes in those other systems. Among these systems are coat color, dentition, locomotor skills, feeding skills, and, most importantly, communication skills.

These observers generally distinguish three stages in the young primate's relationship with his mother. The first (Infancy I) is a period of essentially constant physical contact between mother and infant. Both infant and mother play a role in maintaining this contact, the mother through physical constraint and the infant through physical activity such as clinging, and through motor and vocal signals such as squealing when he suffers loss of contact or support. The infant begins to develop basic locomotor skills, although he only practices these when mother is resting. During this period, the only communication skills which the infant displays in a predictable or stable fashion are those signals relating to fright, pain, hunger, and separation from his mother. However, toward the end of this period, he begins practicing those signals relating to interaction with his mother over short distances. At this point, the infant begins to initiate exploratory bouts off the mother, although she tends to restrict him in this movement. Generally, this stage corresponds to Bowlby's first three phases in the development of human infant–mother attachment.

The second stage (Infancy II) usually begins with a color change in the infant's coat. By this time his milk dentition is complete, and while he still nurses he also begins to eat solid foods. He locomotes independently of the mother except when the troop is moving. The amount of time spent in physical contact with the mother decreases during this period as the infant spends more and more time playing with peers. However, mother and infant keep essentially constant visual contact with each other. The attachment behavior of mother and infant becomes increasingly meshed, or integrated, with the infant being primarily responsible for proximity while using his mother as a secure base for exploration. This increased integration is primarily the result of the infant's increased ability to emit and respond to signals that are relevant to interaction with the mother across a distance. Finally, during this period the infant continues to receive preferential treatment from adult troop members, while he begins practicing those communicative skills which will be required of him as a fully integrated member of the troop.

The third period (the Juvenile Stage) begins as the youngster is weaned, and becomes completely independent of the mother for locomotion and feeding. His communication skills have developed to the point where he emits and responds to the entire range of social signals predictably and appropriately enough to become an autonomous troop member. As Jay (1965) states:

> Threat gestures directed by a large juvenile to an adult are responded to with threat or aggressive behavior. Similarly, a submissive gesture may avert impending adult threat or aggression. The juvenile's skill in displaying gestures and its longer consistent sequences of gestures and vocalizations contribute to effective communication of the juvenile's emotional state, whereas the infant intersperses recognizable social gestures with random, often play, behavior. (pp. 229–230)

During this period, the youngster's relationship with his mother undergoes a major change: Except in extreme circumstances the relationship loses its protective function. In some species the relationship appears to be severed completely, while in others (e.g., chimpanzees) it changes to a close relationship based on friendship and mutual respect.

Thus, the young primate's relationship with his mother passes through three major phases between birth and his full autonomy within the larger troop. While each phase is structurally different, there is one invariant aspect which is maintained throughout. This invariant is the youngster's protection from all expectable sources of danger. Initially, this protection is almost totally the mother's responsibility, but her role constantly decreases as the youngster's increases. The increase in his own responsibility is not merely the result of increased size and locomotor skill, but at least as much an increased skill in social communication.

The basic underlying hypothesis in this study is that these same functional relationships hold in the case of human mother–child attachment. Thus, we would expect three major phases in the child's relationship with his mother between birth and school age. During each phase the relationship would be organized in a way that complements the lack of certain behavioral skills on the part of the child, so he is always protected. As these behavioral skills, and especially his communication skills, develop, the child's relationship with his mother also changes. Each of these changes should result in an increased integration between the attachment behavior of mother and child. As in the case of nonhuman primates, the first phase should be organized so physical proximity and contact are the predictable outcomes of the infant's behavior (Bowlby, 1969). The second phase should also be organized with respect to physical proximity, although the increased integration of the partners' behavior should result in a decrease in the absolute amount of this proximity (cf., Hinde, 1974). During this phase, the youngster should spend more and more time using his mother as a secure base for exploring his physical and social environment. Finally, a major change should take place during the third phase. No longer should physical proximity and contact provide the primary basis for the relationship. Unlike some primate species, the relationship is obviously not completely servered at this point, but instead should undergo a qualitative change. Perhaps, as with chimps, it changes in the direction of reciprocal friendship and respect (Van Lawick-Goodall, 1968). The remainder of this chapter consists of an attempt to outline a more detailed model of these changes, and to present preliminary evidence in support of the model.

Post-Infancy Changes in Mother–Child Attachment Behavior

The specific questions that are being asked in this chapter stem from the following four assumptions, or propositions:

1. The basic unit of observation, analysis and conceptualization is the relationship itself, defined in terms of the two partners, and the various interactions between them. Within this, one can conceive of the individual as a more or less autonomous subsystem, whose existence is nevertheless dependent on the relationship as a whole.

2. The existence of an enduring relationship implies the existence of certain invariant, reciprocal relations between the partners. These invariant relations should be specifiable in terms of the outcomes, or effects, of the reciprocal interactions of the partners, and can be conceived of as points of balance, stability, or equilibrium which are maintained despite various disturbances. In a relationship where one or both partners are themselves changing, these points of equilibrium may also change, but should continue to be specifiable in terms of the outcome of the partners' interaction. Bowlby (1969) has argued convincingly that proximity and contact are such points of equilibrium or invariance in the infant–mother relationship. A qualitatively different point will be proposed later in this chapter characteristic of the relationship between the mother and the older preschool child.

As a corollary to this proposition, it is proposed that as the child develops, he comes to internally represent, or interiorize (Inhelder & Piaget, 1958), the relations which exist between himself and other social and physical objects. As a result, he becomes able to behave in a way that achieves many of these relations in a purposive or goal-directed way (Piaget, 1952; Miller, Galanter, & Pribram, 1960; Bowlby, 1969).

3. Any stable social structure, from the level of the troop or society to the level of parent and offspring, is best defined in terms of the reciprocal control which results from communication among its members (Carpenter, 1964; Altmann, 1965). This implies that changes in the mother–child relationship can be defined and studied in terms of changes in the forms of communication and reciprocal control of behavior which characterize the relationship and which maintain the above-mentioned points of equilibrium between the partners.

   4.   By observing the patterns of communication between the individuals in
a relationship in varying contexts, one is able to infer those conditions which the
individuals are attempting to maintain in a goal-directed manner. Since any
goal-directed activity implies the existence of an internal representation, or conception, of the goal-state, one is also able to infer each individual's conception of
the relationship by carefully observing his patterns of communication within the
relationship.

   These propositions are seen as being particularly important for the study of
attachment behavior past infancy. Specifically, since the infant's conceptualization of his social and physical world is at best exceedingly primitive, studies of
his relationship with his mother can rely almost solely on observable behaviors.
However, nearly all of the published statements concerning this relationship in
older children imply that the child's increasing cognitive or symbolic activity
plays an important role in any changes in the relationship. The problem arises of
how one can infer what this symbolic activity consists of, how it is structured,
and how it plays a role in these changes. Ideally, any model of these cognitive or
symbolic activities should be based on, or at least related to, observable behaviors. Thus, the problem becomes one of inferring internal events from observable behaviors. As suggested by the four propositions presented above, the
position taken in this chapter is that one can make such inferences by observing
the patterns of communication within the relationship. The specific questions in
the study then become: (a) what are the major changes that take place in the
attachment relationship between mother and child as the child develops through
the preschool years; and (b) how do developmental changes in the child's communication skills affect the relationship, and account for changes in it?

   The only work on humans that comes close to addressing the issue of the
relationship between mother–child attachment and the child's communication
skills is the work of John Bowlby (1969, 1973). Bowlby proposes that before the
age of about 8 months, a baby can make no goal-directed, planned attempt to
bring about the conditions that will terminate his attachment behavior. "Either
the necessary conditions obtain, in which case he is content, or they do not, in
which case he is distressed" (1969, p. 350). While the young infant's attachment
behavior is not yet goal-directed, the mother usually behaves in such a manner
that proximity and contact are the predictable outcomes of his attachment behavior.

   By the time a baby nears his first birthday things have changed. Certain
cognitive changes that have taken place enable him to conceive of the conditions
that will terminate his attachment behavior, and he is now able to execute a plan
which will achieve these conditions in a goal-directed, or intentional, manner.
For example, the baby can now conceive of being in contact with mother even
though he is in a different room and can decide to execute a plan, e.g., locomotion, which will result in that contact. There is no implication here that the baby
has only one specific goal or plan with respect to his mother: indeed the particu-

lar goal, the particular plan employed to achieve the goal, and the particular environmental circumstances which will terminate his attachment behavior will all vary according to the situation, the state of the baby, and the quality of the relationship between mother and baby. In each case, however, the goal, and the plans for achieving that goal, should be specifiable.

One of the major ways in which the baby's plans may vary is in the extent to which they are designed to influence the behavior of his attachment figure. If mother and baby are in different rooms of the house, and the baby wants proximity, all he need do is locomote to mother. In this case there is no need to influence her behavior. However, if the mother is reading a book, or talking on the phone—and if the baby wants to be on her lap—his plan must include elements designed to make mother behave in a certain way.

Bowlby suggests that the baby's earliest goal-directed attempts to change the mother's behavior are quite primitive, e.g., pushing or pulling mother in certain directions, pulling the book off her lap. In other words, these early attempts consist of directly controlling the mother's behavior in a physical manner. As he continues to develop, he constructs more and more sophisticated means of affecting his mother's behavior, and in turn is able to be affected in more and more sophisticated ways by his mother's behavior. These new developments should further change the organization of the relationship between mother and baby.

It seems reasonable to suggest that one of these changes in sophistication should occur as the youngster develops the ability to (a) inhibit his goal-directed behavior, and (b) communicate his goals and plans verbally. Given that the young preschooler is developing more and more complex plans for achieving a particular goal, then as his language ability develops it should be possible for either mother or child to insert one of her/his own goals or plans into the goal and plan structure of the other (cf., MacKay, 1969). For example, should the child want to sit on the mother's lap while she is engaged in some activity, she could now tell her child that he can sit on her lap as soon as she is finished. If the child accepts this and temporarily inhibits his goal-directed behavior, what the mother has done in effect is to communicate or insert one of her own plans into her child's plan for contact. The child's plan now becomes: wait until mother is finished, and then climb on her lap. In effect, child and mother are now able to change one another's behavior indirectly by directly affecting each other's goal and plan structures through communication. Of course, in order for this tactic to be effective over the long run the mother must allow her child's plans to be carried to completion with some degree of consistency. For example, in this case she must allow him to sit on her lap when she is finished. This process can also be carried out in reverse, i.e., through communication the child can insert some plan or goal of his own in mother's plan or goal structure. Finally, this form of behavioral integration should apply not only to mother–child attachment behavior, but also to interaction in other contexts.

In order to assess this idea operationally, a sample of 16 children at each of ages 2, 3, and 4 years (48 children in all) was observed in two standardized situations, one of which is relevant to mother–child interaction in general and the other to attachment behavior specifically.[2]

The Cookie Test

The first, designed to assess the possibility of the mother's inserting one of her own plans into that of her child, was as follows: the mother showed her child a cookie and told him he could have it as soon as she finished writing a letter. She then placed the cookie out of the child's reach, but within his sight, and began writing the letter. She continued to do so for 3 minutes. During this period she was to handle her child's response in any way she wished. However, she was asked to wait until the period was over before allowing him to have the cookie. At a signal from the observer, the mother put down her pen and told her child he could have the cookie. The situation was conducted in the child's home, and was recorded on videotape. The tapes were then scored on the basis of the following behaviors of the children: crying; reaching for the cookie; interrupting the mother by vocalizing about the cookie or about not writing the letter; interrupting the mother through some physical intervention; discussing the contents of the letter with the mother; and otherwise occupying himself while the mother was writing.

Results and Discussion.   Almost all 2-year-olds in this situation attempted to get the cookie before the mother finished her letter. Within this age-group, 81% of the children displayed some combination of crying, attempting to reach the cookie, trying to interrupt the mother at her task by pushing her hand away from the paper, grabbing her pen, slapping at her, etc. The 3- and 4-year-olds, on the other hand, almost invariably accepted the situation immediately: only 25% of the 3-year-olds, and none of the 4-year-olds, displayed any of the behaviors typical of the 2-year-olds. The remainder of these older children either watched the mother write the letter, talked with her about it, or otherwise oc-cupied themselves and made no attempt to get the cookie until the mother indicated that she was through. While there were no significant differences between the 3- and 4-year-olds, the differences between the 2- and 3-year-olds were highly significant ($p < .01$, Fisher's Exact Test).

These results are interpreted as suggesting that in a somewhat extreme situation such as this (where the plan the mother is attempting to insert in her child's plan hierarchy is antithetical to the child's own), it is not until sometime between 2 and 3 years of age that children's communicative skills, and their ability to inhibit their goal-directed behavior, are integrated to the point where they can take on one of the mother's plans with no loss of composure. Another way of stating this is that the 3- and 4-year-olds are able to inhibit, or delay

[2]Most of the data reported in this paper were taken from the author's unpublished doctoral disserta-tion (Marvin, 1972). The analyses, however, are different.

executing, a particular plan until the appropriate circumstances obtain, these circumstances depending very much on the mother's behavior and being at least implicitly agreed upon by both mother and child. These results are also consistent with Bowlby's notion that some of the earliest attempts to change a mother's behavior will take the form of direct, physical control.

As stated earlier, this situation is not directly related to mother–child attachment. However, it is probable that interpersonal, social–cognitive skills like this one are generalized skills which can be applied in a wide range of contexts. Thus, if 3- and 4-year-old children are able to inhibit the execution of a plan in the sort of situation just described, and thereby incorporate one of the mother's plans or activities into their own plan for achieving a goal, then one might expect children of this same age to be able to inhibit their attachment behavior until they perceive that the appropriate circumstances exist.

The Strange Situation

In order to make the appropriate observations, this same sample of children was videotaped in Mary Ainsworth's "strange situation" (Ainsworth & Wittig, 1969). This is a standardized, 21-minute situation involving two brief separations between mother and child. It is composed of seven episodes, each 3 minutes long and presented in a single order. To determine how differential the child's attachment behavior is toward the mother *per se,* an adult female stranger is present during three of the episodes. The specific sequence of episodes is as follows:

Episode 1. Mother and child present. Child explores while mother sits in her chair.

Episode 2. Mother, child, and stranger present. Stranger speaks with mother and then interacts with child.

Episode 3. Child and stranger present. Mother leaves and stranger interacts with child, comforting him if necessary.

Episode 4. Mother and child present. Mother reenters, stranger leaves, mother responds to child's reunion behavior, reinterests child in toys, and returns to her chair.

Episode 5. Child present. Mother leaves and child is alone.

Episode 6. Child and stranger present. Stranger reenters and interacts with the child, consoling him if necessary.

Episode 7. Mother and child present. Mother reenters, stranger leaves, and mother behaves in the same manner as she did in Episode 4.

Only episodes 5 through 7 are analyzed in this chapter. Also, in this version, when the mother leaves in Episode 5 she says to her child, "I have to make a phone call; I'll be back." This statement was seen as being particularly important for this study because it informs the child of the mother's plan, which includes making a phone call and then returning. This provides the child with the opportunity to insert the mother's plan into his own plan for proximity. Furthermore, it affords the child the opportunity to demonstrate his ability to inhibit his goal-directed attachment behavior until the circumstances are appropriate to both mother and himself, i.e., until mother returns.

The behavior of mother, child, and stranger can be coded in many different ways. In this chapter, the data are discussed in terms of the incidence of children at each age displaying crying, sociable, and negative reactions to mother and stranger, and proximity-seeking toward the mother.

Crying. Each child was scored as crying or not crying during each episode. Crying was considered anything from fussing to hard and prolonged crying (in the latter cases, however, the episode was terminated).

Proximity seeking. Each child was scored as to whether or not he sought his mother's proximity during Episodes 5, 6, and 7. During Episodes 5 and 6, a child was scored as seeking his mother's proximity if he went to the door and tried to open it, or called his mother. During Episode 7, proximity-seeking was defined as making one or more full approaches to within arm's distance (or closer) to mother.

Rejecting and sociable behavior. A child was scored as responding negatively to the stranger if he displayed any angry, avoidant, or rejecting behaviors toward her. Specifically, the behaviors included were the following: refusing to respond to the stranger's vocalization, gaze averting when she attempted some interaction, locomotor withdrawal, refusing or batting down a toy she offered, rejecting contact with her, or vocalizing negatively toward her, e.g., telling her to leave, telling her that he doesn't want to play with her or do as she suggests, etc. Otherwise, the child was scored as being sociable.

Results and Discussion.[3]   Fifty-six percent of the 2- and 3-year-olds, and 44% of the 4-year-olds, cried when the mother left them alone in Episode 5. There were only slight differences in seeking the mother's proximity in this episode, with the older children tending to do so less than the younger ones. It is important to distinguish between those children who did and did not cry in this episode, since their subsequent behavior followed different patterns. When the stranger entered the room in Episode 6, 89% of the 2-year-old children who had been crying continued to cry, rejected the stranger, and continued to seek the mother's proximity. Of the 2-year-olds who did not cry in Episode 5, only one rejected the stranger. The remaining children played happily with her.

The 3- and 4-year-olds, on the other hand, responded differently. Sixty-seven percent of the 3-year-olds, and 86% of the 4-year-old children who cried when alone in Episode 5 ceased crying and played happily with the stranger in Episode 6. With one exception at each of these ages, those children who did not cry in Episode 5 also played well with the stranger. While the differences between the 2- and 3-year-olds was significant ($p = .024$, Fisher's Exact Test),

---

[3]A more detailed version of these results is contained in Marvin and Greenberg (in preparation).

among those who had cried in Episode 5, those between the 3- and 4-year-olds were not.

Two interpretations of this data can be made. First, the fact that many 3- and 4-year-olds cried when left alone in Episode 5, yet went on to play happily in Episode 6, suggests that it is important to distinguish between being separated from the mother and being left completely alone. Not surprisingly, it appears that being left alone in a novel setting such as this is upsetting to, or disturbs the equilibrium of, many preschoolers of all ages. It would be difficult to determine whether the behavior of a solitary child is organized toward regaining proximity to mother specifically, or whether he would be satisfied with proximity to a wider range of friendly conspecifics. Thus, it is probably not a good idea to use a child's response to being left alone as an index of his attachment to mother. A much better index is his behavior when with a friendly stranger versus his mother. This leads to the second interpretation of the data.

A number of children at all ages displayed no proximity-seeking toward their mothers while they were with the stranger in Episode 6, which suggests at first glance that whether or not they were upset by being left alone, their goal with respect to proximity to their mothers had not been disturbed. On the other hand, with one exception, those 2-year-olds who cried in Episode 5 rejected the stranger in Episode 6 and continued to seek proximity to their mothers. This suggests that these children's goals with respect to their mothers had been disturbed, and that they were unable to inhibit their attachment behavior either when alone or with a friendly stranger. On the other hand, the fact that most of the 3- and 4-year-olds played well with the stranger whether or not they had cried during Episode 5 suggests that either their goals with respect to their mothers had not been disturbed by their absences or once they were no longer alone they were able to inhibit their attachment behavior until the appropriate circumstances existed, i.e., their mothers' return. In order to determine which is the case, we must look at their behavior when their mothers returned.

When the mother returned in Episode 7, 63% of the 2-year-olds approached her (67% of those who had cried in Episode 5, and 57% of those who had not). Seventy-five percent of the 3-year-olds approached their mothers (equal percentages of those who had and had not cried), and 44% of the 4-year-olds approached them (86% of those who had cried, and 11% of those who had not). This further supports the interpretation that in the case of most 2-year-olds, their goal with respect to proximity with their mothers had been disturbed, and that they were unable to inhibit their attachment behavior while she was absent. They tended to be upset during any episode in which their mothers were not present, they rejected the stranger, and they actively sought their mothers' proximity when they returned.

In the case of the 3-year-olds, the fact that so many of them approached their mothers when they returned suggests that their goal with respect to proximity had also been disturbed. However, the fact that they played well with the stranger in Episode 6 and displayed attachment behavior only when their mothers returned suggests that, once no longer alone, they were indeed able to inhibit this system of behavior until the appropriate conditions existed for both the children themselves and for their mothers. Finally, the 4-year-olds also seemed able to inhibit their attachment behavior until their mothers returned. However, the fact that so many of the 4-year-olds who had cried in Episode 5 approached their mothers when they returned, and that with one exception those who had not cried did not approach her, suggests a further change in the organization of attachment behavior in these 4-year-olds.

To summarize thus far, I propose that in his development to this point, the youngster has progressed through two major phases in the development of attachment behavior.[4] First, as a young infant, his attachment behavior was elicited and terminated in a somewhat automatic fashion, with proximity to his mother being predictable outcome of his behavior (Bowlby, 1969). Then, sometime before his first birthday, his attachment behavior becomes goal-directed. He now possesses an internal, cognitive representation of a variable but specified degree of proximity or contact with his mother, and a set of behavioral plans which he can execute in order to achieve that state. We can say that from the child's point of view his relationship with his mother is now represented in physical-spatial-temporal terms. Comparing this model to the primate model that was presented earlier, this child has now made the transition from Infancy I to Infancy II. In Piaget's terms, the child is entering the preoperational period.

As the young preschooler continues to develop through this second period, his conceptual and communicative skills develop to the point where a new form of mother-child relationship is possible. Due to the child's increased communication skills, both mother and child are now able to communicate their respective goals and plans to one another, in effect sharing common goals and plans. In addition, the child's developing ability to inhibit his own goal-directed behavior allows his plans for achieving any particular goal to become increasingly complex. One form of this increasing complexity is that he can now intentionally take his mother's probable behavior into consideration before engaging in some activity, and can therefore treat her plans or behavior as an element in his own plan. He can now inhibit his attachment behavior until the circumstances conform to the plans and goals of both his mother and himself. His attachment behavior should thus become less intense and frequent generally, in that the proximity he desires is more integrated within the ongoing interaction, and ongoing plans and goals, of both mother and child. The two now share what Bowlby calls a partnership (Bowlby, 1969).

It is probably not useful to attempt to pinpoint a particular age at which this ability develops, since it almost certainly develops first in very simple contexts, and is gradually applied to increasingly complex and varied situations. In any event, the data from this study suggest that, for this sample in these two situations, the ability becomes functional sometime between 2 and 3 years of age.

[4]The first of these encompasses the first two phases in Bowlby's model (Bowlby, 1969).

Another important point is that this child's relationship with his mother is still represented in physical–spatial–temporal terms, and that separations which are not directly under his own control continue to disturb his goal-representation with respect to his mother. This is evidenced by the behavior of the 3-year-olds when their mothers returned in the last episode of the strange situation. The reason that this child doesn't become upset during many of these brief separations is that he is now able to inhibit his attempt to reinstate the goal (i.e., he is able to inhibit his attachment behavior) until such time and circumstances as are appropriate to both mother and child. Just how prolonged or extreme these circumstances can be must remain an unanswered question for the time being. However, the fact that so many 2½- and 3-year-old children are able to attend half-day nursery schools and play groups attests to the fact that the period of separation can extend to at least a few hours under the proper circumstances.

Further Changes in Mother–Child Attachment Behavior

This section considers what appears to be yet another phase in the development of attachment behavior during the later preschool years. The additional aspects of the model, and the data presented to support it, relate to the question of what happens to the human mother–child relationship as the need for relatively constant proximity continues to decline. Does the close relationship cease to exist at some point in the youngster's development? While this appears to be the case in many species of nonhuman primates, it is obviously not so in humans. Is any further change, then, merely one in which the child, now an older preschooler, is able to insert more and more complex elements of his mother's goal and plan structures in his own? Is he merely able to wait for longer and longer periods of time before executing his attachment behavior? Or does the organization of his attachment behavior change in a further, qualitative mannner such that interaction in proximity and contact are no longer the key to their relationship?

Most parents of school-age children will maintain that they now have a very different relationship with their child than they did when he was two or three years old (Marvin, 1972). This older child is able to withstand—and even initiates—separations of hours or days with little or no loss of security. In fact, proximity and contact are no longer the really important issues in the eyes of these parents. Other behaviors and characteristics of the child and of their relationship with the child now give the parent both joy and frustration. While reinforcement of these new behaviors may partially explain the context in which the change takes place, it is hardly an adequate description or explanation of the change itself. From the point of view of this study, the important questions are—how is this new relationship organized behaviorally, how does the child conceive of it, and what cognitive and communicative changes take place in the child to make this new relationship possible?

There has been very little empirical research on parent-child attachment in older preschoolers and school-age children. What little there is suggests that a major change takes place sometime around four years of age. For example, Shirley and Poyntz (1941), and Blurton Jones (1972) both report that the largest decline in amount of crying when children are introduced to nursery schools occurs about this age. Konner (1973), in his study of the Zhun-twa hunter-gatherers, points out that in that culture mothers and children maintain very close ties until three or four years of age, after which the child's ties seem to shift to a multiaged peer group. Eibl-Eibesfeldt (personal communication) has noticed the same in a number of cultures.

A central hypothesis in this chapter is that the mother-child relationship does undergo a specific qualitative change in the later preschool years, which can be operationalized, and which again involves changes in the child's cognitive abilities and in specific communicative skills. The change is most easily introduced by returning again to Bowlby's theory of the partnership.

In discussing how a child comes to learn that the best way to change his mother's behavior is to attempt to influence her goals and plans, Bowlby focuses primarily on a communicative skill which has received much attention in the developmental literature recently, i.e., the ability to see things from another person's perspective, or role- or perspective-taking (See Flavell, Botkin, Fry, Wright, & Jarvis, 1968, 1974; Shantz, 1975). Bowlby suggests that as the child grows older he begins to realize in an explicit fashion that his mother has goals and plans of her own, and that these may differ from his. Eventually, he will develop the necessary sophistication at inferring what his mother's goals and plans are to attempt to change them in a goal-directed fashion: to formulate a plan the explicit purpose of which is to change his mother's goal or plan.

While a two- or three-year-old child might have developed to the point where his mother is able to insert one of her own behavioral plans into her child's plan structure, this younger child is probably unable to conceive of his mother's plans as thoughts that occur in her mind. Presumably, he conceives of her plans as behaviors she engages in, rather than thoughts she possesses. At some point, however, the child is able to make these inferences about internal events on his mother's part. To develop to this point, the child must overcome a large degree of his egocentrism: his tendency to assimilate everyone's point of view to his own. As he loses his egocentrism and develops the ability to see things from others' points of view, his partnership with his mother, and his ability to cooperate in general, will become much more sophisticated.

This model, as far as Bowlby develops it, generates a number of hypotheses concerning the child's increasing ability to integrate his attachment behavior with his mother's goals and plans. For example, one would expect that as a child becomes able to see things from his mother's point of view he would become more skillful at assessing the likelihood that a specific plan for proximity would be successful. In addition, many of the plans and goals his mother attempts to implement would seem much less arbitrary to this child, since he could relate them more to his mother's ongoing point of view, rather than assimilating them to his own. However, the model has little or nothing to say concerning what happens to the overall mother–child relationship as the child's demands for proximity and contact continue to decline as he approaches and enters the school-age, or juvenile period. Still, the model holds the key to understanding this further change—and that key is the notion of perspective-taking, or the process of attributing internal, mental events to the mother.

Stated briefly, the idea is that whereas the young preschooler conceives of his relationship with his mother in terms of interaction within physical contact and proximity, the school-age child conceives of their relationship more in terms of internal perspectives. While the 1- or 2-year-old is able to maintain with his mother a balance or equilibrium of a physical nature in a goal-directed fashion, this older child is able to maintain an equilibrium of a much more abstract sort. This new equilibrium consists of shared ideas, values, attitudes, goals, and plans, and the shared or reciprocal control that these internal events have over each other's behavior. When this older child's goal is disturbed (i.e., when he perceives a mismatch between his perspective and his mother's), he will engage in behaviors designed to reestablish this new, more abstract match. In doing so he will engage in behavior or communication which will either bring his mother's perspective into balance with his, his own perspective into balance with mother's, or some combination of the two. What this amounts to is goal-directed cooperation. If this older child perceives a lack of cooperation in an area that is important to him, he will make an attempt to reestablish that cooperative balance. This is not to say that the young school-age child will be able to maintain a cooperative relationship with his mother in a very sophisticated manner. However, beginning in simple situations that are biologically and psychologically important to him, this ability will improve with experience.

The major implication of this model for further changes in mother–child attachment is the following. To the extent that a child is able to conceive of his relationship with his mother in these more abstract terms, he should be able to recognize that there is a relative invariant in their relationship that is not dependent on physical proximity or contact. In other words, if I know that you and I share common attitudes or plans, then I should be able to recognize that you and I have a definite, specifiable relationship whether we are in proximity or not. In fact, most adults would probably tell you that while they enjoy being in proximity with loved ones, the more valued part of their relationship is the shared internal events or qualities.

To return to the child, what is being proposed is that at some point the child assumes this more abstract balance or invariant as the goal in his relationship with his mother. If this child's mother leaves him in the strange situation, then to the extent that his primary goal is no longer that of physical proximity, his goal will not be disturbed. Therefore, he should display little or no attachment behavior either during his mother's absence or when she returns. On the other hand, should the child perceive his mother as not cooperating—as not playing her part in maintaining this more abstract relationship—then the child's goal (the more abstract goal) will be disturbed, and he should attempt to reassert the balance.

In order to support this idea, at least four questions must be answered. First, what communicative skills, or, more specifically, what perspective-taking skills, are necessary for this development? Second, can an empirical relationship be established between the development of those communicative skills and some measureable attenuation of attachment-behavior? Third, can patterns of behavior relevant to a close mother-child relationship be identified which would either be predicted by, or conform to, this proposed change? And fourth, in order to support the functional argument on which this entire presentation is based, can it be demonstrated that both of these changes take place at an age when children normally begin initiating extensive daily separations from their attachment figures?

To date, very few studies have been conducted that appear to be relevant to this proposed change. The next two sections of this chapter report data that have been collected on children's abilities to see things from their mothers' (and others') perspectives, and some patterns of behavior in the strange situation which are relevant to the proposed change.

The Early Development of Perspective Taking

There are at least four closely related perspective-taking skills that are especially pertinent to this developmental change. (a) The child must be able to recognize that his mother possesses these internal events; that his mother has thoughts, goal, mans, attitudes, values, etc. (b) He must be able to distinguish between his mother's point of view and his own: he must realize that their points of view are, or at least can be, different from one another. (c) He must be able to assess the degree of coordination between their respective points of view. That is, he must at least be able to tell when his mother's point of view is the same as, or different from, his own. (d) He must learn what factors influence his mother's point of view, and be able to influence that point of view in a goal-directed way.

Interestingly, when one reads the literature on the development of perspective-taking with an eye toward relating it to the attenuation of attachment behavior, he immediately encounters the following problem: the vast majority of studies on the development of this ability conclude that a child cannot engage in perspective-taking until he is between 6 and 8 years of age. This is the age at which Piaget says that children make the transition from the preoperational to the concrete operational periods. Yet it is obvious that children are able to spend hours at a time away from their attachment figures at least 2 or 3 years earlier. Recently however, John Flavell and his associates (e.g., Flavell, 1974) have presented data supporting the argument that children are able to conceive of another's perceptual point of view, i.e., what another person sees, hears, etc., by the time they are 3 or 4 years of age. But essentially no studies have been able to demonstrate that children are able to conceive of another's conceptual point of view, i.e., his thoughts, attitudes, plans, etc., before the age of 6 (e.g., Selman, 1971).

Based on the conviction that the tasks utilized to assess these abilities are much too complex and unrealistic for very young children, we have developed a number of tasks which are: (a) as simple as possible while still requiring the child to conceive of another's perspective in a nonegocentric fashion; and (b) designed to require the child to conceive of his mother's point of view rather than, or in addition to that of a total stranger. In the simplest task (the Birthday Game), the same sample of children who were observed in the strange situation were asked four questions of the following sort: (a) Which do you think your mommy would like for her birthday—a toy doll or a new dress? (b) Which do you think your mommy would like for her birthday—a picture for the wall or a new toy truck? In each case the child was given a binary choice, one choice appropriate for mother and the other for a child, and the order of presentation within each binary choice was randomized. A child's overall response was scored as egocentric if he chose the child-appropriate article in more than one case out of the four (Marvin, 1972).

In a more recent study, a sample of 80 children between the ages of 2½ and 6½ years was administered a number of conceptual perspective-taking tasks. Two of these tasks were also administered to the same sample that was earlier observed in the strange situation. A comparison of the results across the two samples yielded no differences, thus allowing generalizations to be made with some assurance across the two samples.

One of the tasks was a Secret Game in which mother, child, and a relatively strange experimenter participated (Marvin, Greenberg, & Mossler, 1976). The task was designed to assess the following abilities: (a) to conceive of the fact that each of the participants has an internal point of view; (b) that each of the participants' point of view is independent of those of the others; and (c) that, depending on the circumstances, each participant's point of view may be the same as, or different from, the point of view of each of the other two participants.

The game was as follows. Mother, child, and experimenter sat in a circle on the floor of the child's living room. In the middle of the circle were two toys. The experimenter hid his eyes while mother and child jointly thought of a single toy to have as their secret. Mother and child left the toy on the floor so the experimenter wouldn't know which one they picked. When they had chosen, the experimenter uncovered his eyes and asked the child the following questions: (a) "Do you know what the secret is?" (b) "Does Mommy know what the secret is?" (c) "Do I" (the experimenter) "know what the secret is?" (d) "Do you and Mommy have the same secret, or different secrets?" In case the child did not understand the meaning of the word "secret," he was also asked, "Do you know which toy you and Mommy are thinking of," etc. The game was repeated twice, so that each participant took a turn hiding his eyes. In each case the child was asked the same series of questions. Finally, the child's responses were scored according to whether he correctly inferred who did and did not know the secret in each case.

   Results.   In the Birthday Game, none of the 16 2-year-olds answered any of the questions in a nonegocentric fashion. They either did not understand what was expected of them, or they invariably responded with the child-appropriate article. Only 20% of the 3-year-olds were judged as nonegocentric, while 75% of the 4-year-olds were judged as nonegocentric. This difference was highly significant ($p = .003$; Fisher's Exact Test).

   The results of the Secret Game were essentially identical to those of the Birthday Game. Again, the 2-year-olds were generally unable to play the game. Those 2-year-olds who were able to play the game, and 85% of the 3-year-olds, thought that everyone knew the secret in all three versions. In the age-groups from 4 to 6½ years, at least 95% of all subjects had no trouble distinguishing who did and did not know the secret. The difference between the 3- and 4-year-olds was again highly significant ($X^2 = 60.32$, $df = 4$, $p < .001$). Finally, it was sometime between 4 and 5 years of age that the children were consistently correct in assessing whether or not the participants had the same secret (or perspective).

   These results were interpreted as indicating that between the ages of 3 and 5 years children develop the ability, in simple situations, to recognize that others have such internal events as thoughts and goals. They are also able to recognize the independence of a given person's internal perspective, and to recognize when two such perspectives are either similar or different. We have not yet developed a task designed to assess young children's abilities to influence other's points of view so as to bring them into line with the child's own.

   Thus, it appears that 4-year-old children possess at least most of the proposed skills underlying the ability to conceive of this more abstract relationship based on shared internal perspectives. The question that remains is whether or not these 4-year-olds display behavior in the strange situation which also supports the conclusion that they have formed this new relationship with their mothers.

Observations of Further Changes in Mother–Child Attachment Behavior

   From the performance of the four-year-olds on the perspective-taking tasks, it was expected that they would display little or no proximity-seeking behavior when their mothers returned. The actual results were quite unexpected. At least two distinct groups emerged within this age group. Consistent with the model presented above, one group made no attempt to seek their mothers' proximity. The other group sought their mothers' proximity, and maintained it, more than any other age group. This was most puzzling, so further study was made of the patterning of each child's behavior from the beginning of Episode 5, when his mother left the room, through Episode 7, when she returned. The detail and consistency within the two groups is quite compelling, in spite of the small sample.

As a mother departed after telling her child that she had to make a phone call and that she would be back, 7 of the 16 4-year-olds (Group I) said, "OK," "Unh-huh," or a similar comment of acceptance. As Figure 1 shows, none of

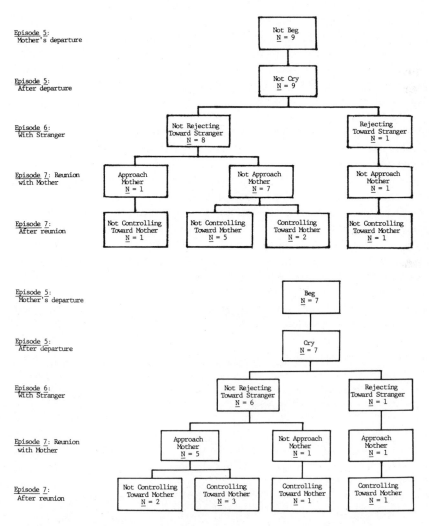

Fig. 1. Patterns of behavior in the strange situation: 4-year-olds — this figure includes the 4 children in Groups III and IV (see text).

these children cried when alone, and all but one played well with the stranger: only one of these children reacted in a negative or rejecting manner as defined earlier. When the mother returned in the last episode, one child approached her, hugged her quickly and happily, and then immediately returned to the toys. The other six greeted their mothers vocally but made no attempt to approach them. All seven then continued playing, occasionally talking to their mothers in a relaxed, happy manner.

Group II, consisting of five children, displayed the following sequence of behaviors. When the mother said that she was going to make a phone call and would be back, these five children immediately rushed to the door, asking their mothers to let them accompany them. Each mother refused. All five children then began to beg their mothers to let them go with her, saying such things as, "But there's no one here to stay with me!" or "But then I'll be alone!" or "Please let me go with you: I'll be good!" The mothers again refused to let the children come, stepped out of the room, and closed the door. All five children then cried while alone during Episode 6. Interestingly, their crying seemed quite different from that of the 2- and 3-year-olds. While no formal tests were conducted, it appeared to the observers and to many of the mothers that the crying of these children was more controlled and angry than apprehensive or scared. It seemed forced and purposeful.

When the stranger entered in Episode 6, all five immediately stopped crying, and four of the five played well with the stranger: only one of these children rejected the stranger. Finally, when the mothers returned in the last episode, four of the five children approached them and remained in their proximity for some time. All five children, whether they approached or not, then engaged in a very curious sort of behavior. All five became very insistent toward their mothers, making demands that seemed quite out of context, and making them repeatedly in spite of the mother's insistence that she could not fulfill them at the moment. Moreover, all five children continued to make them in an exaggerated tone of voice, whining and fussing the entire time. The following is an example from one of the transcripts:

> (First of all, this child approached mother as soon as she entered the room. Mother sat in her chair and the child followed her and stood right in front of her. During the ensuing interchange the child climbed on mother's lap, stretched out in what appeared to be a very uncomfortable position, and continued talking to mother. The course of the conversation went as follows):

> C   "I want a glass of water!"
> M   "Pretty soon, as soon as we leave."
> C   "I want it now!"
> M   "They don't have any water in here."
> C   "Yes they dooo!" (It was quite obvious that we didn't.)
> M   "Well, you can have some as soon as we leave."
> C   "Noooooo, now!"
> M   "We can't just go wandering around this building looking for water."
> C   "But I need a drink of waterrr!"

C   "I want to get up on you."
M   "But look at all the toys to play with."
C   "But I want to get up on you! Help me!" (Mother helps her child up at this point.)
M   "OK, you can sit on my lap."
C   "No, I wanna glass of water!"
M   "You can have some as soon as we leave: it'll only be a minute."
C   "I want some beer!"
M   "Beer?! Beer isn't for little girls."
C   "Yes, it is!"
M   "No, it isn't."
C   "Yes, it is!"
M   "No, it isn't."
C   "Yes, it is!"

At this point the situation was terminated. While this example is somewhat more extreme than the other four, it does illustrate the sort of interaction that took place in all five cases.

Due to the small sample size, a relatively simple statistical technique was employed to determine whether these two, very different patterns of behavior can be considered independent of one another. First, each child's sequence of behaviors was divided into five segments, each of which had one of two possibilities. Then Fisher's Exact Test was computed for the relationship between the first segment and each of the remaining four. The segments were defined in terms of the presence or absence of the following behaviors: (a) begging when the mother left the room; (b) crying while alone in Episode 5; (c) rejecting the stranger during Episode 6; (d) approaching the mother in Episode 7; and (e) engaging in the demanding, controlling behavior described above.

As Table I indicates, the differences are significant in all but the relationship between begging and whether or not the child displayed rejecting behavior toward the stranger in Episode 6. Here, there appears to be no difference whatsoever. Thus, with this one exception, the two groups appear to be truly independent of one another in their patterns of behavior.

These two groups account for 12 of the 16 4-year-olds. The remaining 4 children fell into two more groups, each containing 2 children who displayed similar patterns of behavior across these three episodes. The 2 children in Group III also ran to the door and begged their mothers to let them accompany them. In each case, the mother immediately interrupted her child before he or she could finish the plea. In one case the mother merely left and closed the door; in the other case the mother diverted her child's attention to a toy and then left. Neither of these children rejected the stranger in Episode 6. When the mother returned in Episode 7 each child approached her, remained in her proximity for a few moments, and then returned happily to the toys. Neither displayed the demanding behavior toward the mother which was characteristic of Group II.

Group IV, also consisting of two children, displayed absolutely no response when their mothers left them alone in Episode 5. They continued playing with the toys, neither looking at their mothers nor saying anything. When the stranger

Table I. Sequential Behavior Patterns of 4-Year-Olds in Strange Situation[a]

		Episode 5		
		Beg	Not beg	
Episode 5	Cry	7	0	$p < .001$
	Not cry	0	9	
Episode 6	Reject stranger	1	1	$p = .525$
	Not reject stranger	6	8	
Episode 7	Approach mother	6	1	$p < .001$
	Not approach mother	1	8	
Episode 7	Controlling toward mother	5	2	$p < .05$[b]
	Not controlling toward mother	2	7	

[a]Computed by Fisher's Exact Test.
[b]Fisher's Exact Test, with Tocher's modification (Siegel, 1956).

entered in Episode 6, neither child rejected her. Finally, when the mother returned in the final episode neither child approached her. In fact, both children completely ignored her: neither looking at her nor talking to her.

Before discussing these results one final question must be answered. Specifically, if the behavior of the 4-year-olds in the perspective-taking tasks and in the strange situation is truly indicative of this new relationship with the mother, then the behavior patterns that were displayed by the first two groups of 4-year-olds in the strange situation should not have been displayed by many of the three-year-olds. As Figure 2 indicates, this appears to be the case.

Two of the 3-year-olds said, "OK," when the mother left the room. Neither rejected the stranger or displayed the controlling behavior toward the mother when she returned. However, both children approached the mother when she returned, and maintained that proximity for a period of time. With one exception, the 4-year-olds who said, "OK," did not approach their mothers.

Five of the 3-year-old children begged their mothers to let them go with her. Similar to the 4-year-olds, four of these children played happily with the stranger in the next episode. However, unlike the 4-year-olds, these children were not consistent either in whether or not they approached the mother when she returned, or in whether or not they displayed the controlling behavior. Three of the five approached mother, and one displayed controlling behavior. However, none of the five displayed the combination of approach and controlling behavior characteristic of the second group of 4-year-olds.

The modal response of the 3-year-olds was to display no response to the mother's departure other than looking at her as she left, and continuing to look at the door for a moment after she had left. Seven 3-year-olds displayed this pattern. Two of these children then cried while they were alone in Episode 5, and two rejected the stranger when she entered. The remaining children in this group played happily with the stranger. Five approached their mothers when they returned, one withdrew from her briefly, and none displayed controlling behavior toward her. In summary, no 3-year-olds displayed the patterns of behavior characteristic of the first two groups of 4-year-olds.

Discussion. The behavioral patterns of the first two groups of 4-year-olds conforms closely to the proposal that was presented earlier. In fact, the results support that proposal more than if none of the 4-year-olds had sought the mother's proximity in the final episode. Based on the results of the perspective-

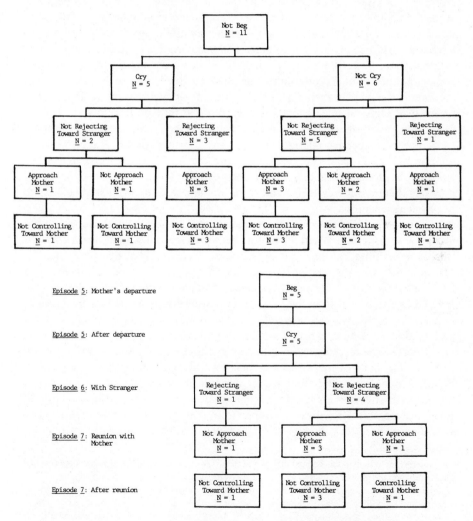

Fig. 2. Patterns of behavior in the strange situation: 3-year-olds.

taking tasks, we begin by assuming that the 4-year-olds have developed the ability to maintain a more abstract relationship with their mothers which is based on a goal-directed, cooperative balance of internal perspectives and reciprocal control of behavior. The difference between Groups I and II can then be explained in the following manner.

When a mother left the room after telling her child that she would return, the children in the Group I said "OK," and did not cry while alone. This suggests that their goals with respect to their mothers were not disturbed. It also indicates that being alone in this situation did not upset their equilibrium. These children then played happily with the stranger when she entered. When their mothers returned in Episode 7, these children neither sought their proximity, nor engaged in any controlling behavior. Instead, they continued to play happily. This conforms to the proposal because it is only when a child's goal with respect to the mother is disturbed that he should engage in behavior that is designed to reestablish that state. Since they neither cried while they were alone with the stranger nor sought their mothers' proximity when they returned, we can presume that the predominating goal in their relationships with their mothers are no longer represented in physical-spatial terms. Assuming that they do have a goal in their relationships with their mothers, the facts that (a) they performed nonegocentrically on the perspective-taking tasks, and (b) no aspect of the strange situation appeared to upset them, are consistent with the idea that their goal is a more abstract one, based on shared internal perspectives. Only with such a goal could they feel that their relationships with their mothers remained undisturbed in spite of physical separation.

For the children in Group II, it appears that some goal with respect to the mother was disturbed. When the mother started to leave the room, these children tried in a goal-directed way to alter her plans. Every child in this group tried to reason with his or her mother, stating the reasons why he wanted to come with her, and some even tried to make a cooperative agreement with her. From what the children said, and from the fact that they were happy as soon as the stranger entered the room, we can conclude that what upset their equilibrium was the anticipation of being alone, rather than separation from mother *per se*.

Because the mothers had been instructed that their children were to remain in the room, none of them allowed their own plans to conform to the goals of their children. Thus, the mothers had temporarily disturbed the equilibrium— the balance—between their own internal points of view and those of their children. In fact, in their refusal to cooperate in coming to some resolution of this goal-disturbance, they had even undermined the very process by which the equilibrium is maintained.[5]

[5]It is interesting to note in this context that two of the 4-year-olds in Group I had initially approached the door when the mother started to leave, and asked the mother to allow them to go with her. These mothers leaned over, explained their reason for leaving in more detail, and asked their children if they would be willing to stay in the room. The children both paused for a moment, said "OK," returned to the toys, and subsequently displayed the same pattern of behavior as the remainder of the first group. It appeared that these mother–child pairs had established a cooperative balance—or equilibrium—on the spot.

This would seem to be very arbitrary or unreasonable behavior from the point of view of a child who is able to maintain such an equilibrium in a goal-directed manner, and in fact some of these children appeared angry.

Thus, the crying displayed by this group of 4-year-olds is attributed to the apparently arbitrary manner in which the mother left. The stranger's entrance in the next episode reestablished that part of the equilibrium related to being in the company of another person, and the children returned happily to the toys. However, the disequilibrium induced by the mother's lack of cooperation related specifically to the mother herself, and was not corrected by the stranger's entrance. Therefore, when the mother entered the room again in the final episode, the child approached her in a very controlling fashion. The model presented earlier would suggest that these children were trying to reestablish the equilibrium which the mother had previously disturbed. This attempt took the form of engaging in behavior which itself was overly controlling. It is important to note that in every case the children displayed behavior which predictably functions to indirectly control another person's behavior by directly influencing his goal and plan structures.

The behavior patterns of the children in Groups III and IV are not as readily explained by the model presented. The two children who asked their mothers to let them accompany them and were interrupted cried briefly while alone, played happily with the stranger, and then approached their mothers after they returned in the final episode, without, however, engaging in controlling behavior toward them. Perhaps these two children merely were not as upset by being alone as those in the second group. Perhaps they were secure enough in this more abstract relationship with their mothers that their goal in the relationship was not disturbed by the mother's lack of cooperation in this instance, i.e., they were willing to change their own plans to fit their mothers'. Or perhaps the mothers' interruption functioned to curtail their attempts to establish a cooperative agreement at such an early stage in the process that the children did not perceive their mothers as being unfair. Whatever the reason, basing a conclusion on the behavior of two children would be premature, and further observations are obviously necessary. The same is true for the two children who made *no* response when their mothers left.

Summary and Conclusions

In this study, the behavior of 2-, 3-, and 4-year-old children was observed in contexts relevant to their attachment relationship with their mothers. Three ideas served as the basis for the study: (a) Social relationships can be defined and understood in terms of the communicative acts which structure those relationships (e.g., Altmann, 1965; Carpenter, 1964). (b) Ontogenetic changes in the relationship between two or more individuals can be described and understood in terms of changes in the communicative skills of the individuals, and in terms of the conceptual structures which underly those skills. (c) By observing the conditions which activate and terminate an individual's communicative and other behavioral acts within a relationship, one is able to specify the equilibrial state which one or both individuals are attempting to maintain in a goal-directed manner *vis-a-vis* one another.

An extension of Bowlby's (1969) model of infant-mother attachment was presented to map postinfancy changes in the mother-child relationship. Data relevant to this model was obtained from a sample of 2-, 3-, and 4-year-old children in three situations: the Cookie Test, the Strange Situation, and a number of perspective-taking tasks.

The model expands Bowlby's theory of stages in the development of attachment. Specifically, it focuses on Bowlby's fourth stage, i.e., the partnership, and divides it into two distinct substages. After the baby's attachment behavior becomes goal-directed and he begins constructing plans for achieving proximity and contact (Bowlby's Phase III), he will also begin constructing plans the purpose of which is to change his mother's behavior in a way which will allow him to terminate his attachment behavior. As the child's language skills develop and he becomes able to inhibit his goal-directed behavior (Phase IV), both mother and child will be come able to communicate their plans and goals to one another, in effect inserting those goals and plans into each other's goal and plan structures. As a result, both mother and child will now be able to inhibit their goal-directed behavior until the circumstances are appropriate for both. This increased behavioral integration constitutes the beginning of what Bowlby calls the "partnership."

As with Ainsworth's 1-year-olds, the 2-year-olds in this sample appeared not to have reached this phase. These children tended to interrupt the mother as she was writing her letter during the Cookie Test, and were unable or unwilling to wait until she was through before obtaining the cookie. Of this same group, those who were upset when the mother left the room in the strange situation tended to reject the stranger and continue executing their attachment behavior until the mother returned and the circumstances existed for the termination of that behavior. Thus, these 2-year-olds appeared to be unable to delay or inhibit the execution of their goal-directed behavior in contexts relevant to both their attachment to the mother and at least one other situation not directly related to this system of behavior. They appeared unable to incorporate one of the mother's verbally stated plans into their own plan for action, thus demonstrating an inability to carry out one of the most basic functional forms of human communication and behavioral integration. Finally, the fact that so many of these children rejected the stranger and continued to seek the mother's proximity suggests, as with 1-year-olds, that their goal in their relationship with their mothers is still represented conceptually in terms of proximity and contact.

The 3-year-olds behaved quite differently. They were not at all upset during the cookie test, and were quite willing to wait until their mothers had finished writing their letters. In the strange situation, they were quite content as long as they were not alone. The fact that they did not continue to seek their mothers' proximity while the stranger was present, along with their behavior in the cookie test, suggests that these 3-year-olds were able to inhibit their goal-directed behavior and incorporate one of the mother's plans into their own. This is consistent with evidence suggesting that only toward the end of the preschool years do children achieve the neurological maturity required to inhibit ongoing behavior to the point where they can consider factors which are not immediately present (Bronson, 1965; Bowlby, 1969).

An important point related to the above is that the 3-year-old's goal in his relationship with his mother remains basically the same as that of one- and two-year-old children. He still conceives of his mother in physical-spatial-temporal terms, and his goal remains one of interaction within some specified degree of proximity or contact. Thus, separations which are not of his own initiative continue to disturb his equilibrium, and while he may not be especially upset, that equilibrium will not be completely regained until he has again achieved some specified degree of proximity. This idea is supported by the fact that while the three-year-olds tended not to seek the mother's proximity while alone with the stranger, they did tend to do so as soon as she returned. It is also supported by the fact that they were generally unable to perform nonegocentrically on the perspective-taking tasks, suggesting that they do not yet have one of the skills most basic to the next phase.

The next major change in the mother–child attachment relationship (Phase V) comes at that point when the child is able to conceive of the mother's internal point of view. The realization that mother has her own thoughts, goals, and plans, which are independent of his own, yet which have a certain degree of match or mismatch with respect to his own, opens up a whole new world in terms of the child's conception of his relationship with her. The realization that he and his mother share the same (or complementary) goals or plans allows the child to conceive of a relationship with his mother which is not dependent on physical proximity; a relationship that endures and can be maintained whether they are together or apart. Beginning in relatively simple situations, this older child will be able to construct plans to maintain some cooperative balance in terms of both internal perspectives and reciprocal control of behavior. To the extent that this child maintains a more abstract relationship of this sort in a goal-directed manner, his equilibrium should not be disturbed by physical separation from his mother. This development accounts for both a major, further attenuation of the child's proximity-seeking behavior, and a relationship with his mother which is increasingly based on cooperation and consideration for each other's feelings, goals, and plans.

However, in a manner which is formally similar to the 1-year-old's goal-directed proximity-seeking behavior, this older child should become upset if he perceives this more abstract relationship as not being maintained; if he perceives either a mismatch between his perspective and his mother's, or an imbalance in the control of the relationship. If such a mismatch occurs, this older child will execute a behavioral plan to reestablish that match. This plan could include many different sorts of behavior, including motor or communicative acts which predictably function to bring his and his mother's internal perspectives back into balance, or perhaps he may even revert, or regress, to the use of proximity-seeking behaviors. These behaviors will be executed until such conditions exist which allow the child to perceive a match between his goal representation and the real, perceived relationship between his mother and himself.

The behavior of the four-year-olds in the three situations offers convergent support for the conclusion that they do seem to have the prerequisite skills required for this more abstract relationship with their mothers. Similarly to the 3-year-olds, the 4-year-olds were quite willing to wait until the mother had finished her letter before attempting to obtain the cookie. They were also content in the strange situation as long as they were not alone. However, their performance on the perspective-taking tasks and their rather unexpected behavior in the strange situation both suggest a major difference between them and the younger children.

Almost all of the 4-year-olds performed nonegocentrically on the perspective-taking tasks. This indicates that they have at least most of the cognitive skills underlying the proposed new relationship with the mother. In the strange situation, this age group was characterized by two major patterns of behavior. The children in the first group consented to the mother's departure and played happily while alone. They continued to play happily when the stranger entered, and when the mother returned in the final episode, they greeted her casually and continued playing without approaching her. This pattern is consistent with the proposed Phase V in that the lack of goal-directed behavior when the mother returned indicates that their goal with respect to her had not been disturbed by her departure. Assuming that they do have a goal in their relationship with the mother, the conclusion is that it is not dependent on physical proximity or contact. Their performance on the perspective-taking tasks constitutes convergent evidence that their goal is based on, or represented in terms of, internal perspectives and the effects of these perspectives on behavior.

The proposal is supported even more by the second group of 4-year-olds. As the mother left, these children ran to the door, asking the mother to let them accompany her. When the mother refused, these children attempted further to affect the mother's plan by stating reasons why they wanted to accompany her, promising good behavior on their own part in exchange for being allowed to go, etc. In other words, these children attempted in a goal-directed manner to change some aspect of the mother's internal perspective, i.e., her plan. When the mother rejected this attempt and departed, these children became upset. Similarly to the first group of 4-year-olds, they played happily with the stranger when she entered the room, and did not reject her.

When the mother returned in the final episode, these children behaved very differently from those in the first group. Most approached the mother, and all engaged in exaggerated verbal behavior which appeared controlling and, at first glance, rather inappropriate to the circumstances. In each case, the behavior appeared designed to change either the mother's point of view, or her behavior, as they related to the child himself. It appeared that these children were attempting in a goal-directed manner to establish some control over the mother's behavior, with no willingness to cooperate or compromise. This behavior is consistent with the notion that these children were attempting to reestablish the balance in control which the mother had earlier upset by her apparently arbitrary mode of departure.[6] Presumably, this attempt could only be possible with a child who is able to conceive of the integration or balance between the internal perspectives and the reciprocal control of behavior characteristic of a continuing relationship.

In terms of the issues raised, this study is obviously only a beginning: much more research will have to be conducted before the value of the approach can really be assessed. The results of the study suggest a number of questions which should be answered in assessing the proposed model. In the case of some of these questions, the model (or qualifications of it) suggests certain hypotheses to be tested.

1. It was suggested above that after the mother returned in the final episode, the second group of 4-year-olds attempted to reestablish the balance in control which the mother had upset by her mode of departure. In order to demonstrate that a given behavior pattern is a goal-directed attempt to achieve some outcome, it is necessary to show that the behavior terminates, or ceases, when that outcome is in fact achieved. In this case it would be interesting to see if those children whose mothers allow them to assume this control do stop the behavior after a short period of time, whereas those children whose mothers do not allow them to assume the control do not stop the behavior (or that they switch to some other means of control). While this suggestion did seem to apply in a couple of cases from this sample, the final episode was probably too short, and the mother's behavior too constrained, to allow the question to be answered from this data. In any case, this question cannot be answered merely by looking for certain behaviors on the child's part. It can only be answered by considering the child's behavior in the context of the mother's behavior: the basic unit of analysis must be the relationship, not the individual.

2. The most important proposal in this study is that sometime in the later preschool years children develop a new relationship with their mothers which is based on a balance, or integration, of internal perspectives. While this balance is maintained, the child should feel secure, or be in a state of equilibrium. Should the balance be disturbed, the child should try in a goal-directed way to reestablish it.

What is needed to fully assess this proposal is information on just what classes of circumstances constitute both a balance and a disruption of the balance

[6]Note the formal similarity between this behavior and the exaggerated proximity-seeking, clinging, etc., of many 1- and 2-year-olds when their mothers return in the last episode.

in this relationship. In this chapter, the emphasis has been on shared perspectives as constituting the balance. However, this has been largely a matter of convenience: There are numerous ways in which two perspectives can be in harmony. In some cases, the harmony consists of identical perspectives; in some, it consists of complementary perspectives; and in others, it consists of opposite perspectives. Just what circumstances constitute a balance or disruption (or, in terms of the child's goal-representation, a match or mismatch) is an empirical question which can be answered on the basis of the conditions which disturb or reestablish his security, or equilibrium.

Exactly the same argument applies to the plans the child executes in order to reestablish that equilibrium. We need to identify the classes of behavior the child employs as means to this end, and the conditions under which he selects one behavior over another. The situation used in this study permitted a very narrow range of behaviors to emerge: in his day-to-day relationship with his mother, the child certainly displays a much wider range of such behavior patterns, and also displays developmental and individual differences. Identifying the circumstances which constitute this balance, and the plans employed to achieve it, would be a difficult task requiring much observation and experimentation. However, it is in principle no more difficult than identifying the plans and goal-states in the 1-year-old's relationship with his mother. In fact, many of the same approaches to answering these questions can be used at both developmental points.

3.   Related to the two questions that have already been discussed is a third which concerns any student of cognitive development, especially those working within a Piagetian framework. Specifically, it is assumed that if a child is able to work in a goal-directed way toward some end, or is able to conceive of some relationship between himself and his social and/or physical environment, then he must have some identifiable cognitive structure, or scheme, for that relationship. This implies that the 4-year-old children in this sample must have some cognitive scheme corresponding to their newly developed relationships with their mothers. Furthermore, this scheme should not be restricted to this specific relationship, but should be a generalized structure applicable to various concrete versions of the relationship.

To my knowledge there is no published research relevant to such a scheme: Nearly all of the research on this age-range concentrates on what the child cannot conceive of. However, it seems that the basis for this scheme would be the ability to represent the fact that any two individuals or processes which interact with one another are going to have an ongoing, reciprocal effect on one another, resulting in a state that is independent of either one of the individual processes considered by itself. A scheme of this sort would be a true, albeit simple, "operatory scheme" (Inhelder & Piaget, 1958), in that two individual, internal operations would be coordinated through reversibility by reciprocity. A further discussion of this proposed scheme, of its relationship to mother–child attachment, and of a Piagetian-type task designed to assess the child's ability to apply this scheme to the relationship between physical objects, is presented elsewhere (Marvin, 1973).

4. This chapter has proposed in a number of places that as the child becomes able to conceive of a relationship with his mother which is based on a balance of internal perspectives, he should realize that there is an invariant to the relationship which is independent of physical proximity. It proposed that as the child takes this more abstract invariant as the goal in his relationship with his mother, physical separations from her should not disturb his equilibrium.

In fact, this is almost certainly an oversimplified statement of the change. The model should not be interpreted as suggesting that once a child develops to this point, he will no longer require any physical proximity to his mother. It is meant to imply that physical proximity becomes less important, relative to a balance or integration of goals, plans, attitudes, etc. At the same time proximity will certainly remain an important part of this loving relationship, as is true with all close, emotional relationships. In the first place, even this more abstract relationship cannot be maintained over very lengthy periods of time without occasional periods of proximity in which the partners communicate with one another and realign their perspectives. In situations where the child does not perceive a match between his perspective and his mother's, it is highly likely that he will fall back on the security he knows he can obtain from physical proximity and contact. Finally, physical proximity and contact are enjoyable at all ages, not merely for the security they offer, but also for the simple pleasures involved. This suggests that the goal of proximity and contact will not disappear; rather, it remains part of the relationship while taking on some (perhaps subordinate) relationship with the goal of integrated perspectives. As psychoanalysts have always recognized, attachment behavior remains important throughout the lifetime of the individual.

5. Another way in which the model, as presented, requires qualification concerns the nature of the transition from the phases in which physical proximity is the child's major goal to that in which some relationship between internal perspectives is his major goal. As presented, the model is not meant to imply that this new relationship emerges suddenly, in mature form, at 4 years of age. Rather, it is more likely that by 4 years the child has developed the skills most basic to this new relationship, and that at this point he can apply these skills in relatively simple and familiar contexts. Then, over the next few years, the skills, and the relationship, become increasingly extended, consolidated, and mature. Flavell (1971) has examined the implications of a similar model for cognitive development in general.

6. One particularly important series of questions concerning this proposed new relationship between mother and child is the following: just what is this relationship which Bowlby calls the partnership. Is it something in the relationship between mother and child, something in the child himself, or merely something in the mind of the observer. Should we continue to refer to this new

relationship as an attachment, or should we reserve this term for the early mother-child relationship which is based on behavior promoting physical proximity and contact?

My point of view is that the construct of a partnership, as with all scientific constructs, is first and foremost a construct in the mind of the observer. However, with continued research the construct should come continuously closer to accurately representing some phenomenon in the real world. As discussed in Bowlby (1969) and in this chapter, the term partnership refers to an enduring relationship between two individuals, characterized by mutual adjustment of goal and plan hierarchies (Miller *et al.*, 1960) such that over a period of time there is an integration and balance of these hierarchies, and of the control of behavior, which is satisfactory to both individuals in the relationship. This mutual adjustment is normally accomplished through communicating or inferring each other's perspectives, and executing plans the purpose of which is to bring those perspectives (and the behavior controlled by those perspectives) into some specified relationship with one another.

While the partnership is thus something that exists in the relationship between mother and child, the child (as with the scientist) comes eventually to represent it internally in the same way he comes to represent other knowing relationships between himself and his environment. Therefore the partnership, in some sense, also becomes something internal to the child. However, this should not be interpreted as implying that the partnership becomes a trait in the child, as some have mistakenly interpreted Bowlby and Ainsworth's notion of attachment in infancy (e.g., Maccoby and Masters, 1970). It is no more a trait than is the infant's knowledge of the permanent object (Piaget, 1952).

The question as to whether or not the partnership should be considered an attachment is more difficult. Certainly it is part of the close, loving relationship between mother and child, and therefore could be considered an attachment. However, the term attachment has come to refer to a relationship that is based on physical proximity and contact, and since the partnership refers to a relationship that is based on a balance of internal perspectives, perhaps the two should be considered as being in some sense independent. Bowlby integrates these two arguments by stating that:

> . . . the capacity to form partnerships is to be considered as a general purpose skill, like walking or talking, and is thus not comparable in kind to attachment behavior. Appropriate questions are whether or not attachment behavior is, in a particular child, organized in terms of a partnership, and whether or not the skill can be developed except within the context of an attachment relationship (Bowlby, personal communication).

This "general purpose skill" is the human version of cooperation, and its application in the mother–child relationship is only one of many. For example, children form partnerships with peers as they begin to integrate their play in terms of roles (Iwanaga, 1973), and as they form dominance hierarchies (Omark

& Edelman, in press). At the same time, the partnership between parent and child is probably the first, and certainly one of the most emotion-laden of all partnerships. Perhaps it would be appropriate, as Bowlby is suggesting, to consider the mother–child partnership as in some sense a subset of attachment in older preschoolers, rather than equating it with attachment.

In concluding, perhaps the most important implication of this study concerns our basic orientation toward developmental changes in any behavior system: are these changes to be conceived of in terms of changing frequencies in individual behaviors, or as changes in the organization of complex systems? With respect to mother–child attachment behavior specifically, the question is even more basic: Do mother and child gradually become less and less attached, with the child and mother displaying decreasing frequencies of attachment behavior, or would it be more useful to conceive of their relationship as continuing (and perhaps becoming even closer in some sense), while at the same time undergoing significant qualitative changes? The point of view taken in this chapter is that the most important changes in this relationship are of an organizational or qualitative nature, and that without this orientation we will miss the essence of both the relationship and changes in it.

The child, as with any other biological organism, is seen as a complex system consisting of a number of subsystems with relationships among them. These subsystems interact in a way that compensates for disturbances to the system, and ensures certain outcomes, invariants, or points of equilibrium necessary to the organism's survival (Ashby, 1952; Bowlby, 1969). In turn, the child is structured within a larger system consisting of the child, his mother, and the relationships between them. The parts of this larger system also interact in a way which maintains these biologically necessary invariants. Bowlby bases his theory of mother-infant attachment on one such necessary outcome, i.e., the physical proximity and contact between mother and infant, which fulfills the biological function of protecting the infant. To understand this system at either of these levels, it is not adequate merely to describe frequencies of behaviors, and the contexts in which these behaviors are displayed. Rather, it is necessary to describe each part of the system and the relationships among them. It is necessary to describe the behavior of various subsystems of the child, the behavior of both mother and child, the conditions which activate and terminate the behavior of each, the behavioral outcomes which constitute the invariants or points of equilibrium, and the conditions under which the behavior of one part of the system compensates for a disturbance to that or another part. Thus, the relationships between mother and child, or between parts of the child (e.g., his attachment behavior and his communication skills) become just as important as the parts themselves.

The same framework can be extended to include changes in the mother–child relationship which are initiated by developmental changes in the child himself. Given the above, it follows that developmental changes will consist of coincidental and functionally related changes in numerous parts of the child himself, and in numerous parts of the mother-child relationship. At the same time, these changes will be organized in a way that continues to maintain the biologically necessary invariants.

Now, assuming that at some point during his childhood the youngster begins spending a predominant proportion of his time among peers out of physical proximity of his mother, there are at least two important implications of this framework. First, since the mother can no longer play the major role in protecting the child, this responsibility must be assumed by the child himself, and by his integration within his peer group and the larger social structure. Second, it implies that numerous changes must take place within the child himself, and that they must take place in specific ways which ensure that the child will be able to assume this responsibility. In other words, as the child's attachment behavior changes developmentally, other changes must take place which compensate for, or complement, that change so the biological necessity of protection is maintained. There are certainly many such complementary changes, and the results of this study conform to the hypothesis that one important area of change is the child's communication skills. That this complementary relationship may have roots deep in our evolutionary past is suggested by Goodall's discussion of the role which the mother chimpanzee plays in the development of her infant:

> Finally, she protects . . . [her infant] from social encounters with other individuals until it is able to react correctly to the various expressive calls and movements of the adult (Lawick-Goodall, 1968, p. 235).

Thus, however correct or incorrect the model presented in this paper may be, what is absolutely necessary is that we approach this changing mother–child relationship from the point of view of a complex system undergoing qualitative changes which interact with each other in a way that continues to maintain certain functions necessary for the child's survival. Only in this way will we develop a theory which reflects at the same time both the complexity of the developing child, and his biological and psychological continuity.

ACKNOWLEDGMENTS

The research reported in this chapter was supported by the following grants: USPHS-5 TO1-MH08502, HEW USOE-S/C NPECE-70-002, and NIMH 1-RO3-MH25815-01. The author wishes to thank the following individuals for their helpful comments, criticisms, and assistance during various phases of this project: Mary D. S. Ainsworth, Mark T. Greenberg, Cherri N. Marvin, Elizabeth A. Bates, and Mark H. Bickard. This chapter is an extension of a paper presented at the Erindale Symposium on Communication and Affect, Toronto, March 1975.

References

Ainsworth, M. D. S. *Infancy in Uganda: Infant care and the growth of love*. Baltimore: Johns Hopkins University Press, 1967.

Ainsworth, M. D. S. Object relations, dependency and attachment: a theoretical review of the mother-child relationship. *Child Development*, 1969, **40**, 969–1025.

Ainsworth, M. D., & Wittig, B. A. Attachment and exploratory behavior of one-year-olds in a strange situation. In B. M. Foss (Ed.), *Determinants of infant behavior*, Vol. 4. New York: Wiley, 1969.

Altmann, S. A. Sociobiology of rhesus monkeys. II: Stochastics of social communication. *Journal of Theoretical Biology*, 1965, **8** 490–522.

Anderson, J. W. Attachment behaviour out of doors. In N. Blurton Jones (Ed.), *Ethological studies of child behaviour*. London: Cambridge University Press, 1972.

Ashby, W. R. *Design for a brain*. New York: Wiley, 1952.

Bell, S. M. V. The development of the concept of the object as related to infant-mother attachment. *Child Development*, 1970, **40**, 291–311.

Blurton Jones, N. Categories of child-child interaction. In N. Blurton Jones (Ed.), *Ethological studies of child behaviour*. London: Cambridge University Press, 1972.

Blurton Jones, N., & Leach, G. Behaviour of children and their mothers at separation and greeting. In N. Blurton Jones (Ed.), *Ethological studies of child behaviour*. London: Cambridge University Press, 1972.

Bowlby, J. *Attachment and loss*, Vol. 1, *Attachment*. New York: Basic Books, 1969.

Bowlby, J. *Attachment and loss*, Vol. 2, *Separation*. New York: Basic Books, 1973.

Brannigan, C. R., & Humphries, D. A. Human non-verbal behaviour, a means of communication. In N. Blurton Jones (Ed.), *Ethological studies of child behaviour*. London: Cambridge University Press, 1972.

Bronson, G. The hierarchical organization of the central nervous system: implications for learning processes and critical periods in early development. *Behavioral Science*, 1965, **10**, 7–25.

Carpenter, C. R. *Naturalistic behavior of non-human primates*. University Park: Pennsylvania State University Press, 1964.

Clarke-Stewart, K. A. Interactions between mothers and their young children: characteristics and consequences. *Monographs of the Society for Research in Child Development*, 1973, **38**.

Flavell, J. H. Stage-related properties of cognitive development. *Cognitive Psychology*, 1971, **2**, 421–453.

Flavell, J. H. The development of Inferences about others. In T. Mischel (Ed.), *Understanding other persons*. Oxford: Basil Blackwell, 1974.

Flavell, J. H., Botkin, P. T., Fry, C. L., Jr., Wright, J. W., & Jarvis, P. E. *The development of role-taking and communication skills in children*. New York: Wiley, 1968.

Hall, K. R. L., & DeVore, I. Baboon social behavior. In I. DeVore (Ed.), *Primate behavior*. New York: Holt, Rinehart & Winston, 1965.

Hinde, R. A. *The biological bases of human social behavior*. New York: McGraw-Hill, 1974.

Hinde, R. A., & Atkinson, S. Assessing the roles of social partners in maintaining mutual proximity, as exemplified by mother/infant relations in monkeys. *Animal Behaviour*, 1970, **18**, pp. 169–176.

Inhelder, B., & Piaget, J. *The growth of logical thinking from childhood to adolescence*. New York: Basic Books, 1958.

Iwanaga, M. I. Development of interpersonal play structure in 3, 4, and 5 year-old children. *Journal of Research and Development in Education*, 1973, **6**, 71–82.

Jay, P. The common Langur of North India. In I. DeVore (Ed.), *Primate behavior*. New York: Holt, Rinehart & Winston, 1965.

Konner, M. J. Infancy among the Kalahari Desert san. Paper presented at Burg Wartenstein Symposium No. 57: Cultural and Social Influences in Infancy and Early Childhood, Vienna, June 1973.

Lawick-Goodall, J. van. The behaviour of free-living chimpanzees in the Gombe Stream Reserve. *Animal Behaviour Monographs*, 1968, **1**, 164–311.

Lee, S. G. M., Wright, D. S., & Herbert, M. Aspects of the development of social responsiveness in young children. Report to Social Science Research Council, United Kingdom, 1972.

Maccoby, E. E., & Feldman, S. S. Mother-attachment and stranger-reactions in the third year of life. *Monographs of the Society for Research in Child Development*, 1972, **37**.

Maccoby, E. E., & Masters, J. C. Attachment and Dependency. In P. Mussen (Ed.), *Carmichael's manual of child psychology*. New York: Wiley, 1970.

MacKay, D. *Information, mechanism and meaning*. Cambridge: MIT Press, 1969.

Marvin, R. S. *Attachment-, exploratory- and communicative behavior in 2, 3, & 4 year-old children*. Unpublished doctoral dissertation, University of Chicago, 1972.

Marvin, R. S. The attenuation of mother–child attachment and the child's cognitive development. Paper presented at a conference of the Mathematical Social Science Board. Monroeville, Pa., October, 1973.

Marvin, R. S., Greenberg, M. T., & Mossler, D. G. The early development of conceptual perspective taking: distinguishing among multiple perspectives. *Child Development*, 1976, **47**, 2.

Marvin, R. S., VanDevender, T., Iwanaga, M. I., LeVine, S., & LeVine, R. A. Infant-caregiver attachment among the Hausa of Nigeria. In H. McGurk (Ed.), *Ecological factors in human development*. Amsterdam: North-Holland Publishing Co., in press.

Miller, G. A., Galanter, E., & Pribram, K. H. *Plans and the Structure of Behavior*. New York: Holt, Rinehart & Winston, 1960.

Omark, D. R., & Edelman, M. S. Development of attention structure in young children. In M. R. A. Chance & R. Larsen (Eds.), *The social structure of attention*. New York: Wiley, in press.

Piaget, J. *The origins of intelligence in children*. New York: Internat. Univ. Press, 1952.

Selman, R. Taking another's perspective: role-taking development in early childhood. *Child Development*, 1971, **42**, 1721–34.

Shaller, G. *The mountain gorilla: Ecology and behavior* Chicago: University of Chicago Press, 1963.

Shantz, C. N. The development of social cognition. In E. M. Hetherington (Ed.), *Review of child development research* Vol. 5. Chicago: University of Chicago Press, 1975.

Shirley, M. & Poyntz, L. The influence of separation from the mother on children's emotional responses. *Journal of Psychology*, 1941, **12**, 251–82.

Siegel, S. *Non-parametric statistics for the behavioral sciences* New York: McGraw-Hill, 1956.

CHAPTER 3

Establishing New Social Relations in Infancy

Hildy S. Ross and Barbara Davis Goldman

Department of Psychology
University of Waterloo
Waterloo, Ontario, Canada

This chapter will explore a relatively neglected topic in child development, the process whereby infants establish new social relations. It is important to state at the outset that new relations need not be contrasted with the infant's attachment to his mother or parents; rather, these relations can be examined as an independent but related aspect of social development. The neglect of this process in the psychological literature of infancy can perhaps be understood in terms of widespread opinions concerning the nature of infants' social behavior. First, it has often been stated that the infant shows very little interest in his peers, that his play is solitary, that he treats his peers as inanimate objects (yet he happily explores and shows great interest in inanimate objects), or that the principal form of social interaction between peers involves impersonal struggles over toys. For example, in 1943 Gesell and Ilg wrote:

> The 18-month-old tends to treat another child as an object rather than as a person. He resorts to experimental poking, pulling, pinching, pushing and sometimes hitting (p. 158).

Second, the infant's reactions to new adults have often been characterized not merely as lack of interest, but rather as fear, sometimes as terror, and at the very least as wariness.

These opinions have been amplified over a period of time as psychologists have searched for simple, resounding summary statements for textbooks and other secondary sources. The 1974 revision of the section from Gesell and Ilg on peer interaction quoted earlier exemplifies this process:

The usual 18-monther is not much interested in other children. He has nothing to say to them and very little to do with them. He is primarily interested in himself and his own concerns. To a large extent, so long as opportunity is available for him to express his own drives and wishes, other people in social and play situations are quite unnecessary (p. 292).

Given that the infant is uninterested in his peers and afraid of strangers, he can hardly be expected to become friends with either category of new people. As a result, the process of forming new social relations could not possibly be an important part of his social activities. This may account, at least in part, for the relative neglect of such processes.

The data we will describe here come from two studies. The first examined the infant's interactions with adult strangers; the second concerned his early peer relations. The new relations established by subjects in these studies could last only a short period of time as they were confined to an encounter of less than 30 minutes in a laboratory situation. They demonstrated, however, that extensive social interaction with new people is possible in infancy.

Stranger–Infant Study

With an adult, as well as with a peer, some degree of social interaction would seem to be a precondition to establishing a more lasting friendship. Yet the literature on reactions to strangers has concentrated almost singlemindedly on the phenomenon of fear of strangers. The possibility of other responses has been largely neglected. Similarly, theoretical explanations have been concerned chiefly with accounting for the presence of fear reactions to a stranger; in many cases these theories would require radical revision if other, friendlier reactions were found as well. And such evidence is beginning to accumulate.

Harriet Rheingold and Carol Eckerman in their recent review (Rheingold & Eckerman, 1974) convincingly demonstrated that fear of strangers is neither universal nor typical. The findings from their own study indicated that nearly all 8-, 10-, and 12-month-old infants would look at, smile at, and play happily in the presence of a stranger. Most also allowed the stranger to pick them up and hold them while their mothers left the room, all in the virtual absence of any apparent signs of distress or fear, such as fussing, crying, or clinging to their mothers. This chapter has increased the sensitivity of other researchers to evidence in their own data that infants can be friendly toward strangers. For example, George Morgan (1973) reanalyzed his data and reported that the percentage of infants who showed some positive reactions to the stranger was very high at all ages tested in the first year. Unambiguously positive responses included smiling, happy vocalizations, and reaching toward or touching the stranger.

Nevertheless, the extent to which the infant initiates interaction with a stranger and the course of this interaction remain to be documented fully. Carl

Corter's (1973) work indicated that infants will remain away from their mothers for longer periods of time if this enables them to see a stranger; yet approach to and interaction with the stranger were all but absent. Similarly, Eckerman and Rheingold (1974) reported some increased approach to a responsive stranger (who smiled and talked to the infant) as compared to a nonresponsive stranger; however, here, too, social interaction was minimal. In my own study on the effects of increasing the familiarity of an adult stranger (Ross, 1975), infants also spent relatively little time near or in physical contact with the adults. In all of this research, however, the adults remained relatively passive; passive both in the sense of not approaching the infant or initiating play with him, and also of failing to indicate that they were willing to play with the infant, or would react positively to any of the infant's overtures. Where small changes were made in the behavior of the adult, as in Eckerman and Rheingold's responsive stranger, small changes occurred in the behavior of the infants.

Our aims in this study of infant-stranger interaction were threefold. First, we wanted to demonstrate that a situation could be devised in which the infant, of his own initiative, would approach an adult stranger; second, we tried to describe the course of relatively extended interaction between infant and stranger. To achieve these first two aims we created one particular version of an *active* stranger; a young girl who remained seated (so the infant could approach her), but who talked, gestured, smiled, and looked at the infant. She held out or offered the infant a series of small toys, and once the infant had approached, she continued to offer or manipulate the toys, talk to the infant, attempt to direct his play, imitate him, or interact reciprocally. Our third purpose was to demonstrate the infant's sensitivity to the behavior of the stranger, and so the reactions of our active-stranger group were compared with those of a passive-stranger group. When the stranger was passive, she sat quietly, looking and occasionally smiling at the infant. Directly in front of her were the toys that the active stranger had offered the infant.

Sixty-four normal 12-month-old infants served as subjects for this study; four young women whose ages ranged from 20 to 24 were the strangers. There were four trials and a different toy was used on each trial. The toys were all commercially available, brightly colored, and contained many small parts. The strangers' behavior was consistent across the trials—either active or passive. The stranger was already seated on the floor in one corner of the room when the mother entered carrying her infant and sat in the opposite corner. She placed her infant on the floor in front of her to begin the trial. A mother could look or smile at her infant, offer him physical support, or say a few words when he was nearby. She was not to encourage, discourage, or direct her infant's behavior, nor to initiate any interaction with him. Rather, the infant was to be free to do as he wished within the constraints of the experimental situation. Each trial ended when after 4 minutes the experimenter reappeared and asked the mother to carry her infant out of the room, where they remained for approximately one minute until a new trial began as before.

Our first aim was to create a situation in which infants, on their own initiative, would approach a stranger. As Table I shows, our findings indicated that this occurred.

Of the 32 infants in the active-stranger group, 30 approached the stranger; 21 infants approached on all four trials, and the average number of trials on which the infants approached the stranger was 3.4. Approach was only when the infant entered a circular area extending 1.25 meters from the center of the stranger's position. A smaller area with a radius of .75 meters within this outer area defined close proximity to the stranger. Generally, when the infant was in the outer area, both he and the stranger could touch and play with the toy; when the infant was in the inner area, he could touch the stranger as well. Another area with a .75-meter radius marked the mother's position and was used to determine how long the infant stayed near his mother and when he left her.

Infants in the active-stranger group left their mothers after 110 seconds and approached the stranger with a mean latency of 204 seconds. They spent an average of 244 seconds near their mothers and 580 seconds near the stranger—257 seconds in close proximity to the stranger. Thus, they spent considerably more time near the stranger than near their own mothers. Figure 1 shows the circular areas which surrounded the stranger as well as a series of infants who remained near the stranger.

Our second aim was to describe the social interaction patterns shared by the infant and the adult, as Table II shows. The categories derived for that purpose were based on repeated observation of videotape records of the trials and thus come from the data themselves. They were scored only when the infant was near the stranger, an average duration of slightly less than 10 minutes.

Infants spent a considerable amount of time looking at the stranger. They frequently glanced at her face (for example, Figure 1a), but more often they watched the stranger's activity with or manipulation of the toy (Figures 1b and 1e). The mean duration of these classes of visual activity was 28 and 131 seconds respectively.

Infants and strangers spent relatively little time in physical contact. Although 25 of the 32 infants did touch the stranger, the average duration of contact

Table I. Infants Approach an Active Stranger

Number who leave their mothers	31/32
Number who approach the stranger	30/32
Number of trials stranger approached	3.4/4.0
Latency to leave mother	110 sec
Latency to approach stranger	204 sec
Time near mother	244 sec
Time near stranger	580 sec
Time in close proximity to stranger	257 sec
Total duration of the four trials	960 sec

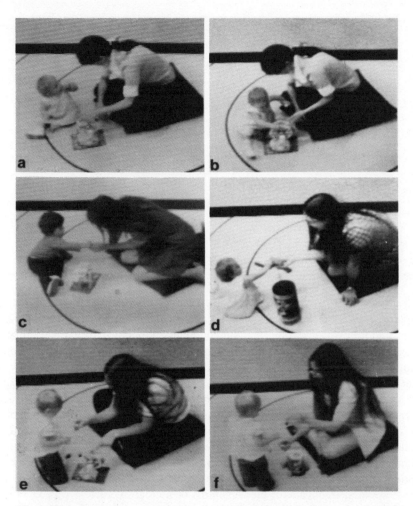

Fig. 1. Examples of infant–stranger interaction at 12 months. (a) Looking at the stranger's face. (b) Mutual toy contact. (c) The strangers give and (d) the infants take toys. (e, f) The strangers model actions with the toys.

throughout the entire session was only 4 seconds. Mutual contact of the toys, however, was far more common (Figures 1b, 1c, and 1d); its average duration was 94 seconds, and all subjects who approached the stranger engaged in some joint contact of the toys.

Other interaction patterns were best characterized in terms of their average frequencies. The infants took the toys offered by the stranger 13.6 times (Figures 1c and 1d); the infants offered and the stranger accepted the toys 1.4 times. The strangers modeled actions with the toys and often encouraged the infant with

Table II. Infant-Stranger Interaction Patterns in the Active-Stranger Group

Response	Mean duration (in seconds)
Time near the stranger	580
Visual regard of the stranger's face	28
Manipulation of the toys	131
Physical contact of the stranger	4
Mutual contact of the toy	94

Response	Mean frequency
Stranger gives and infant takes a toy	13.6
Infant gives and stranger takes a toy	1.4
Infant imitates the stranger	12.1
Stranger imitates the infant	0.9
Infant follows stranger's directions	1.3
Mutual games	6.5
Total social interaction	33.0

words or gestures to imitate these (Figures 1e and 1f); the infants imitated 12.1 times, and followed directions that did not include a modeled response 1.3 times. Longer, reciprocal sequences of interactions also took place, in which each partner responded in turn and repeatedly to the actions of the other. These "games," as we have labeled them, could involve either similar activities on the part of each participant (for example, pushing a turtle back and forth to each other), or quite different activities on the part of each participant (for example, two or more repetitions of a sequence in which the infant picked up a block and handed it to the stranger, the stranger accepted the block and dropped it into a container). Games occurred, on the average, 6.5 times with each infant. When scoring redundancies, such as those between imitation and games, are eliminated, the total frequency of these patterns of mutual interaction was 33 in the 10-minute period that subjects, on the average, spent near the stranger; that is, about three explicit social interactions in each minute. Thus, a wide variety of patterns of mutual interactions was observed, and with relatively high frequencies, especially considering that the alternatives for the infants were staying near their mothers, playing relatively exclusively with a series of novel toys, or, indeed, carrying those toys to their mothers and playing with them there.

Our third research question involved the influence of the stranger's behavior on the infant's reactions to her. Did the infants react differently to our active and passive strangers? Were they sensitive to this behavioral difference between individuals? Was the stranger's behavior responsible for the fact that the infants in the active-stranger group so frequently approached and interacted with her? The answers to these questions were all yes, as Table III shows.

Reliable differences between the two groups were found for the time subjects spent near their mothers, their latency to approach the stranger, the time they spent near and in close proximity to the stranger, the number who touched the stranger, their latency and duration of contact of the toys, and their latency and duration of fussing or crying. One of the few measures not to show a reliable difference between these groups was the infants' latency to leave their mothers.

When the stranger was passive rather than active, the infants spent more time near their mothers, approached the stranger later, and spent less time near her. Fewer subjects touched the stranger. They took longer to touch the toys and played with them less; they began to fuss or cry earlier and spent more time doing so.

Thus, the behavior of the strangers had a dramatic and extensive impact on the reactions of the infants. The consistent pattern of findings indicated that the infants were sensitive to the behavioral differences between the strangers and were themselves more friendly when the strangers were more friendly and more interesting.

The study as a whole demonstrated that far more variety and complexity exist in infant–stranger interaction than a rating of the degree of fear would have enabled us to detect. Most patterns of response showed the infants were friendly, active, and highly interested in interacting with the stranger. These findings also suggested that the infants' sole purpose in approaching the stranger in the active-stranger group was not merely to gain access to the toys. In addition, the lengthy period spent near the stranger and the high frequency of social interaction indicated that the stranger herself, the stranger's activities with the toys, and especially the games were important incentives in attracting the infant.

Table III. The Influence of the Strangers' Behavior on the Infants' Responses[a]

Response	Active	Passive
Time near mother	244	639[b]
Latency to leave mother	110	186
Latency to approach stranger	204	592[b]
Time near stranger	580	148[b]
Time in close proximity to stranger	257	65[b]
Number who touch stranger	25	2[b]
Latency to touch toys	213	667[b]
Time touching toys	578	167[b]
Latency to fuss or cry	830	613[c]
Time fussing or crying	9	98[c]

[a] The probability levels were derived from F values in analyses of variance, except the number who touched the stranger, where a Chi Square test was used, and the latency and duration of fussing and crying, where Mann-Whitney U tests were used.
[b] $p < .001$.
[c] $p < .01$.

Peer Study

These factors were also important in establishing and maintaining peer interaction, an aspect of social behavior that was ignored for many years by those who were concerned with infancy. *The Competent Infant* (Stone, Smith, & Murphy, 1973) is a massive compilation of more than 200 studies of the infant up to the age of 15 months. Three hundred pages are devoted to a section entitled "The Social Infant," yet no study of the human infant's social interactions with his peers is included. There is, however, a passing reference to early peer interactions in young rhesus monkeys, who became depressed following separation from their peers. The editors' statement concerning this finding reflects the prevailing opinion: "Though there may be parallel peer-deprivation effects in older human children, these findings cannot, obviously, be extended to young human infants, whose peer relations are virtually nonexistent" (p. 985). It is our intention to demonstrate that relations with peers not only exist in infancy, but that such relations reveal an ability for subtle, complex interactions which may necessitate a rethinking of the current definition and domain of infant social development.

Despite our flag-waving tendencies, we do not want to contribute to the erroneous impression that there has been no research in the area of early peer relations. On the contrary, there is a very recent resurgence of interest in peer interaction. At least a dozen researchers have, in the last few years, presented firm evidence of the sociability of infants with their peers. Further, a considerable amount of data were accumulated between the late 1920s and the early 1940s on early peer interaction. Yet this early work was either forgotten or misquoted or misread. For a quarter of a century, child development researchers seemed to assume that peer interactions were nonexistent, generally negative, or at least not worthy of attention, until the child approached three.

Blurton-Jones (1974) blamed the influence of Parten's (1933) categories of play for the failure to consider early social interaction. It seems more truthful to accuse the less-than-careful readers of her work who have apparently neglected to look at her actual data. For Parten's two-year-olds, her youngest group, parallel play was the most common activity, but the combined categories of associative group play and cooperative play were also common. These two highest levels of social play were observed 25% of the time. Further, while it is true that "solitary play is most common at two and one-half years" (p. 263), it was not the most frequent interaction pattern of the children in this age range; it was just more frequent in this age range than in the others.

In addition, it is likely that initially interested readers were dissuaded from this area due to a poor choice of terminology. Though perhaps due to the translation, the use of the term *interfering* in Charlotte Buhler's 1933 review of the literature is a particularly striking example. She refers to a 6- to-10-

month-old "... *interfering* with the other by *touching* him, *exchanging toys* with him, or pushing or pulling him" (p. 375; emphasis added). An even more unusual use of the term "interfering" occurs in her summary of the developmental sequence of peer interaction. "Besides the initiation of contacts, the children were observed to interfere with each other by taking away or offering toys, by inhibiting the other's movements, by warding off another's attack, and by cooperating in play" (p. 378).

That cooperative play, or giving a child toys would be termed interference is unfortunate, but perhaps even more unfortunate is the selectivity of her readers; many of her statements in a 1935 publication, *From Birth to Maturity,* would, if read, certainly encourage subsequent research, but we have yet to encounter a single researcher in early peer relations who has referred to this source. In discussing the predominance of positive social behavior toward other humans in the first year, she notes:

> At six and seven months the infant tries eagerly to include anyone who is present in its play. Objects are given and received from others, and the child enjoys especially those games that include a partner, hide and seek, exchange of toys, etc. The partner's gestures are observed at the latest in the fifth month and at eight months there is an astonishing capacity for interpreting and understanding them. Children of this age have been observed trying to comfort a frightened or crying child (pp. 55-56).

So much for egocentrism in the first year.

Thus, it is obvious that there was research in early peer interaction, and that the data indicated that this was an interesting, rich, and potentially important area of investigation. But for some reason the research ceased. From 1940 onward, babies must have smiled and vocalized to each other from their respective carriages, strollers, and grocery carts, and infants in day and residential nurseries, and twins and triplets in homes, must have continued to pat each other and share toys, but either no one watched with much interest or those who watched didn't record their observations. Thus, if in 1970 you decided to study peer relations in human infancy, your literature search would have had to go back more than thirty years before you would find a useful reference, except for Faigin's (1958) study of kibbutzim children.

My own interest in peer interaction stemmed from watching the incredible speed and persistence of my own, barely-walking one-year-old as he disappeared repeatedly into our neighbor's yard; her two children and the others who congregated there were the chief attraction. This experience, along with my impression that peer relations was an almost totally ignored class of social behavior—I had yet to read the early literature—prompted me to begin to collect some pilot data on the topic. The day that Barbara Goldman and I met, I had just observed for the first time in our laboratory the peer interaction of two 1-year-old boys. We had planned a 10-minute session, but continued for 45 because of the obvious delight of these two infants in each other, and our delight in watching this incredible phenomenon. I kept repeating, in my amazement, that so much rich and exciting interaction had taken place. I also had the foresight to at least note that I did not know how we would ever characterize or describe it, much less count it. I was repeating these two phrases when Barbara, then a new graduate student, found me; she was innocently unaware that she would be the person most responsible for our efforts to describe the course of peer interaction. She cannot accuse me of failing to warn her from the start.

The design of our peer interaction study was fairly simple. We used 48 different children, 16 at each of 12, 18, and 24 months. Each 18-month-old came to two sessions, a week apart. One was with an older and one with a younger same-sexed peer. The 12- and 24-month-olds participated in one session each. For 25 minutes, the two children were free to act as they wished in a laboratory playroom, in the presence of 10 toys and the two mothers. The mothers were instructed beforehand to feel free to interact with each other, but to refrain from guiding the children's behavior in any way. All sessions were videotaped, and descriptions of the two children's behavior were recorded on audiotape by two observers.

To obtain data on social interaction, each tape was viewed repeatedly along with its audio commentary. The sequence and duration of all social behavior the infants directed to each other was recorded.

In general, our data indicated that unacquainted infants and toddlers, paired with children slightly older or younger than themselves, were definitely sociable. In a total of 800 minutes, the children directed more than 2000 intentioned, explicit social overtures to each other. Most frequent among these were positive vocalizations, attempts to give a toy—holding it out to offer, tossing to, or placing it in the other child's lap, smiling or laughing, and reaching for or attempting to take an unoffered toy. Table IV shows that negative vocalizations were less frequent than positive ones; negative contact was less frequent than positive contact.

The particular data this chapter will focus on indicated, in a slightly different way, the sociability of unacquainted infants and toddlers. The skills which underlie or support social interaction generally have not been dealt with in any detail in the research on early peer interaction. These skills, however, are considerable, and enabled the children in our sample to engage in complex, ex-

Table IV. Frequencies of Social Behaviors (32 Dyads: 800 Minutes)

All attempts to give a toy	364
All attempts to obtain an unoffered toy	316
Expression of positive affect: smiles and laughter	340
Positive vocalization	531
Negative vocalization: angry yell, fret, cry	103
Show, demonstrate, or point at a toy	237
Positive physical contact: touch, hug, or lean on	212
Negative physical contact: hit, push, pull	52

tended, well-formed, and patterned interactions which we called games. The games varied in length from a few exchanges to 3 minutes of continuous interaction within one game. A study of the game-playing skills of the entire sample reveals a sophisticated social repertoire possessed by children who are between their first and second birthdays, and it is this repertoire which may allow for the establishment of new social relations in infancy.

It should be noted that there was no specific intention to study social games when we began our peer interaction study. The presence of games within the larger context of peer interaction became obvious, however, while viewing the actual sessions. At this point, we are not entirely sure that we are able to fully describe all interaction skills that are involved in game-playing. Perhaps part of the problem is that across the 12-month age range of our sample, marked differences occurred in the style, the pacing, the types of games, and the clarity of the signals involved in initiating and then maintaining the games. For example, with the younger dyads, the 18- and 12-month-olds, positive affect, such as smiling and laughing, did not seem to serve as a form of metacommunication, that is, to signal "this is a game," but in the older children's interactions, positive affect definitely did serve this function. Of the 31 instances of smiling or laughing among the 12-month-olds, none was within the context of games or game overtures. For the 18-month-olds, 25% of their smiles and laughter with the 12-month-olds was within such contexts; and 33% of their smiling and laughing with the 24-month-olds was during games. In contrast, 72% of all smiles and laughter by the 24-month-olds occurred within games or game overtures. So the usefulness of smiles and laughter as a cue to identifying the presence of a game depended on the ages of both children involved.

There did, however, seem to be interaction skills or features that were common to all of the peer interactions which we felt should be called games. Only further research will indicate whether the following list contains the necessary and sufficient skills for early peer interactions. Parenthetically though, the similarities to games between the infant and the adult stranger noted earlier, and to the verbal games of 3- to 5-year-old children recently described by Catherine Garvey (1974), provide some support for their generality.

The most general feature of games is that both children must be clearly involved in the interaction; each child performs some action in response to the action of the other child. If one child throws a ball, looks at the other, smiles, and waits, but the other child just continues watching, or doesn't even notice, this might be classified as a game overture (in fact, a quite common one) but not a game. If the other child were to laugh, or bounce up and down, or chase the ball and throw it back each time it was thrown, then a game would be occurring, though a traditional ball game would be noted only for the last possibility.

Following directly from mutual involvement are the set of skills, or features, of acting in turn and repetitively. Alternation of turns is crucial for mutual involvement; it is a skill in that one child must leave room for the other to respond. Repetition is required in order to signal that the activities involved are not meant literally, but playfully, to serve as a means for a game. The most obvious examples occurred with games involving exchanges of objects, primarily blocks and balls. To illustrate, if a child requested the ball from the other child and received it, it appeared to us as observers, and to the child who originally had the ball, that the first child intended a real object exchange. If, however, after receiving the ball, the child then offered, or rolled, or threw it back, then waited, arms outstretched, requesting it again, it became apparent that the action was meant nonliterally, as a game. Further, a vocalization often had the function of an attention-getting device, and, when used as such, was a literal communication. But if the children were already in mutual, eye-to-eye contact, and one child vocalized, followed by the other's vocalization, with repetition of this sequence, then the vocalization was nonliteral, and a game was in progress.

Turn-taking, or action-alternating signals in our sample ranged from simply pausing after an action completion; to actions such as throwing the ball, looking at the other child, looking at the ball, looking at the other child; to verbal statements such as "I'll get it, I'll get it," to mark one's own turn; to encouraging the other child to throw the ball, as one 24-month-old girl said, "Go, baby. Go," while waving her on. One of the most difficult aspects of turn-taking seemed to be giving sufficient time for the other to complete his turn. Receptive skills are obviously necessary here also, as a child, viewing another child act and then pause, must realize that this is a cue for his own turn. Figure 2 illustrates the use of visual gaze direction and pausing to signal turn-taking in a ball game between an 18- and 12-month-old.

Games frequently ended for all age groups when one child took too long to perform his turn or failed to perform his turn at all. Though a game might be reestablished by the other child repeating his turn, at times he apparently felt constrained not to take two turns in a row and the game would end. Sometimes, however, games were stopped by mothers, as they readjusted the children's clothing, repositioned them, or verbally directed an interaction to stop. Object-exchange games terminated through all the above turn-taking rule deviations, but also through redefinition of the interaction as literal. In these cases, extended, nonliteral exchanges of blocks, or of the ball, would suddenly be terminated by one child keeping the object, rather than relinquishing it, often accompanied by "no, mine," or turning away, or going to his mother with the toy.

Thus, the games were maintained by turn-taking rules, and often terminated if these rules were broken, which is another indication of the highly organized, rule-governed structure of game interactions. Perhaps some indication of the diversity among the 36 games the children's skills allowed them to initiate and maintain is now in order. There were 12 traditional ball games, where the children were able to reverse roles, to chase and catch, then to throw and wait. The ball games differed in the particular ways the children chose to exchange the ball, rolling, throwing, offering, handing it directly, bouncing it off the wall, and

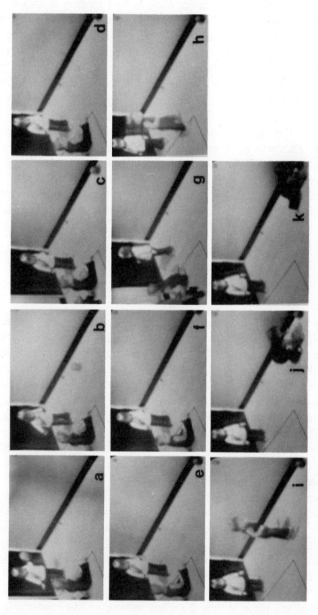

Fig. 2. Alternation of gaze direction and pausing as a turn-taking signal: This sequence of video stills of a single exchange of turns, within an ongoing ball game, occurs during the fourth minute after the two children met. The child standing in the first pictures is an 18-month-old male, the other is 12 months old. (a) 03:35, 18 holds up ball and looks at the baby, (b) 18 throws ball, looks at ball, (c) looks at the baby, (d) looks at the ball, (e) looks at the baby, (f) looks at the ball, (g) 03:42, watches baby get up, (h) watches baby walk toward ball, (i, j, k) continues watching baby retrieve ball, 03:55.

so forth. There were 9 games involving imitation of physical action or of vocalization, or of a combination of the two. Each of the 9 games involved a different imitated act as the basis for the interaction, such as foot-tapping or kicking the barrier. Games with complementary but nonreversing roles were the most varied and numerous. These 15 games included tickling, touching, repeated giving of a series of objects, lopsided ball games, and action and vocalization games where the role of one child was to laugh at the antics of the other.

Thus, children between their first and second birthdays, upon meeting for the first time, actively chose to interact frequently, competently, creatively, and with sophistication. A large part of our effort in this study has been to characterize the essential and unique features of the interactions we have observed among our infants. This was most difficult when it came to understanding the signals, skills, and structures of games. After a year's time, we still are not certain that our verbal descriptions capture the essence of these events. Yet games, and the skills which underlie them, may constitute the most important components available to the infant for establishing new, and continuing, social relations with a peer.

Discussion

Our findings indicated that infants are active participants, in fact, active initiators of complex social interaction with both peers and adults. These actions could readily form a basis for establishing new social relations in infancy; at the very least, the high level of social interaction observed is a dramatic illustration that the infant is neither uninterested in nor predominantly afraid of new people. With these two barriers to the study of the full range of infant social behavior removed, the propositions that infants are capable of forming more lasting and extensive new relations, and, in fact, frequently do so, can be examined. Our data do not yet provide firm evidence to fully document the characteristics of this process; however, we can and will offer further speculation, hypotheses, and questions, to create a direction for additional study.

Much of the social interaction we observed could be characterized as a system of specific interaction patterns. These contained within them individual responses by each participant that were performed repeatedly. We propose that these specific interaction patterns form the raw material for the development of new social relations. In other words, the activities of the two individuals and the patterning of these activities form the basis of their emerging relationship. The system could not be static, but must continue to develop and change as interaction continues; yet at any point in time the relationship could be characterized in terms of past or current patterns of interaction. This hypothesis implies that if the two individuals met after a period of separation, the games that they initiated would show some similarity to those that occurred between them in previous encounters.

Moreover, it follows that these specific patterns of interaction will differ, depending upon the characteristics of the individuals involved and the situations in which they find themselves. Our infant-adult data clearly demonstrated that the extent and nature of the interaction depended in large measure on the activity of the adult—one member of the dyad. Individual differences were apparent, as well, among the infants.

However, it seems reasonable to expect individual differences in the system of interaction that cannot be explained readily in terms of differences in only one of the partners. Not only is a particular action or overture important in determining how an interaction sequence will develop, but the perception of that overture by the other member of the dyad must be taken into account. His response, in turn, and its perception by the first actor, all combine to create a system that quickly becomes so complex and interdependent that the independent influence of one member of the dyad cannot be isolated. This was particularly apparent in the peer study, where both children acted without constraints on their behavior. Thus, it might be more profitable to speak of differences in the dyad, in the development of patterns of mutual interaction, or in the emerging relationship, rather than attempting at the outset to attribute these to specific characteristics of the individuals involved.

This leads to the question of how much diversity could be created in a new social relation. The physical and cognitive capacities of the individuals involved constitute a very obvious set of limitations. Other restrictions might also exist in the kinds of overtures that each partner will understand and respond to, and in the complexity of the sequences that might be involved. For example, a stranger would not be well advised to approach the infant rapidly and rather artificially in the so-called six steps designed to elicit fear of strangers; neither should a new person, adult or child, sit passively in the corner of a room, even if he does show some readiness to look and occasionally smile at the infant. More activity is required—but must this activity be of a specific nature? Have we been very fortunate in selecting mutual play with a toy as a situation in which to observe the infant and stranger? How important is the toy as a lure or as a distracting agent from more direct confrontation? Similarly, how important was the environment and the particular objects it contained in creating the kinds of peer interactions we observed? Would more activity on the part of the mothers have altered the likelihood of the games? What was the role of the small toys or the ball that were so easily exchanged or incorporated into games? Could relations develop that are based on other forms of play—rough and tumble play or chasing games for example, verbal games or contact-mediated interaction such as holding, hugging, or kissing? Finally, we might ask if there is a particularly good or appropriate sequence of different interaction patterns that can combine to create a relation between two individuals. Should the interaction patterns be ones involving closer and closer physical proximity? Should they involve more and more vigor or activity? Should they incorporate progressively greater levels of novelty or complexity? These are not issues that lend themselves readily to simple research paradigms, but they could be investigated.

Finally, because the child's attachment to his mother is one of his most important social relations in infancy, it would be a very great oversight to begin the study of new relations as a phenomenon completely apart from the knowledge already existing concerning attachment. Where might we look for the interface between these two processes or systems?

In the first place, qualitative features of the infant's attachment to his mother may be related to his ability to form new relations with others. One such distinction that readily comes to mind is Ainsworth's patterns of secure and insecure attachment (Ainsworth, Bell, & Stayton, 1971). A securely attached infant uses his mother as a base for his exploratory activity, and the stresses of separation heighten his attachment. An infant whose attachment is insecure either remains near his mother or may avoid his mother and relieve his insecurity through independent play. It follows, then, that an infant who is secure in his attachment can more readily establish new relations, both because he is more exploratory and because he has a history of associating with a sensitive, responsive individual, his own mother. The confidence he holds in the responsiveness of one human should generalize to other people he meets.

Second, the presence of the mother and her reactions to the stranger, the new peer, or even the other mother may set the tone for the infant's interactions. It is easy to envision two extreme cases in which the mother may seriously impede the establishment of new relations, either by ignoring or being hostile to the new person, or, alternatively, by so completely occupying either the infant or his potential friend as to allow little opportunity for friendship to develop. Similarly, it seems possible for the mother to act in such a way as to promote the establishment of new relations, by providing the infant with a secure base for his explorations of the stranger, by increasing the stranger's confidence in his ability to interact with, or amuse her infant, and by knowing when her active participation will benefit, and when it will interfere with a growing relationship. One important place in which the mother may play a role is as an interpreter and promoter of peer interactions. The mother may be better able to interpret, and therefore clarify her child's signals so that the two infants can more easily establish games and other mutually satisfying interaction patterns. She may perform a similar role with an adult stranger, thus making his task of reading the infant's sometimes ambiguous signals a little less bewildering.

A third point of contact between attachment and new relations may involve the direct transfer of patterns of interaction from one realm to the other. The infant may initiate games or interaction sequences with a new person that he developed originally with his mother. The process may be conceptualized along the lines suggested by Piaget, and more recently expanded and applied directly to the situation in which an infant meets a stranger by Sandra Rafman (1974). The infant may, in a sense, try out or practice established schemas with the new person. We may have capitalized inadvertently on just such a tendency by having our active stranger play with the infant and the toy; possibly this is a common enough situation for it to be a prevalent feature of mother–infant attachment. Yet even greater similarity to things the mother does with her infant, and greater sensitivity (perhaps with the mother's intervention or interpretation) to the particular pattern of interaction that the infant is attempting to initiate may greatly facilitate the establishment of new relations. Rafman has recently reported findings demonstrating this process: strangers approached 9- and 13-month-olds, first using the typical procedure of increasing proximity that constitutes a test of fear of strangers, and then imitating a specific behavior pattern suggested by the mother as a part of the mother-child interaction patterns. All of the eleven infants who displayed negative affect as the stranger approached in the standard sequence reacted positively once they began to play their own parts in the games. Similar borrowed patterns may be excellent ways of beginning a relation with infants; further, the infant himself may actively attempt to initiate the process as he searches for means of determining who the new person is and whether it would be to his benefit to make the stranger a friend.

We may also look for similarities in the processes involved in establishing a new social relation, and the continuing process of forming an attachment to the mother. The formation of an attachment could be considered a continuing process in that new sequences of interaction are continually becoming part of the mother–infant relation. An example drawn from my own interactions with the current object of my mother–child attachment illustrates this point. Corey Ross was 28 months old when, at his initiative, we developed the game we might call "Uncle Stanley." I played the role of Uncle Stanley, Corey played himself, and we generally took a trip in Uncle Stanley's car and visited Corey's grandparents. Some repeated features of the game involved waiting impatiently for Auntie Rosie who takes a long time to "get herself together," and searching for Guelpher, Rose and Stanley's bulldog, who has chosen just this moment to make his dash for freedom. Corey initiated this game repeatedly and enthusiastically. He only played Uncle Stanley with me—he never asked his father or friends or other relatives to play this with him—indeed he didn't even play this game with Uncle Stanley himself. It was an exclusive part of his relation with his mother. In fact, this game, combined with many other diverse patterns of interaction, may form one cornerstone of our attachment relation. Yet it was a game that developed fairly recently and relatively rapidly. It was also the kind of interaction pattern whose formation one can readily envision as the infant establishes a new relation with a stranger or peer. The evidence is anecdotal, but it is used merely to illustrate a speculation rather than to verify an hypothesis. The processes involved in forming a new relation may be parallel, at least in part, to those by which the attachment relation is continually developing. Differences may also be present of course, based on entire histories of interaction with the mother, yet these differences do not make the discovery of both similarities and divergences any less interesting or instructive.

Thus, at first glance, there are at least four ways in which the child's attachment to his mother may play a role in advancing our understanding of his establishing new social relations. Certain qualitative features of his attachment may predispose him to actively seek new relations. The mother herself could play a role in promoting the establishment of new friendships. Certain patterns of interaction may be directly borrowed from the mother-infant repertoire. There may be similarities in the processes involved in establishing new relations and in continuously reestablishing the mutual attachment of mother and child.

So we are committed to the proposition that the infant not only has the capacity to be attached to one particular person, but is open to developing new relations with adults and with peers. Indeed, he may initiate much of this process on his own.

ACKNOWLEDGMENT

This chapter was presented at the Erindale Symposium on Communication and Affect, Toronto, March, 1975.

References

Ainsworth, M. D. S., Bell, S. M. V., & Stayton, D. J. Individual differences in strange-situation behaviour of one-year-olds. In H. R. Schaffer (Ed.), *The origins of human social relations.* New York: Academic Press, 1971, 17–57.

Blurton-Jones, N. G. Ethology and early socialization. In M. P. M. Richards (Ed.), *The integration of a child into a social world.* New York: Cambridge University Press, 1974, 263–293.

Bühler, C. The social behaviour of children. In C. A. Murchison (Ed.), *Handbook of child psychology.* New York: Russell & Russell, 1933, 374–416.

Bühler, C. *From birth to maturity: an outline of the psychological development of the child.* London: Routledge & Kegan Paul Ltd., 1935.

Corter, C. M. A comparison of the mother's and a stranger's control of the behavior of infants. *Child Development*, 1973, **44**, 705–713.

Eckerman, C. O. & Rheingold, H. L. Infants' exploratory responses to toys and people. *Developmental Psychology*, 1974, **10**, 255–259.

Faigin, H. Social behavior of young children in the Kibbutz. *Journal of Abnormal and Social Psychology*, 1958, **56**, 117–129.

Garvey, C. Some properties of social play. *Merrill-Palmer Quarterly of Behavior and Development*, 1974, **20**, 163–180.

Gesell, A. & Ilg, F. L. *Infant and child in the culture of today: the guidance of development in home and nursery school.* New York: Harper & Row, 1943.

Gesell, A., Ilg, F. L., Ames, L. B. & Rodell, J. L. *Infant and child in the culture of today: the guidance of development in home and nursery school*. New York: Harper & Row, 1974.

Morgan, G. Determinants of infants' reactions to strangers. Paper presented at the meeting of the Society for Research in Child Development, Philadelphia, Pennsylvania, March, 1973.

Parten, M. B. Social play among preschool children. *Journal of Abnormal and Social Psychology*, 1933, **28**, 136–147.

Rafman, S. The infant's reaction to imitation of the mother's behavior by the stranger. In T. G. Décarie (Ed.), *The infant's reaction to strangers*. New York: International Universities Press, 1974, 117–148.

Rheingold, H. L. & Eckerman, C. O. Fear of the stranger: a critical examination. In H. W. Reese (Ed.), *Advances in child development and behavior*. New York: Academic Press, 1974, 186–222.

Ross, H. S. The effects of increasing familiarity on infants' reactions to adult strangers. *Journal of Experimental Child Psychology*, 1975, **20**, 226–239.

Stone, L. J., Smith, H. T., & Murphy, L. B. *The competent infant*. New York: Basic Books, Inc., 1973.

CHAPTER 4

Brief Separation and Communication between Infant and Mother

Carl M. Corter

Department of Psychology
Erindale College, University of Toronto
Mississauga, Ontario

This chapter deals with the behavior of 10-month-old infants while they are away from their mothers for brief periods in a number of laboratory situations. Before presenting the results, I will set the background with a discussion of two general topics: first, the nature of separation and second, the relation between responses to brief separation and attachment.

The Nature of Infant–Mother Separation

The topic of infant–mother separation has tragic connotations. It brings to mind pictures of infants wasting away in institutions from lack of maternal love and the trauma of tearing the young child from his mother when either partner is hospitalized. I have nothing to say about such separations except to wonder whether these pictures, drawn years ago, are coloring present ideas about the effects of separations that are radically different from the sometimes tragic circumstances I have just mentioned.

A brief laboratory separation seems so different from institutionalization that applying the term separation to both situations may seem useless. Yet the equation has been made explicit by a number of people including John Bowlby in his volumes on attachment (1969) and separation (1973). I will discuss Bowlby's ideas in some detail since his view of attachment is one of the most comprehensive and influential and because he has devoted much thought to the nature of separation. Bowlby states that the absence of the mother in both laboratory and long-term separations produces the feeling of fear and overt signs of distress that differ only in intensity, not in form. He also argues that distress is due to the mother's departure and absence per se, and not to distressing events which are sometimes associated with separation, although such events intensify the distress. Separation protest and anxiety are thus to be expected when an infant is separated from his mother, even in the course of everyday life in the home. Bowlby's thinking about the effects of separation in everyday settings is reflected in the following passage on the developmental course of separation responses:

> During his first year an infant protests especially when put down in his cot and, a little later, on seeing his mother disappear from sight. Subsequently a child who, when his mother leaves him, is otherwise engrossed, begins to notice that she is gone and then protests, thenceforward, he is keenly alert to his mother's whereabouts. . . .During his eleventh or twelfth month he becomes able, by noting her behaviour, to anticipate her imminent departure, and starts to protest before she goes. (1969, p. 204)

At other points in his writing Bowlby states that beyond the first year, following may replace vocal distress as a response to the mother's departure (1969), but in both cases the responses are accompanied by feelings of fear and anxiety (1973).

These are strong, categorical statements about separation. Bowlby makes them on the basis of his theory of attachment and various kinds of evidence. His theory of attachment is complex since it represents a synthesis of Freudian, ethological, Piagetian, and control-systems theory. In Bowlby's own words "the child's tie to his mother is a product of the activity of a number of behavioural systems that have proximity to mother as a predictable outcome" (1969, p. 179). He goes on to say that the nature of the system is such that it would keep the infant and mother together constantly were it not for competing systems of behavior such as exploration. Bowlby describes attachment behaviors as instinctive because they are exhibited by almost all year-old infants reared under normal circumstances and since the behaviors have obvious survival value. Thus, infants are genetically biased to seek and maintain proximity to the attachment figure. Of course, learning has a place in the theory. The infant learns the characteristics of his attachment figure in early infancy. The infant learns increasingly more about his environment and his mother as he builds mental models which modify his attachment behavior; for example, as noted earlier, he learns to predict his mother's departure. He learns too about alarming events, which may activate attachment behavior.

Nevertheless, the nature of the innate predispositions Bowlby sees underlying attachment are very clear in his analysis of separation responses. In his view, the departure and absence of the mother almost inevitably activates attachment behavior. The immediate activation is mediated by the infant's innate sensitivity to "being alone as a natural clue to danger" and "nothing increases the likelihood that fear will be aroused more than that" (1973, p. 118). In fact, a recent and sympathetic review of Bowlby's work summarized the thrust of his ideas under the title, "The Terror of Solitude" (Hogan, 1975). Bowlby is not alone in his ideas. Bell and Ainsworth (1972) write that the infant is genetically programmed to cry when he is out of contact with his mother, as if it were a matter of life and death. Scott (Scott, Stewart, & DeGhett, 1973) states that separation distress is based on a built-in mechanism of emotional distress upon separation from the familiar. These claims show that Bowlby is not unique in the strong conclusions he draws regarding separation.

Bowlby gathers a wide range of research evidence to support such conclusions. Most relevant for this paper is the evidence from studies of brief laboratory separations. The evidence Bowlby reviews seems fairly clear. A number of studies show that when the mother leaves her year-old infant in a laboratory playroom and shuts the door behind her, the infant commonly cries, ceases playing, and may attempt to follow. The distress is fairly immediate, usually coming as soon as the infant realizes the mother is gone.

Bowlby also finds clear evidence in these studies that the distress is due to the mother's departure and absence and not to the laboratory setting, since infants play and explore contentedly in the same setting when the mother is present. Thus, he describes the mother as serving as a base of exploration; the infant may venture away confidently provided he leaves with the certain knowledge of his mother's location and his ability to return to her, but exploration ends abruptly if the mother moves away.

The evidence suggests to Bowlby and others (Ainsworth, 1964; Lewis and Ban, 1971) that the infant's leaving the mother is a very different situation than his being left, and Bowlby reserves the term separation for the mother's departure and absence. A complication in Bowlby's definition of separation is that absence is a relative term and depends on the child's interpretations about his mother's accessibility. If a child interprets that his mother is really available even though she has departed, the situation does not qualify as a separation. Furthermore, the mother may even be physically present but emotionally absent. This cognitive hedging makes an objective definition of separation difficult, but Bowlby seems to imply that these mental complexities apply to the behavior of young children and not to year-old infants. The year-old infant in Bowlby's view has only recently mastered the idea that an absent object still exists and is not yet capable of complex interpretations about the absent mother's accessibility. By the time the three-year-old goes to nursery school, mental interpretations about the mother's accessibility and her certain return allow the child to adapt with little distress, and so the mother's absence is no longer a separation. Nevertheless, in describing the one-year-old's response to his mother's departure and absence, Bowlby has given us a picture of inevitable distress.

Leaving aside the mental complexities, it is still obvious that separation is a broad term which may be defined in many different ways in brief separations depending on the characteristics of the mother's departure and absence as well as on the characteristics of the environment in which the infant is left. In laboratory studies of separation, the mother's absence has been defined by her being visible but inaccessible (Goldberg & Lewis, 1969), out of sight but accessible (Corter, Rheingold, & Eckerman, 1972), and even absent except for her voice (Turnure, 1971). However, the most common separation procedure in laboratory studies is the mother's leaving and shutting a door behind her (e.g., Ainsworth & Bell, 1970). Bowlby, in fact, limits his consideration to laboratory separations defined in this way.

In our own studies, the mother leaves the infant, but does not shut a door as she enters another room. In these circumstances we do not find that distress is inevitable. Instead, we find that following is more common, that the infant's play does not cease as soon as mother leaves, and that reunions are not tearful affairs. In short, we find that infants are content to stay away from their mothers for a time, and that the duration of time away provides a useful measure of the effect of variations in the separation situation.

Attachment and Responses to Brief Separation

In turning to a consideration of the relation between responses to brief separation and attachment, I should note that Bowlby assigns great importance to separation responses in understanding attachment since the goal of proximity maintenance is clearest in responses to separation rather than in responses to the mother's presence.

In fact, since Schaffer and Emerson's (1964) pioneering longitudinal study of the development of separation protest in everyday situations, vocal distress upon separation has often been used as a means of assessing the infant's attachment to his mother. Schaffer and Emerson stated that the response is not itself an attachment response but, rather, evidence that an attachment exists. In this statement they foreshadowed the relatively recent spate of criticism of separation protest as a useful index of the attachment of infant to mother.

The nature of the criticism depends on the view of attachment adopted by the critic. Some researchers have conceived attachment as a trait of the infant and examined individual differences in various behaviors to determine the pattern of intercorrelations across behaviors, ages, and situations (e.g., Coates, Anderson, & Hartup, 1972). The strategy is to determine which behaviors intercorrelate to a degree that would warrant their use as indices of the attachment trait. The finding and the criticism concerning separation responses is that they do not correlate with responses to the mother's presence and therefore are not part of the attachment trait. However, this criticism is weakened by Masters' recent critique of trait validation procedures in attachment research (Masters & Wellman, 1974). Masters argues that there is little evidence for attachment as a trait even when consideration is limited to responses to the mother's presence. He states that the correlations reported are often more artifacts than evidence for a trait; for an example, he singles out the high correlation in one report between proximity to the mother and touching her.

Other critics of separation protest as an index of attachment do not necessarily assume that there is a trait to be measured, but do point out that separation protest may be a relatively indirect response to the mother. Gewirtz (1972) argues that emotional responses upon separation may not be behaviors that reflect positive stimulus control by the mother; in other words, such responses may not have the effect of producing discriminative stimuli from the mother which signal reinforcement, an effect that Gewirtz believes is a useful way of defining a class of direct attachment behaviors. He does say that operant crying has the effect of bringing the mother to the child, but that separation protest does not always reflect such control. Instead, it may reflect other factors such as individual differences in thresholds for emotional responding and situational differences in the degree of interference with the child's normal response sequences.

Others argue in different terms along the same lines: separation protest as a response to the mother is complicated by situational and individual differences, which in turn are due to cognitive variables rather than anything to do with attachment. For example, one line of argument is that the infant's lack of understanding of discrepant events may lead to separation protest. The discrepancy involved in separations may be due either to the novelty of the environment or the nature of the mother's departure. Thus, a widely cited study of separation protest in the home showed that among the small proportion of infants who cried, crying was more common when the mother left through a rarely used exit such as a closet or cellar door (Littenberg, Tulkin, & Kagan, 1971).

Finally, a number of people have pointed out that the infant's level of object concept development, in Piaget's terms, will affect his separation responses. If he cannot respond to hidden things, he cannot respond to his absent mother (e.g. Lester, Kotelchuck, Spelke, Sellers, & Klein, 1974). Separation responses to the mother are therefore complicated by individual and age differences in cognitive level.

While most of these criticisms are directed at separation protest as a measure of the infant's response to the mother, they may be extended to other separation responses, such as cessation of play and looking or following to the point of the mother's disappearance. Thus, the question becomes whether separation situations provide any useful information about the infant's attachment to his mother. My feeling is that the criticisms also apply to responses to the mother's presence; there are no "pure" responses to the mother. Situations involving the mother's presence vary and have various effects on the responses the infant may direct toward her. Within a situation involving the mother's presence, infants may vary in their responses as a function of individual differences in such variables as temperament, cognitive level, or previous learning history. The criticisms of separation responses, thus, simply become complexities requiring analysis in any full account of the infant's responses to his mother.

Given these complexities, how should we go about defining attachment? The ultimate answer will probably be framed in terms of the dyadic perspective that Cairns calls for in Chapter 1 of this volume. Traditionally, however, attachment has been approached from the infant side as either an entity underlying responses to the mother or a response class having certain features. There is little agreement about the nature of the entity among those who use such a conception of attachment, and as Gewirtz (1972) states, the nature of the entity is often not specified at all. Perhaps the clearest specification along these lines is the concept of attachment as a unidimensional trait, but the usefulness of this approach is not at all clear in the data that have been collected to support it.

There is greater agreement among writers when the definition of attachment is approached at the level of a response class. Attachment behaviors are commonly defined in terms of two major attributes. Firstly, they are behaviors that increase or maintain proximity between infant and mother. Secondly, they are selective in the sense that they are controlled more by the mother, or attachment object, than by other people.

Using these simple criteria, it becomes possible to determine which responses to separation fit the definition. Both separation protest and following have been studied in these terms and seem to fit, so at least at this simple level separation can tell us something about attachment. However, there are a number of limitations of the definition that apply both to separation responses and responses to the mother's presence. First of all, if we limit our study to responses that fit the definition, we neglect useful information provided by other responses, including those directed to the mother and to the inanimate features of the environment. I will argue later that the infant's looking and playing behaviors after his mother has left provide an understanding of the nature of the infant's subsequent following of his mother. Following fits the definition of an attachment behavior, but looking does not seem to be selective in most accounts, and play or its absence certainly does not fit the definition.

A second limitation is that not all behaviors assumed to fit this definition have actually been shown to have these two attributes. For example, although following obviously has the effect of bringing the infant closer to the mother, separation protest does not necessarily have the effect of bringing the mother to the child, even though our intuition and some descriptive evidence tells us that it may. Likewise, behaviors are sometimes assumed to be selective in the absence of any clear evidence. In some cases, the selectivity of the responses would seem to be impossible to test. It is relatively easy to present the infant with the mother and another person to determine the selectivity of something like smiling; it is more difficult to imagine a meaningful test to determine whether the sucking behavior of a breast-feeding 10-month-old is selectively directed toward the mother.

A final limitation of attempts to define a class of attachment responses is that the class must be qualified by the age of the infant and the situations in which the responses are studied. Thus, a response may be one that produces proximity and is selective for most infants only at particular ages and only in certain situations.

Research Strategy

The reason for pointing out these limitations is to argue that inquiries regarding infant–mother interaction should go beyond assembling a list of attachment responses. Situational differences may be interesting in themselves and not simply hindrances to the study of attachment. The series of studies that will be described in this chapter represent an attempt to understand some situational determinants of the infant's response to brief laboratory separations. I hope to show that such a strategy may have implications for understanding the general nature of infant–mother interaction as well as for understanding attachment responses which selectively bring infant and mother together.

In order to deal with situational complexities I've chosen to simplify the research in other ways. One main way has been to limit the study to ten-month-old infants rather than to deal directly with developmental issues. Another way has been to generally ignore individual differences. Still another way has been to focus on the infant's, not the mother's, response. In all but one study, the mother's behavior is carefully constrained by the experimental procedure and her behavior is not under study. Before dealing with the results of our studies, I will describe some of their common features.

Subjects are approximately 10 months old and range in age from 9.5 to 11.0 months. An additional selection criterion is the infant's ability to crawl well enough to move from room to room. The samples are predominantly middle class as judged by parental education.

The test environment for the studies consists of a suite of two or three large laboratory rooms. The rooms have one-way windows and ceiling microphones which allow recording from an adjacent observation room. The test rooms are unfurnished aside from a cushion or chair for the mother to sit on while she is away from her infant.

The procedure for the studies begins with a 10- to 15-minute adaptation period in a reception room prior to the observation of separation. During this period we explain the mother's role to her and give the infant toys. The mother then carries her child into the test rooms where we briefly point out where she is to place her infant and where she is to sit. As soon as the experimenter leaves, the mother places her infant in one room and then without pause and without speaking moves to a position in an adjoining room. The mother is instructed to sit silently while the infant is away, but she may look and smile at her infant when he is in sight.

The measures of behavior vary somewhat, but the major focus has been on the length of time an infant is content to stay away from his mother before following; following is defined simply as the infant's crossing the threshold as he moves to the mother's room. In order to assign some meaning to this measure, we record a number of other responses during the time the infant is away from mother as well as after he has moved to her.

By recording play behavior and vocal distress during separation we can make judgements about the affective state of the infant. In addition to following, other responses directed to the mother are also useful in assessing the effects of separation. Thus, we record the infant's looking in his mother's direction, smiling to her, and touching her upon reunion.

Recording is generally done by observers who look through the one-way window and use an Esterline-Angus event recorder to continuously record the behavior categories. Vocal behaviors are recorded at a later date, from audiotapes. To check interobserver reliability, two observers record the majority of our observations. The mean percentages of agreement for measures within the various studies range from 79% to 100%.

The Role of Nonsocial Stimuli

Study 1

In Study 1 (Corter *et al.*, 1972), we examined the infant's response to separation as a function of variations in the nonsocial stimuli in the separation environment. In particular, we examined the effects of presence or absence of a toy and the relative novelty of the toy in delaying the infant's following of his mother.

The method in Trial 1 involved placing one group of ten infants in a bare room, and another group of ten infants in the same room with a single toy. In a second trial, infants in the Toy Group of Trial 1 were placed with the same familiar toy, and infants in the No-Toy Group of Trial 1 were also placed with the toy, which for them was novel. In all four conditions, each mother walked away and went out of sight in another room. Figure 1 shows the layout of the experimental setting.

Both the presence and relative novelty of the toy had clear effects in delaying following. Figure 2 shows the latency to follow in the four conditions. Infants left with a toy in Trial 1 played with it and took almost ten times longer to follow than infants left without a toy. In Trial 2, infants left with the novel toy took significantly longer to follow than infants left with the familiar toy.

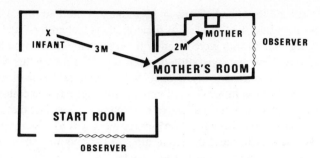

Fig. 1. The experimental setting for Study 1. In Trial 1, infants were placed in the start room with no toy or with a single toy. In Trial 2, infants were placed with either a novel or familiar toy.

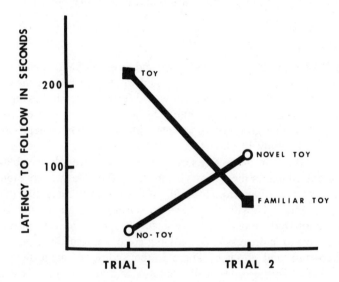

Fig. 2. Delay of following mother in the four conditions in Study 1.

As for the infants' affective state in Trial 1, 14 out of 20 emitted no vocal distress during the time they were away from their mothers. Furthermore, 14 out of 20 smiled at their mothers upon seeing them when they reached the doorway. Social interaction across a distance and exploration of the mother's room often intervened between the infant's arrival at the doorway and further movement toward the mother. The amount of time between arrival at the doorway and touching the mother averaged approximately 1½ minutes for all infants in Trial 1.

In Trial 2, only 3 infants in the Novel-Toy Group fussed and none cried during the 5-minute observation which included both separation and reunion with the mother. On the other hand, 8 out of 10 infants in the Familiar Toy Group cried, usually after they had moved to their mothers. Therefore, distress was common only for infants who were faced with an unchanging environment.

These results show that separation distress is not the rule in this setting and that following is not automatically evoked by the mother's departure and absence. The patterns of the infants' reunion behavior suggests that following was not a flight from separation or an aversive environment. The fact that following was immediate only when the separation environment was bare suggests that the infant may leave simply because the environment offers nothing so interesting as the mother. Thus, following need not always be a flight but may instead be a movement to the mother because she is a source of social stimulation providing complex feedback in different modalities. Characterizing movement to the mother as a movement to security as Bowlby (1969) and others have done may miss an important point in the nature of infant–mother interaction.

Study 2

Study 1 demonstrated that the presence and novelty of a toy delayed following. In Study 2 (Corter et al., 1972) we asked whether increasing the complexity of toys in the separation environment would further delay following.

Complexity was manipulated simply by leaving one group of 13 infants with 1 toy, and another group of 13 infants with 6 toys. The general procedure was the same as in Study 1.

Although infants in the 6-Toy Group stayed somewhat longer before following than did infants in the 1-Toy Group, the difference was not significant. The general patterns of behaviors for both groups was very much like that of the Toy Group in Study 1, with little distress during separation, and generally positive behavior upon reunion. These results support the conclusions from Study 1 that separation distress and following are not automatic responses to the mother's departure and absence. There is the additional suggestion in these results that there may be limits to the amount of time an infant is content to remain away from his mother in an unchanging environment.

The Role of Social Stimuli

Study 3

Study 3 (Corter, 1973) was designed to test the role of social stimuli in controlling the infant's separation responses. The focus of the study was on the infant's social responses across a distance to either his mother or a strange female. Thus, we inquired whether following, separation distress, looking, and smiling are selectively directed to the mother in a separation situation, and whether they qualify as attachment responses in that sense.

To make statements about selectivity, we compared responses to the presence and absence of both mother and stranger, and we compared responses to mother and stranger when both were present at a distance. The design thus entailed three groups of 10 infants. For the Mother–Stranger Group the infant was placed with a toy, and the mother and stranger then left and sat in separate rooms where the infant could see them. Figure 3 shows the setting for the Mother–Stranger Group. In a second group, the Mother Group, the same procedure was followed except that the stranger left and shut the door, leaving only the mother present at a distance. In the Stranger Group, this procedure was reversed so that only the stranger was present at a distance. Both mother and stranger were allowed to look and smile, but not to call to the infant from a distance.

Fig. 3. The experimental setting for Study 3. In the condition illustrated, both mother and stranger were present at a distance. In a second condition, the stranger shut the door to her room so that only the mother was present. In the third condition, the mother shut her door and only the stranger was present. (Copyright, 1976, by the American Psychological Association. Reprinted by permission.).

The general findings concerning the selectivity of social responses can be summarized quickly. When both mother and stranger were available, following was directed to the mother but looking and smiling were directed almost as often toward the stranger as toward the mother. When only the mother was present, the infant followed her, but when only the stranger was present the infant did not follow. Most infants cried when the mother was absent, but most did not cry when the stranger was absent.

An important question in considering these findings is whether the selectivity of following and separation distress reflect aversive qualities of the stranger or positive control by the mother. Evidence for the latter is provided by the finding that the majority of infants looked and smiled toward the stranger when both adults were present. Furthermore, infants in the Mother–Stranger Group took significantly longer to follow the mother than did infants in the Mother Group who did not have the opportunity to interact with the stranger across a distance. Thus, the provision of a novel person, as well as a novel toy, delays the infant's following of his mother. Again, following in this situation appears not to be a flight but rather movement reflecting more positive control by the mother.

The Role of the Mother's Departure and Absence

Study 4

The first three studies demonstrated that the characteristics of social and nonsocial stimuli in the separation environment affect the infant's response to separation. Study 4 (Corter, 1976) examined the effects of variations in the nature of the mother's absence. The effects of two factors were examined in a 2 × 2 design: whether mother or infant initiated the separation and whether the mother was visible or not during the infant's stay away from her.

The importance of both factors in determining whether or not an infant is content while away from his mother is suggested by the concept of the mother as a secure base for exploration. Ainsworth, for example, writes that the infant's "confidence in leaving the secure base is in remarkable contrast to his distress if the secure base gets up and moves off on her own initiative" (1964, p. 54). In this view, the effects of mother's absence depends on who leaves whom.

Similar suggestions are made in the literature regarding opportunity to see the mother; seeing the mother provides security which allows the child to explore and play away from the mother's side. Two-year-olds in a play room with the mother spend more time playing with toys at a distance when the mother is facing the toys rather than facing away or sitting behind a screen (Carr, Dabbs, & Carr, 1975). Even young rhesus monkeys explore more when a surrogate mother is visible but inaccessible in a plexiglass box rather than absent altogether (Mason, Hill, & Thomsen, 1970).

In order to test such suggestions, we observed the behavior of infants while they played in a room away from their mothers under four conditions. In the Mother Departs–Mother Visible (MD-MV) Group, the infant was placed in the room with several toys, and the mother then left and sat down in a position in the adjoining room where she could be seen. In the Mother Departs–Mother Not Visible (MD-MNV) Group, the mother also left her infant, but moved to a position in the next room where the infant could not see her as he played with the toys.

In the Infant Departs–Mother Visible (ID-MV) Group, the infant was placed directly in front of the mother and allowed to move on his own to the toys in the next room and the mother was visible to the infant as he played away from her. Finally, in the Infant Departs–Mother Not Visible (ID-MNV) Group, the infant left on his own, but the mother was not visible once the infant had moved to the toys. Figure 4 shows an infant leaving his mother in the ID-MNV Group. There were 10 infants in each of the four groups.

Fig. 4. The experimental setting for Study 4. In the condition illustrated (ID-MNV), the infant was allowed to depart from the mother's side to play in an adjoining room with toys which were out of sight of her. In a second condition, (ID-MV) the infant left to play with toys within sight in the adjoining room. In a third condition (MD-MNV), mother departed after placing her infant with toys, and assumed a position out of sight in the adjoining room. In the fourth condition (MD-MV), she left and assumed a position in the adjoining room within sight of her infant.

    Since all infants in the ID Groups left their mothers to enter the Toy Room,
it was possible to compare the behavior of all four groups during the stay away
from the mother. Figure 5 shows the duration of the stay away for the four
groups.

    The results showed that whether the mother or infant initiated the separation
had no effects. Infants in both the MD Groups who were left in the toy room and
those in the ID Groups who entered on their own, stayed for approximately three
minutes. Furthermore, who left whom had no effects on play behavior, vocal
distress, or smiling while the infant was away.

    In contrast, the mother's visibility had a significant effect on the duration of
the stay in the toy room. Infants in the MV Group who could see their mothers
from the toys stayed away almost twice as long (mean of 245 seconds) as did
infants in the MNV Group who could not see their mothers (mean of 143
seconds). Infants in the MV Groups also spent more time touching the toy during
their stay in the toy room.

    The effects of the mother's visibility on behavior during separation was
mediated by frequent looks to the mother for infants in the MV Groups as they
sat in the square surrounding the toys. They looked at the mother an average of
10 times (range, 0 to 27) for a mean total of 24 seconds (range, 0 to 88). In

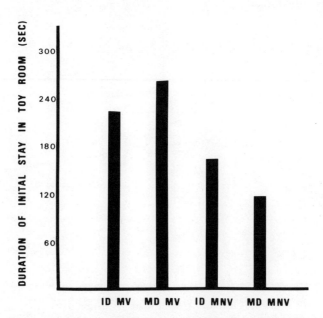

Fig. 5. Duration of time in room away from mother as a function
of whether departure was initiated by infant (ID) or mother (MD)
and whether mother was visible (MV) or not (MNV).

contrast, infants in the MNV Groups looked toward the doorway an average of only 3 times (range, 1 to 14) for a mean of 4 seconds as they sat with the toys.

Although the groups differed in the duration of initial stay and play away from the mother, they were similar in their lack of distress during the separation. Only 4 of 40 infants fussed or cried in the toy room. Smiling was more common than vocal distress. With the mother visible, 10 of 20 infants in the MV Group smiled while playing with the toys. Remarkably enough, 5 of 20 infants in the MNV Groups smiled while sitting with the toys out of sight of the mother.

Comparison of the infants' movement to the mother and to toys adds to the generally "positive" picture of the infants' affective states. Infants in the ID Groups left the mother's room to go to the toy room significantly sooner than infants in the MD Groups left the toy room to go to the mother's room. Infants in the MD Groups who were placed in the toy room stayed for a mean of over three minutes (mean, 196 seconds; range 14 to 558) in the toy room before leaving, while infants in the ID Groups stayed for a mean of less than a minute (mean, 49 seconds; range, 5 to 226) in the mother's room before leaving.

If attachment and exploration are viewed as two behavior systems in balance, the results of this study show that the balance was initially tipped toward exploration. In rooms that were new to the infants and bare except for mother and toys, infants played away from the mother, regardless of whether they were placed there or moved there on their own, and regardless of whether the mother was visible or out of sight.

The findings attest to the pervasiveness of exploratory behavior shown in Rheingold's laboratory and field research on detachment, or the infant's leaving his mother (Rheingold & Eckerman, 1970). Nevertheless, the mother is still a part of the settings of these studies and other research (e.g., Rheingold, 1969a; Corter, 1973) shows that infants do not explore or play contentedly in the same settings when separated from the mother by a closed door. What conditions, then, are necessary to evoke playful exploration rather than separation distress?

One suggestion in the literature is that the infant must leave on his own. However, the findings of this study show that whether the mother or infant initiated the separation had no effect on the infant's behavior once he was in the play room. If the mother is a secure base for exploration she is not a base in the sense that the infant must start at her side and move away on his own.

A second suggestion is that opportunity to see the mother should reduce distress and support exploration while the infant is away from her. In this study, infants went out of sight of the mother and remained away after the mother had gone out of sight, but they stayed away longer when the mother was visible. This finding is consistent with the notion that the mother functions as a secure base in a novel setting, but other interpretations are possible. One is suggested by the finding in Study 3 that opportunity to look at a stranger increased the time infants spent in a play room before leaving to go to their mothers; the stranger may have increased time away from the mother by providing interesting visual stimulation. In this study, the mother herself may have increased time away by serving as a source of stimulation rather than security. Thus, the possibility that the mother may be an object of exploration as well as a base for exploration should not be overlooked in analyses of infant-mother interaction.

Study 5

Study 5 was designed to answer two questions: Firstly, does a mother's pausing to say "goodbye" change the generally positive responses we have found during separation, and secondly, what are the mother's predictions regarding her infant's response to a brief separation? Both questions may have some bearing on the ecological validity of our studies. For example, since the mother's departure was programmed in previous studies in a way that may not match her behavior in the home, the infant may not realize that her unusual departure signals a separation. We reasoned that having the mother say goodbye as she left the room would certainly define the situation as a separation for her infant.

An answer to the second question, about mothers' predictions, we assumed might show whether our results are at odds with what mothers observe in the home. Occasionally, mothers had volunteered predictions in our previous studies, and almost invariably the prediction was that the infant would cry immediately. Thus, we wondered about the expectations of mothers as they participate in these studies.

To answer these questions, we observed 14 infants in one condition, since we felt that the previous studies provided a reasonable baseline against which we could judge any dramatic effects of the mother's saying goodbye.

Again, each mother placed her infant with several novel toys, and without pause moved to the doorway of an adjoining room. Before leaving, she turned to her infant and said "goodbye" or "bye bye" until the infant looked at her, and then she went out of sight.

We described the setting and the procedures to the mother prior to the observation and asked her to predict how her infant would behave. Most mothers prefaced their prediction with remarks like "It's hard to say, but. . . ." and two mothers flatly refused to play the game at all. Among the remaining 12 mothers, the most common prediction, made by 8 mothers, was that the infant would play for a while before missing her and the majority of these said the infant would then follow. Three mothers predicted immediate distress and one mother, immediate following. The typical maternal prediction was therefore the same one that we would have made based on our previous studies. In amplifying their predictions most mothers made it clear that they were generalizing mainly from what they had observed in the home.

As for the behavior of the infants during separation, I need only say that the typical maternal prediction was correct. The average duration of the stay away from the mother was 234 seconds, or just under 4 minutes. Of the 14 infants, 10 emitted no vocal distress during the separation, and 13 of the 14 played with the toys. The pattern of behavior here is very much like the pattern in the other studies when the mother leaves without comment.

These simple results show that even in a certain separation, following is not immediate and distress is relatively rare. The mothers' predictions also show that the general picture is in keeping with what mothers expect, even though the picture runs counter to what some psychologists might expect.

Sex Differences in Response to Separation

Individual differences in the response of 10-month-old infants to the separation situations in the first five studies I've described do exist, but the general patterns of response hold for a large proportion of infants within each situation, and for that reason I've been able to generally pursue a strategy of ignoring individual differences in the hope of first clarifying the common ground that exists among infants. One difference that is impossible to ignore, however, is a fairly consistent difference between male and female infants in response to separation. The general finding is that male infants tend to follow after a briefer period away from the mother; females stay longer. The findings that novel toys, a novel person, and an opportunity to see the mother increase time away hold for both sexes, but the stay is briefer for males.

In the first five studies, differences in this direction were found in 8 of 9 conditions presented in a first trial in which the mother was available to follow. Figure 6 shows the latency to follow for males and females in these 9 conditions. In 4 of the 8 conditions in which females stayed longer, the difference was significant and in a fifth condition the numbers of males and females were not distributed evenly enough to test. The single difference in the direction of males staying longer was not significant.

The finding that males followed more quickly is given some support but little clarification by other studies of brief separation. A number of reports show that males are more responsive in moving to, or attempting to move to, the mother (e.g., Goldberg & Lewis, 1969). On the other hand, when response to separation is indexed by vocal distress, no notable sex differences appear.

The finding of a sex difference in movements to the mother thus seems real enough to wonder about. Although the possibilities for explaining sex differences are endless, the use of sex as a marker might eventually provide useful information about other variables that control the infant's response to separation.

To constrain the endless possibilities in some way, I have considered whether sex differences in movement to the mother might reflect differential responsiveness to the mother's departure and absence, differential responsive-

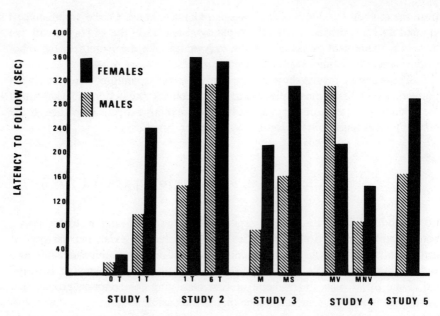

Fig. 6. Sex differences in delay of following mother in Studies 1 to 5.

ness to the situation in which the infant is left, or stable behavioral predispositions that are not unique to either the mother or the situation.

With regard to the latter possibility, there are few sex differences reported in
infancy that are either replicable or stable across situation and age. Although
neonatal males have been reported to be more active than females in terms of a
very limited number of responses (e.g., Bell & Darling, 1965), activity level is
not a stable characteristic across the first year of life (Pederson & Bell, 1970) and
I have found no reports of greater locomotor activity on the part of males in the
first year of life. Thus, it would seem that males do not move to the mother
sooner simply because they are more active.

Another possibility is that males are generally more irritable and therefore
sensitive to any sudden change in their environment. Moss (1974) has collected
impressive evidence that males emit more vocal distress in the first few months
of life and hence concludes that they are generally more irritable than females.
However, we have presented evidence suggesting that under certain conditions
separation need not be considered irritating. Then, too, sex differences are not
usually found in vocal distress upon separation. Sex differences in stable behavioral predispositions do not seem to exist in forms that are directly relevant to
the sex difference at issue here.

Another class of possibilities for explaining the sex difference is that it
might be mediated by less general differences between males' and females'
responses to the features of the situation in which they are left. Perhaps males

respond differently to the overall novelty of the separation environment. The novelty of the room in which the infant is left does not seem to be a factor, however. In our studies, males followed sooner in both first and second trials in the same room, so that increasing familiarity with test rooms did not attenuate the sex difference. In addition, more frequent following among males has been found in the infant's home environment (Stayton, Ainsworth, & Main, 1973).

For the infants in our studies, the most salient aspect of the separation environment seems to be the toys with which the infant is left, so perhaps differences in play behavior might explain the sex difference in response to separation. Nevertheless, Study 1 showed that the difference held when the infant was left with no toys at all. The finding that males respond more vigorously to separation is thus found across a wide enough range of situations to suggest that the mother herself, her departure and absence, may be the stimulus for the sex difference.

A tempting generalization to make from these data is that male infants of approximately a year of age are more attached and females more independent in the sense that males seek the mother sooner. This temptation should be rejected for at least two reasons. First, the evidence that attachment is a unitary construct is too weak to support such statements. Second, when the mother is present in free-play settings, infants' departures and returns to her do not support the generalization. The majority of these studies do not report sex differences (e.g., Rheingold & Eckerman, 1970). In fact, when sex differences are reported, they are in the opposite direction; that is, males stay longer when they leave the mother (e.g. Goldberg & Lewis, 1969). This result is supported by sex differences in our own study comparing differences in time away from the mother as a function of who left whom. Within both groups in which infants left the mothers to enter a play room in Study 4, we found that males spent longer away than did females, although the difference was significant in only one of the two groups. These results suggest that sex differences in time away from the mother may depend on who leaves whom.

This suggestion is perplexing, but strengthens the possibility that there is something about the mother's departure and absence that accounts for the sex difference in response to separation. Thus, it may depend on differences in previously established patterns of interaction between mother and infant in separation situations. Interest in the possibility and a general interest in the mother's response to separation led us to Study 6.

Maternal Response to Separation

Study 6

In this study (Corter & Bow, 1976), we asked whether mothers respond differently to males and females in a separation and, furthermore, whether the infant's vocal distress has an effect on the mother's response. We were interested not only in the mother's behavior during separation but in her retrieval and reunion behavior as well.

Vocal distress seemed an obvious infant variable to examine since it has received so much attention in theoretical accounts of separation and attachment and in studies of the infant's response to separation. Its signaling power in bringing the mother back into proximity to the infant has been widely acclaimed and actually given some research support by descriptive studies (e.g., Bell & Ainsworth, 1972). We hoped to demonstrate the power of vocal distress more directly by actually manipulating it in order to make causal inferences about its effect on maternal behavior.

The onset of vocal distress was manipulated by placing infants in an empty playpen or in the same playpen with several toys. Our assumption was that the provision of toys would delay vocal distress just as toys had delayed following in the previous studies; the assumption turned out to be correct. The study thus involved a 2 × 2 design with the infant's sex and presence or absence of toys as the two factors.

Subjects were 24 infant-mother pairs assigned randomly to the toy and no-toy groups with the provision that the groups be balanced for sex. The observations took place in two rooms connected by an open doorway. The room in which the infant stayed during the separation contained a soft chair with several toys on the seat, a rug, a tripod and TV camera, and a playpen. For one group of infants, the playpen contained three toys; for the other group, the playpen was empty. During the separation, the mother stayed out of sight in the other room which contained a soft chair, a table with magazines and ashtray, and a video monitor showing the playpen in the first room. Figure 7 shows the layout of the test rooms.

During an adaptation period prior to the observations, the experimenter explained the procedures to the mother. The explanation of the study and instructions to the mother were worded to avoid conveying expectancies about how she should act. She was told that the purpose of the study was to look at, first, the infant's response to being left and, second, the nature of the interaction between infant and mother when they were together again. She was told that her behavior and that of her infant would be recorded in the observation rooms. "For example," the instructions went, "we will record whether the baby smiles if you smile at him." Thus, we implied that we were mainly interested in the infant's behavior as a function of the mother's behavior rather than the reverse and that the mother's behavior was of importance only during the reunion.

The mother was instructed to set her infant in the playpen and then to walk immediately into the adjoining room without speaking or calling to the infant at any point during the separation. It was explained that we would let the separation last a maximum of five minutes, but that she could end it at any time. She was told that after returning she could do as she wished—watch the infant, hold him,

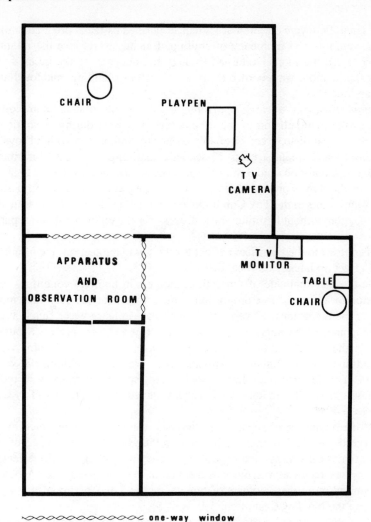

Fig. 7. The experimental setting for Study 6. In one condition, three toys
were available in the infant's playpen during separation. In the second condition, no toys were in the playpen.

play with him, read a magazine—whatever she might typically do in her own
home upon returning to her infant.

The separation trial began when the mother left through the doorway between the rooms and the 5-minute reunion trial began when she returned through
the doorway.

Measures.   Infant distress was a composite of fussing (intermittent whim-
pering) and crying (loud, continuous wailing). Maternal behaviors recorded

during separation were duration of vigilance, defined by facial orientation toward the TV monitor, and frequency of smiling. Latency to retrieve the infant was recorded when the mother returned through the doorway to the infant's room. During the reunion, we recorded the mother's talking, smiling, and touching the infant and the toys.

   Infant Behavior during Separation.   The results of the separation trial show that the manipulation of the infants' vocal distress during separation was successful; vocal distress came reliably earlier for infants left without toys. The mean onset was 1 minute (mean, 77 seconds, and range, 1 to 300) for infants in the No-Toy Condition, and 3 minutes (mean, 187 seconds; range, 30 to 300) for infants in the Toy Condition. Despite their being confined alone in a strange place, four infants in the Toy Condition and two in the No-Toy Condition stayed in the playpen without emitting vocal distress for the entire 5-minute separation trial.

   In contrast to the significant effect for the toy manipulation, the infant's sex had no effect on latency of vocal distress.

   On the maternal side of separation, mothers in both toy conditions looked at the monitor during a large proportion of the separation trial; only three mothers looked at the magazines. Nevertheless, maternal vigilance was a function of the toy factor and of the interaction between the toy and sex factors. Mothers of infants in the Toy Condition spent a greater mean percentage of time viewing the monitor than did mothers of infants in the No-Toy Condition (92 vs. 81). Mothers of males watched slightly more than mothers of females in the Toy Condition (95 vs. 90); mothers of females watched more in the No-Toy Condition (95 vs. 72).

   At the beginning of separation, vigilance was often accompanied by smiling. Overall, 18 of 24 mothers smiled during the separation, but only 5 of the 18 smiled after vocal distress had begun. Frequency of smiling was not affected by the toy or sex factor alone, but was a function of their interaction. Mothers of males smiled more than mothers of females in the Toy Condition (4.0 vs. 1.3) but less in the No-Toy Condition (1.0 vs. 4.5).

   Mothers of infants in the No-Toy Condition ended the separation by entering the infant's room somewhat sooner than did mothers of infants in the Toy Condition, but the difference was not significant. However, there was a main effect of the infant's sex on latency of retrieval. Males were retrieved earlier, at a mean of 166 seconds (range, 12 to 300); females were retrieved at 281 seconds (range, 72 to 300). The difference in latency of retrieval is due to the fact that males were retrieved more often than females. Of 12 males, 7 were retrieved but only 1 of 12 females was retrieved before the end of the 5-minute separation trial.

   During the reunion trial, neither the infant's sex nor the toy manipulation during separation had an effect on the duration of the infant's vocal distress. In fact, vocal distress subsided rapidly during the first minute of reunion. The approach of the mother prior to physical contact ended vocal distress at a mean of 1.3 seconds for 11 of the 17 infants who fussed or cried during the last 20 seconds of the separation. Furthermore, there were no group differences in maternal behaviors during reunion.

Effects of Birth Order and Playpen Use. A final feature of the results is that playpen use, gauged by mothers' reports, did not have any effects on either infant or maternal behavior during either trial. Ten mothers reported that they rarely or never used a playpen and *t* tests comparing this group to the other infant–mother pairs revealed no significant differences.

The overall results of this study can be considered in terms of both the infant's response, and the mother's response, to separation. On the maternal side of separation, this study showed that the mother's vigilance during separation was affected by the infant's vocal distress and sex, and that retrieval was a function of the infant's sex.

Although there were group differences in vigilance, mothers in all groups spent a large proportion of time looking at the video monitor during separation. Early in the trial, and usually before the infants had begun to fuss or cry, most mothers smiled while watching the monitors. Their vigilance early in the separation thus may have reflected the interest and pleasure a mother finds in maintaining contact with her content but active infant (Rheingold, 1969b). Here, then, is the suggestion that the infant may be an object of exploration for the mother.

The group differences in vigilance were not in keeping with our expectation that the greater distress of infants left without toys would evoke greater vigilance from their mothers. In fact, these mothers actually watched the monitor for a lower percentage of time than did mothers of infants whose distress was delayed by the provision of toys. However, this difference was due to differences in mothers of males; mothers of females actually watched slightly more when their infants were left without toys. Our impression was that mothers of males in the No-Toy Group, who began vocal distress early, spent more time looking at the doorway in preparation for or in debating about going to retrieve their infants. The concern of mothers in this group was evidenced by their smiling least of the four groups.

Although the mother's ending the separation by retrieving her infant did not depend on the manipulation of vocal distress, it did depend on the infant's sex. Overall, males were retrieved more often than females, and the difference cannot be explained by differences in the onset of distress, since there were none. It is possible that some other characteristic of vocal distress, such as intensity, or even some aspect of nonvocal behavior transmitted to the mother via the TV monitor may have distinguished males from females. In the data available, however, there are no differences between male and female infants during the separation that account for mothers retrieving males more than females. Therefore, mothers may be more responsive to males because of previously established patterns of interaction which are carried into the laboratory.

Another possibility is that mothers of males were responding to the cultural expectation that a male infant should not cry and were thus motivated to end the infant's vocal distress in the presence of strange experimenters. Nevertheless, the previous findings that male infants are more responsive to separation in many test situations suggest that different patterns of mother–infant interaction in response to separation may have already been established in the home, depending on whether the infant is male or female.

Aside from the possible meaning of the results of this study. I believe it also has something to say about methodology in the study of infant-mother interaction. Although the manipulation of vocal distress did not have powerful effects on maternal behavior, the study at least suggests the feasibility of manipulating the behavior of the infant to test its effects upon the mother's behavior. It may be much easier to program the mother's behavior to test its effects on the infant, but it is still possible to do the reverse.

From the infant's point of view, the successful manipulation of vocal distress provides new information about the effects of brief separations. Distress was postponed by the provision of a few toys, even though the mother was out of sight and the infant was barred from following by the playpen. This finding is another demonstration that the infant's response to separation depends partly on the nature of the nonsocial environment in which he is left.

In turning to more speculative matters, it is notable that the finding held even for infants whose mothers reported that they rarely or never used a playpen. Surely, being left under the circumstances of this study must qualify as a discrepant event for these children, but contrary to predictions made by a discrepancy account of separation (Spelke, Zelazo, Kagan, & Kotelchuck, 1973), they were no more distressed than infants who used a playpen at home. Furthermore, the finding that vocal distress was not usually immediate, even for infants who were left without toys, shows that vocal distress did not come when the discrepancy of the situation should have been highest, that is, at the beginning of the trial before the infant had a chance to become familiar with the features of the situation.

The finding that infants are content for a while when left in a playpen with toys in strange laboratory rooms also poses difficulties for the idea that separation distress depends on whether or not the infant can end the separation by moving to the mother (Bowlby, 1973; Mussen, Conger, & Kagan, 1974). Bowlby's belief that distress should be immediate and intense when the mother is absent and inaccessible is not supported.

Why vocal distress upon separation was less common and less immediate in this study than in other studies in which the mother's inaccessibility was marked by a closed door is not immediately apparent. The finding may require still further refinement of the concept of the mother as a base of exploration. Perhaps the mere possibility of auditory and visual communication with the mother is enough to avert distress and maintain play. Thus, the possibilities of seeing the mother reappear, of hearing her, and of having her respond to nondistress vocal bids may be enough for a time.

The immediate nature of distress in infants faced with a closed door suggests that these possibilities are not worked out on the spot as the infant sits in the laboratory and are no doubt dependent on what he has learned in the home. For example, closed doors may have acquired aversive properties by signalling the termination of interesting social stimulation.

As a first step in investigating such possibilities, Robert Rinkoff, a postdoctoral fellow in our laboratory, is investigating separations involving open and closed doors, in the home and the laboratory.

Conclusions

Taken as a whole, the series of studies I've described show that the situation makes a difference in separation. Separation distress is by no means inevitable and infants do not follow their mothers like imprinted ducklings. The nature of nonsocial and social stimuli in the separation situation and the nature of the mother's absence have clear effects on how long the infant is content to remain away. These findings argue against easy acceptance of theories of attachment that postulate more or less automatic disruption or distress upon the infant's separation from his mother.

The results also suggest to me that a better understanding of infant–mother interaction will depend greatly on a better understanding of the infant's exploratory and play behavior. Simply viewing attachment and exploration as systems of behavior in balance, and describing the mother's role in exploration as a base for infant exploration, may not do justice to the complexity of infant-mother interaction.

The results of the studies show that if the mother is a base, she is a base in a very subtle sense. In order to play and explore away from the mother for a time, the infant does not need to start at the mother's side and move gradually into what would otherwise be a threatening, novel environment. The infant does not need to see the mother at a distance and the mother need not be accessible in the sense that the infant can follow. Perhaps security is provided by the infant's effectiveness in distal forms of social communication, both visual and auditory, and by what he has learned about the nature of physical space, for example, that open doors leave the lines of communication open.

Alternatively, our results suggest that communication over a distance and even following at the end of a separation might just as well be controlled by stimulus change provided by the mother, stimulus change that is not necessarily accompanied by feelings of security. Given the great amount of time infants spend exploring and playing away from the mother in the home, it would be surprising if some of the same functional relationships involved in play and exploration did not hold in infant–mother interaction. Perhaps infants and mothers are objects of mutual play and exploration. This idea is not new; several years ago John S. Watson (1972) proposed a "game" theory of attachment in which the mother comes to signal contingent social stimulation and the contingency involved has the property of releasing strong positive affect for the infant. More recently, others such as Stern (Stern, 1974) and Ross, in Chapter 3 of this volume, have pointed to the importance of infant–mother play in the attachment relationship. While mothers and infants do more than explore each other and play games, this view can serve as a corrective to other oversimplified accounts that miss this feature of infant–mother interaction.

In summary, our research argues against the unqualified acceptance of terms like "separation anxiety" and "separation distress." These terms have obscured the infant's potential for independent activities, just as the term "stranger anxiety" has done. They have also obscured the sophistication of communication across a distance between infant and mother. And, finally, they have obscured the playful or exploratory nature of interaction between infant and mother when they are together.

ACKNOWLEDGMENTS

Studies 4, 5, and 6 were supported by Canada Council Grant S72-0630 and by Erindale College Internal Research Grants to the author.

References

Ainsworth, M. D. S. Patterns of attachment behavior shown by the infant in interaction with his mother. *Merrill-Palmer Quarterly*, 1964, **10**, 51–58.

Ainsworth, M. D. S., & Bell, S. M. Attachment, exploration, and separation: illustrated by the behavior of one-year-olds in a strange situation. *Child Development*, 1970, **41**, 49–67.

Bell, R. Q., & Darling, J. F. The prone head reaction in the human neonate: relationship with sex and tactile sensitivity. *Child Development*, 1965, **36**, 943–949.

Bell, S. M., & Ainsworth, M. D. Infant crying and maternal responsiveness. *Child Development*, 1972, **43**, 1171–1190.

Bowlby, J. *Attachment and loss*. Vol. 1. *Attachment*. New York: Basic Books, 1969.

Bowlby, J. *Attachment and loss*. Vol. 2. *Separation*. New York: Basic Books, 1973.

Carr, S. J., Dabbs, J. M., & Carr, T. S. Mother–infant attachment: the importance of the mother's visual field. *Child Development*, 1975, **46**, 331–338.

Coates, B., Anderson, E. P., & Hartup, W. W. Interrelations in the attachment behavior of human infants. *Developmental Psychology*, 1972, **6**, 218–230.

Corter, C. M. A comparison of the mother's and a stranger's control over the behavior of infants. *Child Development*, 1973, **44**, 705–713.

Corter, C. M. The nature of mother's absence and the infant's response to brief separations. *Developmental Psychology*, 1976, **12**.

Corter, C. M., & Bow, J. The mother's response to separation as a function of her infant's sex and vocal distress. *Child Development*, 1976, **47**.

Corter, C. M., Rheingold, H. L., & Eckerman, C. O. Toys delay the infant's following of his mother. *Developmental Psychology,* 1972, **6**, 138–145.

Gerwirtz, J. L. Attachment and dependence: Some strategies and tactics in the selection and use of indices for those concepts. In T. Alloway, L. Krames, & P. Pliner (Eds.), *Communication and affect.* New York: Academic, 1972.

Goldberg, S., & Lewis, M. Play behavior in the year-old infant: early sex differences. *Child Development,* 1969, **40**, 21–31.

Hogan, R. The terror of solitude. *Merrill-Palmer Quarterly,* 1975, **21**, 67–74.

Lester, B. M., Kotelchuck, M., Spelke, E., Sellers, M. J., & Klein, R. E. Separation protest in Guatemalan infants: cross-cultural and cognitive findings. *Developmental Psychology,* 1974, **10**, 79–85.

Lewis, M., & Ban, P. Stability of attachment behavior: a transformational analysis. Paper presented at the Society for Research in Child Development Meetings, Minneapolis, April, 1971.

Littenberg, R., Tulkin, S. R., & Kagan, J. Cognitive components of separation anxiety. *Developmental Psychology,* 1971, **4**, 387–388.

Mason, W. A., Hill, S. D., & Thomsen, C. E. Perceptual factors in the development of filial attachment. *Proceedings of the 3rd Inernational Primatological Congress,* 1970, **3**, 125–133.

Masters, J. C., & Wellman, H. M. The study of human infant attachment: a procedural critique. *Psychological Bulletin,* 1974, **81**, 218–237.

Moss, H. A. Communication in mother–infant interaction. In L. Krames, P. Pliner, & T. Alloway (Eds.), *Advances in the study of communication and affect.* Vol. 1. *Nonverbal communication.* New York: Plenum Press, 1974.

Mussen, P. H., Conger, J. J., & Kagan, J. *Child development and personality.* (4th ed.) New York: Harper & Row, 1974.

Pederson, F. A., & Bell, R. Q. Sex differences in preschool children without histories of complications of pregnancy and delivery. *Developmental Psychology,* 1970, **3**, 10–15.

Rheingold, H. L. The effect of a strange environment on the behavior of infants. In B. M. Foss (Ed.), *Determinants of infant behaviour.* Vol. 4. London: Methuen, 1969. (*a*)

Rheingold, H. L. The social and socializing infant. In D. Goslin (Ed.), *Handbook of socialization theory and research.* Chicago: Rand McNally, 1969. (*b*)

Rheingold, H.L., & Eckerman, C. O. The infant separates himself from his mother. *Science,* 1970, **168**, 78–83.

Schaffer, H. R., & Emerson, P. E. The development of social attachments in infancy. *Monographs of the Society for Research in Child Development,* 1964, **29**, 3, 1–77.

Scott, J. P., Stewart, J. M., & DeGhett, V. J. Separation in infant dogs. In J. P. Scott & E. C. Servary (Eds.), *Separation and depression.* Washington: American Academy for the Advancement of Science, 1973.

Spelke, E., Zelazo, P., Kagan, J., & Kotelchuck, M. Father interaction and separation protest. *Developmental Psychology,* 1973, **9,** 83–90.

Stayton, D. J., Ainsworth, M. D. S., & Main, M. B. Development of separation behavior in the first year of life. *Developmental Psychology,* 1973, **9**, 213–225.

Stern, D. N. The goal and structure of mother–infant play. *Journal of the American Academy of Child Psychiatry,* 1974, **13**, 402–421.

Turnure, C. Response to voice of mother and stranger by babies in the first year. *Developmental Psychology,* 1971, **4**, 182–190.

Watson, J. S. Smiling, cooing, and "the game". *Merrill-Palmer Quarterly,* 1972, **18**, 323–339.

CHAPTER 5

Experiments on Mother–Infant Interaction Underlying Mutual Attachment Acquisition: The Infant Conditions the Mother

Jacob L. Gewirtz and Elizabeth F. Boyd[1]

National Institute of Mental Health and
University of Maryland, Baltimore County, Maryland

Introduction

The assumption of mutual influence and the instrumental-conditioning paradigm have provided the theoretical bases of an experimental program that we begin to report here. The central assumption is that at the same time a caregiver's behaviors may be conditioning (reinforcing) responses of her infant, the infant's behaviors may be conditioning the caregiver's own responses. Under this conception of mutual learning and reciprocity, mother–infant interactions were manipulated systematically in a contrived situation to highlight critical aspects of the mutual-conditioning process that we have assumed characterize such interchanges in life settings.

This series of experiments represents an attempt to move away from the naturalistic methods of earlier observational studies of parent–infant interchanges in life settings (e.g., Gewirtz & Gewirtz, 1969). Typically, interventions in ongoing interchanges in order to demonstrate causal relationships between behaviors have not been made in such observation studies. Our research tack can permit evaluation of the utility of the operant-conditioning paradigm and the conception of mutual conditioning for ordering the main features of ongoing

---

[1] Authors' address: NIMH Laboratory of Developmental Psychology, Building 15K, National Institutes of Health, Bethesda, Maryland 20014.

mother–infant interaction and, particularly, the two-way flow of influence between infant and mother within the myriad complexities apparent in their reciprocal interchanges. The influence that maternal or caregiver behaviors may have on infant behaviors has abundant experimental documentation. Hence, the present report summarizes the first phase of our research program under the mutual-conditioning conception: the conditioning of the mother's responses by her infant's. Our plan is to investigate simultaneously the mutual conditioning of both mother and infant responses in a later phase of the research program.

The Conceptual Context

Traditional theoretical and empirical approaches to human social and personality development (e.g., psychoanalysis, social learning) were based for the most part on the one-sided assumption that parent (or other caregiver) behaviors are the primary environmental determinants of child behavior and development. If the child's behaviors could at all influence those of the parent, it was assumed that this influence could play but a minor role in the child's socialization. Observed relationships between parent and child behaviors were attributed routinely to the effect of the parent's behaviors on the child's behaviors. Within a social learning approach, this assumption generated numerous demonstrations that selected child responses could be conditioned by actual or simulated parent behaviors (e.g., Brackbill, 1958; Etzel & Gewirtz, 1967; Haugan & McIntire, 1972; McKenzie & Day, 1971; Ramey & Ourth, 1971; Rheingold, Gewirtz, & Ross, 1959; Routh, 1969; Wahler, 1967; Weisberg, 1963). The limitations of this unidirectional model of child socialization have been recognized increasingly during the past quarter century, and the assumption of a two-way flow of influence between parent and child behaviors has come to prevail in diverse theoretical approaches to child development.

In an important instrumental-learning analysis published in 1951, Sears discussed the dyad with its simultaneous focus on the interdependent actions and motives of two or more persons and pointed to instances where the child could influence another's behaviors (in particular, the parent's). Concerned in his analysis primarily with child development as influenced by the social environment, Sears did not elaborate the implications of the dyadic concept either for existing research data or for prospective research. Further, when Sears' paper appeared there may have been an insufficient data base to reinterpret within a bidirectional model of child socialization. It may be for such reasons as these that, at the time it was published, Sears' paper did not have a marked impact on research on the direction of influence in child social development. In the same decade, Bowlby (1958), influenced by ethological rather than learning theory, proposed innate releaser mechanisms whereby species-specific maternal behaviors may be released by such infant behaviors as crying and smiling. Although Bowlby assumed that the "released" behaviors of the mother became organized around her infant (through an unspecified form of learning) to bind her to her infant, in that paper he did not actually advance a mutual influence model for mother–infant interaction.

During the same period, Gewirtz in 1961 made an attempt to fill this gap in Bowlby's and similar approaches. He detailed a conditioning model for the simultaneous acquisition of behavioral attachment of mother to infant and of infant to mother. This model assumed that both mother and infant respond differentially to the other's behaviors. With examples from diverse interaction situations, Gewirtz illustrated how the responses of each could influence (condition) the responses of the other, simultaneously. In this conditioning process, stimuli provided by the appearance and behavior of the mother might acquire discriminative and reinforcing control over the infant's responses, while stimuli from the appearance and behavior of the infant might acquire discriminative and reinforcing control over the mother's responses and denote the acquisition by each of an attachment to the other. Gewirtz' model was open to the operation of unconditioned stimuli (releasers) for species-specific responses, as identified in animal-behavior research and proposed by Bowlby (1958). Paralleling Bowlby's (1958) releaser-stimulus analysis, Gewirtz (1961) analyzed the learning processes that were potentially involved. He detailed how the infant's smiles and cries, being reinforced by a mother's systematic responding to them, in that very same context might be reinforcing other responses of the mother that the infant's smiles and cries followed routinely. He noted also how often this mutual conditioning might occur without the mother's awareness that her responses were changing systematically. More recent statements of this approach to mutual conditioning and attachment can be found in a number of papers by Gewirtz (1969, 1972b, 1976, in press). Other analyses have appeared subsequently that are compatible with this theoretical approach (e.g., Rheingold, 1969).

The above-cited analyses have implications for interpreting directions-of-effects or influence in the literature of parent–child interaction. In that literature, cautions were raised occasionally that correlations did not imply necessarily a unidirectional flow of influence from parent to child (e.g., Sears, Maccoby, & Levin, 1957). However, it was not until well into the 1960s that the issue of the direction-of-influence became central for numerous analyses of early child-development and parent–infant interaction (e.g., Bell, 1968, 1971; Harper, 1971; Kessen, 1963; Korner, 1965; Wenar & Wenar, 1963). It was clear that diverse research results could not be interpreted exclusively as the effect of adult behaviors on child behaviors, and numerous researches were directed subsequently to assess the effects of child features or behaviors on caregiver features or behaviors (e.g., Moss, 1967; Osofsky & O'Connell, 1972; Yarrow, Waxler, & Scott, 1971).

Attachment: Metaphor and Process

In the literature of early human social development, the term "attachment," as in physical bonding, has stood as a convenient metaphor for aspects of the close reliance (often reciprocal) of one individual upon another, expressed in a variety of cued-response patterns. This reliance may involve such pairs as mother and child, wife and husband, lover and loved one, child and child, person and animal, and, on rare occasions, even person and inanimate object or place. Specifically, the attachment concept has been applied to one individual's involvement in what is typically a two-person mutual-influence process in which that individual's sequenced responses have come under the control of cue (i.e., discriminative) and reinforcing stimuli provided by the appearance and responses of another person (Gewirtz, 1961, 1972b, 1976).

For the child, attachment typically labels the complex of response sequences controlled by the cue and reinforcing stimulus characteristics of the behaviors of an adult, usually the mother or main caregiver—termed the primary attachment figure or object. Thus, an attachment can be denoted by the occurrence of child responses under the control of stimuli from the attachment figure, and by the child-maintaining proximity to that person. The attachment metaphor has also been used to order concurrent manifestations of that control process. Hence, it has been denoted by the child's preferential responding to the attachment figure, or by emotional behaviors like crying when separated from her or upon her preparations to depart, or even by an increase in the child's explorations of strange objects or places in her presence (Gewirtz, 1972c). In that same social-development literature, the attachment term has also served occasionally to order adult response patterns under the control of a child's behaviors (e.g., Gewirtz, 1961, 1972b; Klaus, Jerauld, Kreger, McAlpine, Steffa, & Kennell, 1972; Leifer, Leiderman, Barnett, & Williams, 1972). The stimulus–response functions ordinarily denoting attachment are pervasive. Upon disruption, for instance by separation or rejection, these functions can become highly disorganized and often may be accompanied by intense emotional responding. Hence, increasingly, the wide-ranging attachment term has become the central focus of several approaches to social development in humans and animals (Bowlby, 1969, 1973; see also Gewirtz, 1972a, for a survey of five diverse approaches to attachment — Ainsworth, 1972; Cairns, 1972; Gewirtz, 1972b, 1972c; Sears, 1972; Yarrow, 1972).

As discussed here and in Gewirtz' (1961, 1972b) conditioning account of attachment, the dyadic functional relations labeled attachment are not limited to any developmental segment of life or to any particular interaction partners. Moreover, these dyadic functions may involve *several* figures concurrently, in *any* time span. At the same time, the initiations these functions imply need not be reciprocated on each occasion by the attachment-figure. Further, when a dyadic attachment pattern involving a parent, child, or mate is broken, such as by death or divorce, this conception would encompass the acquisition of new (replacement) functions with other partners (Gewirtz, 1961). This conditioning model of attachment is entirely open with regard to such issues as whether or not a positive relation is to be expected between the formation of one or a few primary attachments in early life and the later capacity of the individual to enter close interpersonal relationships, for instance as Bowlby (1969) has proposed. There is little systematic information about the origins and courses of attachments, and even less about the reciprocal influences of one partner's (e.g., a child's) characteristic behaviors on the behaviors of the other partner (e.g., an adult) or about the relation between the formation of attachments in early life and the capacity in adulthood for developing close personal relationships (Gewirtz, 1972b).

It follows from the above that a specific attachment may be denoted by any one of a variety of child-behavior patterns under the control of stimuli from the mother or some other person. In this context, several writers have emphasized the attachment bond in contrast to attachment behaviors. The focus of some of these has seemed to be on attachment as *entity* rather than as organizing concept or metaphor. Thus, for Ainsworth (1972, 1973; Lamb, 1974) emphasis must be on attachment as an enduring bond rather than on the specific behaviors which "mediate" the attachment and indicate its presence. Some pitfalls in such reifications have been noted (Gewirtz, 1972b, 1972c).

Ways in which the attachment concept has been, and can be, used were detailed in the foregoing discussion. In this frame, it is important to note that, as an abstraction, the attachment metaphor may be entirely unnecessary, as when straightforward demonstrations of acquired social stimulus control over instrumental responses are involved. However, the attachment metaphor is used here for the didactic purpose of demonstrating the utility of the conditioning paradigm in the analysis of mother–infant interchange to which that metaphor has sometimes been applied.

Researches on Directions of Influence in Mother–Infant Interchange

This paper will report the results of our studies on the influence of the infant's behaviors on the mother's in an interaction context. To provide a framework for the research designs employed, we present a sample of child behaviors or features that have been reported to influence adult behaviors or features. However, no attempt is made to evaluate the soundness of the studies surveyed, to present the specific results of those studies, or to evaluate authors' inferences about the child's behavioral influence where multiple interpretations of the results are possible. Moreover, as our present research interests are focused on early mother–infant interaction in humans, this summary is limited to humans and is more representative of the mother–child interchange literature in early than in later life. (See Harper, 1971, for a recent review of the infrahuman literature.)

Many of the studies surveyed have employed natural observation or interview techniques to provide data bases for correlations between child features or behaviors and adult features or behaviors. Observational studies in which basically demographic child variables are related to observation-based parent variables include the following: infant gender was related to differential maternal smiling and talking (Thoman, Leiderman, & Olson, 1972), and infant vocalizations by gender were related to differential maternal responses (Lewis, 1972; Moss, 1967); infant fussing and crying by age was related to verbally-stated feelings of maternal attachment (Robson & Moss, 1970), and child age was related to maternal speech (Ferguson, 1964; Snow, 1972); infant developmental level was related to adoptive mother's speech (Beckwith, 1971); and children's membership in clinical or normal population groups was related to personality characteristics of their parents (Bell, 1964; Connerly, 1968; Klebanoff, 1959; Prechtl, 1963).

Several studies reported relationships between infant and parent behaviors: Individual differences in infant behavior were related to differential caretaking behaviors (Osofsky & Danzger, 1974; Yarrow, 1963); and child behaviors (e.g., dependency) were related to positive and negative teacher contact behaviors (Yarrow, Waxler, & Scott, 1971). The results of several studies can illustrate the relationships reported by attempts to preserve the sequential flow and integrity of dyadic behaviors in naturalistic observations of mother–infant interactions: infant fretting and crying was found likely to initiate maternal behaviors of vocalization and rocking (Lewis & Lee-Painter, 1974); infant sucking patterns were found related to maternal movement (Richards, 1971); and conditional probabilities were reported for related shifts in mutual infant and maternal gaze states (Stern, 1974).

A few studies reported the use of experimental or selective sampling techniques to assess parent or adult responses to child features or behaviors as stimuli. In these, only the adult behaviors were bases of the dependent variables; however, in principle, both adult and child behaviors in interchange could be studied simultaneously as dependent variables. Examples of the variables manipulated in these studies follow: Differential adult behaviors were related to IQ-score labels (Rosenthal & Jacobsen, 1966) and to verbal-skill labels (Siegel, 1963) assigned to children with whom the adults interacted. Mothers responded differentially to their own and other children in a structured tutorial situation (Halverson & Waldrop, 1970), and parents responded differentially to those behaviors of their daughters characterized as either independent or dependent (Osofsky & O'Connell, 1972). The quality of infant cries was related to the temperature of the breasts of lactating mother (Vuorenkoski, Wasz-Höckert, Koivisto, & Lind, 1969) and to maternal responsivity to crying (Wolff, 1969). And the behaviors of adults instructed to train a nominal child to learn a task to a specified criterion were conditioned by simulated correct responses of that nominal child (Berberich, 1971).

It has been noted that some studies have employed, as indices of the child's behaviors, such gross variables as gender, age, socioeconomic status, race, developmental level, and clinical population. These gross variables were then related to differential parent behaviors. (We shall not dwell on the fact that sometimes, also, gross adult behavior indices, like those termed personality and responsiveness, have been related to child behaviors as dependent variables.) In these studies, the level of analysis of the independent, child variables is remote from the level of the dependent, parent variables. Moreover, when research is performed under the aegis of a theory, the dependent parent-behavior variables are typically at the level called for by the theory, while the (gross) independent child variables are not and must be reduced to the required level via assumptions that may not be supported by existing data. The use of independent and dependent variables at discrepant levels of analysis may be justified occasionally under a research tactic where the gross variable serves as a first approximation to the appropriate independent variable. Nevertheless, a serious cost of this discrepancy between levels of analysis is that multiple interpretations of the functional relationships reported in these studies become possible, as numerous plausible assumptions can be made to reduce the gross independent variables to the child features or behaviors that, under the theory used, could be controlling the observed adult features or behaviors.

There are also approaches to mother–infant interaction in life settings that would seem to have as their main purpose the complete description or abstraction of the sequential details in naturally occurring interactions. The many details involved in these interchanges include: the number and order of actor turn-taking, the identities of the initiator and terminator of the sequence, the nature and order of response elements within a turn, and the degree of temporal overlap between the actors' behaviors. Given the combinations and permutations of the behavior elements scored, several hours of observation of a few mother–infant dyads can generate myriad unique interaction sequences (as reported by Gewirtz & Gewirtz, 1965, 1969). These approaches that attempt to index "every" feature of a set of mother-infant interchanges may be justified in early hypothesis-generating phases of research. However, such approaches often appear to have ends that are primarily descriptive and to imply research procedures that are more complex than they would need to be to answer important questions under diverse theories.

Occasionally related to these descriptive approaches may be the assumption that the facets of interaction cannot be analyzed functionally because it may be impossible ultimately to analyze simultaneously the influence of the sequenced behavior of one dyad member on the sequenced behavior of the other. However, by long tradition in psychological research, when there are multiple determinants operating in an experimental context, the effects of some factors are held constant while the effects of others are systematically varied. And it has generally proved efficient to assume that the functional relationships resulting from such procedures are operative in a context in which these multiple factors are all free to vary. Therefore, it may often be a fruitful tactic to consider simultaneity of mutual influence at the level of theory under the assumption that the empirical study, at different times, of the influence of the behaviors of each interactor on the behaviors of the other has predictive implications for their behaviors in simultaneous interaction. Going together with this tactic is the view that a functional analysis provides a potentially fruitful approach to the study of mother-infant interaction. In such an analysis, relevant detail is determined by focused questions asked in the context of a theory. Research questions are specified in advance of observations, so that observations can bear directly on them. This logic underlies the research program being reported in this chapter.

A Program of Research on the
Directions of Influence in Mother–Infant Interchange

Pilot observations were made in the contrived interaction setting of the studies. They indicated it would be difficult to achieve the degree of articulation between the responses of the infant and of the mother required to demonstrate the simultaneous conditioning of both interactors' responses. The influence via conditioning of caregiver behaviors on infant behaviors is well documented (e.g., Brackbill, 1958; Etzel & Gewirtz, 1967; Haugan & McIntire, 1972; McKenzie & Day, 1971; Routh, 1969; Wahler, 1967; Weisberg, 1963). Therefore, in the initial phase of the research program being reported, the decision was made to emphasize the conditioning of the mother's behaviors by her infant's. Further, the infant's behavior cue for the mother's response was simulated in order to increase the length of sessions from the 10 to 15 minutes three-month-old infants would tolerate and in order to present that infant behavior cue at a constant rate across treatments. Our working plan is to investigate simultaneously the mutual conditioning of both mother and infant responses in a later phase of the research program.

The specific research questions in the two experiments reported here are: Will an infant's vocalizations (Experiment 1) or head turns (Experiment 2), that appear to be directed to its mother, reinforce the mother's response (to a cue from that infant) upon which the infant's behavior was contingent? An incidental research question in each experiment is: Will the mother be aware that her responses are influenced by her infant's behaviors?

The two experiments are being reported in detail elsewhere (Gewirtz & Boyd, in press; Boyd & Gewirtz, 1976). Their method derives from the "double-agent" design of Rosenfeld and Baer (1970). In that design, the subject is asked to serve as "experimenter" in a study whose nominal purpose is to condition some behavior of a "subject." The subject's responses as "experimenter" are then conditioned by that (simulated) behavior of the "subject." The design of the two experiments being reported differed from the Rosenfeld and Baer design in an important respect: There was *no* explicit instruction to mothers to condition the incidental infant behavior that was to be provided contingent on their responses, and experimenters explicitly avoided giving any indication to mothers that increases in this particular infant behavior were sought.

In the present investigations, each mother was told that the purpose of the study in which she was to serve as "experimenter" was to investigate whether infant "subjects" could learn that their behaviors can have social consequences. Each mother was asked to provide these consequences by saying a short phrase immediately following (simulated representations of) one of her infant's behaviors. These behaviors were head turns toward mother in Experiment 1 and vocalizations in Experiment 2. In each study, another but incidental infant behavior (vocalizations in Experiment 1, head turns toward mother in Experiment 2), also simulated to be that of the mother's own infant, was identified for the mother as merely occurring in the situation. The incidental infant behavior was then presented contingent on one of the mother's verbal and/or expressive responses. The actual purpose of the experiments was to determine the reinforcing effectiveness of these seemingly responsive but incidental behaviors of the infant for the verbal responses or facial expressions of the mother.

Experiment 1

Method

Subjects.   Six mothers of normal 2- to 3-month-old infants (four males and two females) were asked to participate in an investigation of the social awareness of their infants. These mothers were selected from a pool of middle-class mothers who had volunteered to participate in a study of infant social learning. Of the six mothers studied, the results reported here are based on the observations of four mothers, two of male and two of female infants. The observations for two mothers were not completed and their data have been discarded. Because representations of infant head turning to cue the mother's verbal response were presented only when she was not smiling, the high rate of smiling of one mother precluded presenting the minimum rate of head turn cues required for definitive demonstrations of the effects of the infant vocal contingencies. The second mother was not continued beyond two sessions because the vocal repertoire of her infant was judged to be less mature than the recorded infant vocalizations.

Instructions and Experimental Setting.   Each mother was informed that the purpose of the study was to investigate whether infants could learn that their head turns can have social consequences. The mother was asked to provide these consequences by saying a short phrase immediately following each visual representation of her infant's head turns. It was explained that her infant's learning would be denoted by rates of head turning greater than those of infants whose mothers would not be asked to respond specifically to their infant's head turns. Each mother was cautioned that the infant head-turn response requirements would be adjusted routinely as learning progressed. Therefore, changes in the rates of the infant head turn (cue) should not be seen as an index of her infant's learning rate.

The mother was seated in a well-lighted room facing a one-way mirror, as shown in Figure 1. The mother had been shown the infant seat on the other side of that mirror in the adjacent, darkened room where, directly facing her, her infant nominally would be seated for the entire session. Figure 2 shows that view. The mother was told that the light differential, which precluded her seeing her infant, was required to provide the infant with a salient view of her face. It was explained that the infant seat was equipped with a head-turn apparatus that activated automatically a sequence of red lights at the base of the mirror facing the mother whenever the infant turned to look toward her. The light sequence was produced in the infant's room by a row of 6 low-wattage red lights, in a housing 33 cm long and 3 cm high.

Each mother was asked to hold open a microphone switch while she said a one- or two-word phrase to her infant through a microphone, immediately after a sequence of red lights had indicated that her infant turned toward her. The mother was asked to include in her phrase one of four or of six words displayed on a card at the right of the mirror. These words were *what, where, good, nice,*

Fig. 1. A model demonstrates mother's seated position facing one-way mirror that separated mother's lighted room from infant's darkened room.

Fig. 2. View from the darkened infant's room, showing positions of infant (with a doll in infant's seat) and of mother (demonstrated by a model) in lighted room on the other side of one-way mirror.

hi, and *hello* for Mother 1, *where, how, good, nice, hi*, and *hello* for Mother 4, and *big, good, hi*, and *hello* for Mothers 2 and 3. The simulated infant head-turn cue for each response of the mother was presented at least six seconds following the offset of the mother's phrase and when the mother appeared alert with her mouth relaxed.

Each mother was told that, after every one of her verbal responses, the low-fidelity intercom positioned near her opened automatically to her infant's room for one second. It was explained that the intercom could not accept inputs from both mother's and infant's rooms simultaneously. Thus, to insure that she would be prepared to respond immediately each time her infant turned to look at her, the intercom in the infant's room would be opened briefly and sometimes her infant's vocal behavior might seem interrupted. In actuality, the mother's intercom received output from a tape recorder, either of vocalization of an infant (presumably her own) or of ambient room noise denoting ''silence.'' In this way, simulated infant vocalizations could be presented contingent on the verbal and smile responses of the mother that were programmed for reinforcement and simulated ambient room noise could be presented immediately following the responses that were to be nonreinforced. The infant vocalizations were random one-second selections from a continuous tape of recorded vocalizations of several infants, but not including the mother's own child. The low fidelity of the intercom and the brief samplings of often lengthy utterances were designed to make it unlikely that a mother would notice that the vocalizations were not those of her child.

Prior to the first experimental session, each mother practiced opening her microphone switch and saying appropriate verbal phrases in response to the light sequence denoting her infant's head turn. The experimenter remained with the mother for the first six practice trials. On at least one of these trials, the mother's phrase was followed by an infant vocalization over the intercom, and the experimenter noted casually, ''(Infant's name) is talking now.'' Similarly, on at least one practice trial, the ''silence'' was presented and the experimenter remarked ''(Infant's name) is *not* talking now.''

Response Definition and Reliability. The mothers' verbal-response classes were categorized by observers who monitored their responses via earphones. The agreement coefficients for these categories were near unity under all conditions sampled for each mother and therefore, are not presented. Mothers' facial expressions were monitored through the one-way mirror by another set of observers. Facial expressions were scored as *smiles* when they involved movement upward from the corners of the mouth and a deepening of the folds from the corners of the mouth to the wings of the nose. Smiles could also involve an upward bulging of the cheeks that collected under the eyes, and a narrowing of the eyes leading to wrinkles at their outer corners. Only those smiles were counted that occurred during the mothers' verbal phrase or within two seconds of its offset. Within a session, the categorizations of verbal-response content by one observer using earphones together with the categorization of smiles or nonsmiles made by a control observer governed presentation of contingent infant vocalization and silence feedbacks.

Degree of agreement within pairs of independent observers on the occurrence and nonoccurrence of smiles was sampled within each treatment condition for each subject. Observer reliability was determined for complete sessions, as follows: 12 of 18 sessions for Mother 1; 4 of 6 for Mother 2; 6 of 11 for Mother 3; and 16 of 21 for Mother 4. Observer-agreement coefficients were calculated (a) by dividing the number of agreements of smile occurrence and nonoccurrence by the total trials scored and (b) by dividing the number of agreements of smile occurrence by the total of smile occurrences scored. An observer-agreement coefficient was determined for every session sampled, and the median of these coefficients found over sessions for each mother. For the four mothers respectively, the median agreement coefficients for the sessions sampled were .93, .98, .81, and .75 for all trials and .93, .98, .80, and .70 for smile occurrences only.

Conditioning Procedure. Each mother served as her own control under baseline, conditioning, and reversal treatments:

Baseline: During the determination of the initial frequency levels of the mother's verbal responses and accompanying smiles, infant vocalizations were presented randomly on approximately 30% of the trials and silence was presented randomly on approximately 70% of the trials. Both feedbacks were presented automatically two seconds following the offset of the mother's verbal phrase. Words used by the mother were combined into two classes, based on similarity of meaning and of baseline frequencies. Each verbal class could be accompanied, or not, by a smile. Thus, there were four two-component responses: Verbal A with a smile, Verbal A without a smile, Verbal B with a smile, and Verbal B without a smile.

Conditionings and reversals: During the Conditioning 1 phase, the verbal-response class with smiles that had the lower baseline incidence was selected for conditioning. Infant vocalizations were then presented automatically immediately following the smile component of this response. "Silence" (ambient room noise) was presented immediately following smiles that occurred with the other verbal class. On all trials in which the mother's smile did not occur within two seconds of the offset of her verbal response, silence was presented automatically.

A conditioning procedure was continued until, within a criterion number of 15-trial blocks, the frequency of the reinforced response was greater than the frequency of each of the three nonreinforced responses. The criterion ratios were provided by the $p < .05$ values of a one-tail binomial test (Siegel, 1956). For example, if in 7 of 8, or in 12 of 15, of the 15-trial blocks the frequency of the reinforced response class was greater than the frequency of each of the nonreinforced response classes, the criterion would have been met. When this conditioning criterion was attained, the treatments were reversed: Infant vocalizations followed the previously nonreinforced verbal-with-smile response, and silence followed the previously reinforced verbal-with-smile response. Treatments did not change for those verbal responses without smiles. Reversal conditions remained in effect until the criterion increase denoting conditioning in the reinforced verbal-with-smile response was demonstrated. Then, in the Conditioning 2 phase, contingencies in effect during Conditioning 1 were reinstituted until the conditioning criterion was attained. Mothers 1, 2, and 3 all participated in Baseline, Conditioning 1, Reversal 1, and Conditioning 2 phases. Mother 4 participated in two additional conditioning and three additional reversal conditions.

Results

Single-Subject Design. Although 15-trial blocks were used to determine whether or not a mother's performance reached criterion, it is convenient to chart the frequencies of the four responses for individual subjects in successive 45-trial blocks over the treatment-condition series. Within treatments, parallel vertical-line breaks in the curves, corresponding to discontinuous trial-block numbers, indicate that some precriterion data have been omitted from the figure. Figure 3

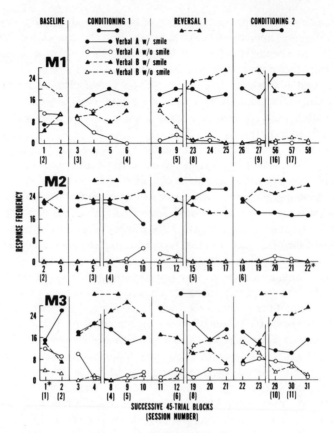

Fig. 3. Frequencies of the four verbal response classes, with and without smiles, for Mothers 1, 2, and 3 under baseline and three successive treatments with incidental infant-vocalization reinforcement.

shows the results for the baseline and three conditioning treatments for Mothers 1, 2, and 3.

For Mothers 1 and 2, the systematic response patterns indicate that the class of simulated infant vocalizations conditioned the verbal, but not the smile, component of those mothers' responses. For those mothers, rates of the verbal categories with smiles increased and reversed appropriately, depending on the contingencies in effect. However, for Mother 1 these smile rates did not reverse to baseline levels when the contingency was withdrawn and Mother 2 smiled on almost all trials independently of the contingencies in effect for smiles with particular verbal classes.

For Mother 3, reinforcer control was shown particularly for Verbal B with smile in Conditioning 1 and Conditioning 2 phases. Some reinforcer control was shown for Verbal A with smile in Reversal 1. When the infant vocal contingency was applied there to Verbal A with smile, its rate increased and was initially high relative to the rate of Verbal B with smile. However, the rate of Verbal A with smile decreased approximately to its preconditioned level (of Conditioning 1) before the infant vocal contingency was withdrawn. The verbal-without-smile curves of Mother 3 under Reversal 1 and Conditioning 2 only suggest that the contingent infant vocalization functioned as a reinforcer to control the smile component of that mother's reinforced response.

Figure 4 shows a pattern of reinforcer control over the verbal plus smile responses of Mother 4 by the contingent infant vocalization, in four successive conditioning and reversal phases.

The scores have been presented for each of the four subject mothers under a *single*-subject design with replications, each mother serving as her own control. The logic of that design was that a treatment continue for each mother until the conditioning criterion was attained for the response. Therefore, systematic score-change patterns all occurred in the appropriate direction under the successive conditioning and reversal treatments. These replicated single-subject data have provided a sufficient basis for the generalization sought: incidental but seemingly responsive contingent infant vocalizations conditioned the verbal phrases of each of the four mothers. Even so, it can be of interest to examine the generalization that could be made under a more conventional *group* design, that employs a routine procedure of statistical inference.

Group Design.   For the group statistical analysis, the four mothers' scores (from Figures 3 and 4) on the response reinforced in the Conditioning 1 treat-

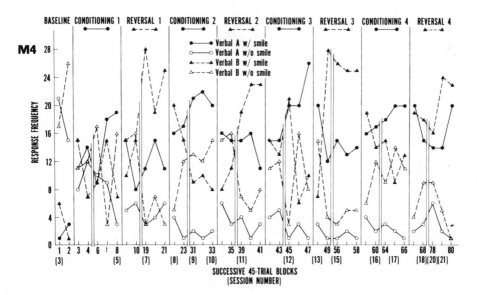

Fig. 4. Frequencies of the four verbal response classes, with and without smiles, for Mother 4 under baseline and eight successive treatments with incidental infant-vocalization reinforcement.

ment were grouped taking the first two and the last three 45-trial blocks of each of the three treatments that all mothers had in common, namely Conditioning 1, Reversal 1, and Conditioning 2. (As only two baseline block scores were available rather than the five required for design symmetry, those baseline scores are omitted from the analysis. Further, because there were only four Conditioning 1 45-trial blocks for Mother 1, the last baseline block score was used as her first Conditioning 1 block score.) These data were subjected to an analysis of variance, of the three treatments by five trial blocks with repeated measures on the two factors. A reliable treatments by trial-blocks interaction effect was found: F $(8,24) = 6.84, p < 0.0002$. (This result was not unexpected, given that training had continued until the reinforced response of each mother had reached criterion.)

Figure 5 shows the mean frequency curves of the response reinforced in Conditioning 1, under the successive treatments. (Broken lines denote the discontinuity between the first two and the last three trial blocks under each treatment.) The reliable treatment by trial blocks interaction effect is due to a systematic increase in the mean response curve under Conditioning 1 when reinforcement for that response was in effect, a systematic decline under Reversal 1 when reinforcement was removed from that response, and an orderly increase once again under Conditioning 2 when reinforcement was reinstated for that response. On this basis, the same general conclusion can be drawn from the group-mean response patterns under Conditioning 1, Reversal 1, and Conditioning 2 treatments as was drawn from the individual response-curve replications charted in Figures 3 and 4.

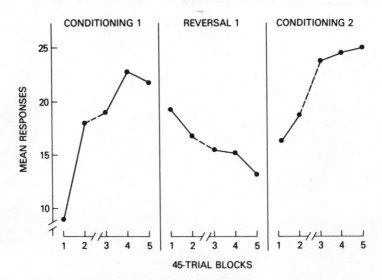

Fig. 5. Mean frequencies of the verbal-with-smile response first reinforced under the Conditioning 1 treatment (Mothers 1, 2, 3, and 4).

Contingency Awareness. Mothers' spontaneous remarks about their infants' performances and postexperimental interview probes suggested that these changes in response patterns occurred without the mothers being aware of the controlling contingencies or that their infants' behaviors had been simulated. For example, following a session in which conditioning had been demonstrated, mothers might remark that their infants had been particularly vocal during the session, or they might note that their infants had not been "talking" following sessions in which the contingencies had been reversed. In the postexperimental interview, Mothers 3 and 4 noticed that their infants were more vocally responsive to one of the words for which contingencies were in effect in the condition immediately preceding that interview. Mother 4 said that, in general, it was easiest to smile when she used this word in a phrase.

Experiment 2

Experiment 2 extended the results of Experiment 1 by *reversing* the functions of the contingent stimulus and of the cue stimulus employed in Experiment 1. Further, different maternal responses, full and partial smiles, nonsmiles, and other facial expressions, were programmed for reinforcement. Each mother was asked to respond with a brief phrase, but this time nominally contingent on her infant's vocalizations, rather than head turns toward her. Simulated representations of the infant's head turns to her, rather than vocalizations, were presented contingent on the mother's expressive responses, to assess the reinforcing effectiveness of her infant's head turns for them. These expressive responses were the full smile, the partial smile, and the nonsmile, or the clipped and sustained oral expression. In one instance (Mother 6), smiles and nonsmiles were crossed with verbal responses.

Method

Subjects. Four mothers of normal 2- to 3-month-old infants (one male and three females) were selected from a pool of middle class mothers who had volunteered in response to announcements of a project on infant social-awareness learning.

Instructions and Experimental Setting. The experimental setting and apparatus was identical to the one pictured and described for Experiment 1 (Figures 1 and 2). The basic instructions to the mother were identical with those given in Experiment 1. Therefore, only those instructions that were unique to Experiment 2 are presented. It was explained to each mother that the study was designed to determine whether infants could learn that their vocalizations can have social consequences. The mother was asked to provide these consequences by saying a short phrase immediately after each of her infant's vocalizations. In addition, the mother was told to expect a sequence of lights to flash frequently at the base of the one-way mirror. It was explained that those lights were activated automatically by the head turn cradle on the infant seat. A relay click would be heard in her room one-third second before the lights were to be activated to signal the appearance of the lights. The mother was told that the lights were in routine use in an entirely separate concurrent investigation to measure an infant's head turns to look toward its mother, and that it was impractical to deactivate the apparatus for every subject in the present study. It was explained that, in the concurrent investigation, a sequence of six red lights flashed in front of the mother whenever her infant turned to look toward her for some seconds during, or soon after, her talking; and that a yellow light indicated that her infant did not turn to look toward her in connection with her talking. Each mother was asked to ignore these lights, as they had nothing at all to do with the present study in which her contingent phrases were to condition her infant's vocalizations. In this context, the red-light sequences denoting infant headturns toward the mother could be presented contingent on the mother's response that was programmed for reinforcement and a yellow-light flash denoting the absence of head turns could be presented following her response that was not to be reinforced.

Further, each mother was told that a voice-operated relay automatically would open a microphone in the infant's room each time her infant vocalized, and that she would hear that vocalization through the low-fidelity intercom positioned near her. The mother was asked to hold open a microphone switch until she completed saying a one- or two-word phrase to her infant immediately following each of her infant's vocalizations. She was asked to include in her phrase one of the four words, *big, good, hi,* or *hello,* displayed on a card at the right of the mirror. She was told it was important for her to respond immediately after her infant's vocalization. It was explained that the intercom could not accept inputs from both the infant's and mother's microphones simultaneously; therefore, the infant's microphone would close automatically after one second to allow the mother to respond immediately. She was told further that, in the beginning, this might occasionally interrupt her infant's vocalization, but that we expected that the infant would learn to emit increasingly shorter vocalizations. In actuality, the infant vocal cues were random 1-second selections from a continuous tape of the recorded vocalizations of several infants, but not including those of the mother's own child. Those simulated vocal cues were presented through the intercom at least 6 seconds following the offset of the mother's expressive response and when she appeared alert with her mouth in a relaxed position.

Prior to the first experimental session, each mother practiced opening her microphone switch and saying appropriate phrases in response to infant-vocalization cues received via the intercom. The experimenter ramained with the mother during the the first six practice trials prior to the first experimental session. The mother's phrase was followed by a red-light sequence on at least one of these trials and the experimenter noted casually, "(Infant's name) turned to look at you while you were talking." Similarly, on at least one of these practice trials, the mother's phrase was followed by the yellow light and the experimenter remarked casually, "(Infant's name) did *not* turn to look at you while you were talking."

Response Definitions and Observer Reliability. The verbal components of the response reinforced for Mother 6 were grouped in one of two categories by observers who monitored her reponses via earphones. As in Experiment 1, the agreement coefficients for these verbal categories were near unity under all conditions sampled and are, therefore, not presented. Mothers' facial expressions were monitored through the one-way mirror by another set of observers. For Mother 5, a *partial* smile was defined as an upward movement of the corners of the mouth and a slight deepening of the nasolabial folds from the corners of the mouth to the wings of the nose; and a *full* smile involved some combinations of the extensive deepening of the nasolabial folds, an upward bulging of the cheeks that collected under the eyes, and a narrowing of the eyes leading to wrinkles at their outer corners. For Mothers 6 and 8, both partial and full smiles were defined as smiles. For all mothers, only those smiles and expressive responses were scored that occurred either during the mother's phrase or within two seconds of the offset of that verbalization. For Mother 7, the *sustained* oral expression was defined as a pursing of the lips, revealing the teeth, that continued following the apparent completion of the verbal phrase; and the *clipped* oral expression involved bringing the lips quickly and tightly together on apparent completion of the verbal phrase. These oral expressions were scored on the basis of facial criteria alone.

Within a session, the categorizations of a control observer governed the contingent light presentations denoting infant headturns or nonheadturns for Mothers 5, 7, and 8. For Mother 6, the categorization of verbal-phrase content by a second observer using earphones together with the categorization of smiles or nonsmiles made by the control observer governed those contingent presentations.

The degree of agreement within pairs of independent observers on the occurrence and nonoccurrence of facial expressions was assessed within each treatment condition for each subject. Observer reliability was determined for complete sessions, as follows: nine of 11 sessions for Mother 5, seven of seven sessions for Mother 6, five of 11 sessions for Mother 7, and seven of nine sessions for Mother 8. Observer-agreement coefficients were calculated (a) by dividing the number of agreements of occurrence and nonoccurrence by the number of total trials scored and (b) by dividing the number of agreements of occurrence by the total occurrences sampled. An agreement coefficient was determined for every session sampled, and the median of the coefficients found over the sessions for each mother. For Mothers 5, 6, 7, and 8, respectively, the median agreement coefficients for the sessions sampled were .82, .94, .82, and .73 for all trials and .74, .94, .71, and .47 only for occurrences of the expressive response being reinforced.

Conditioning Procedure. Each mother served as her own control in the treatment series. After baseline, she served under successive conditioning and reversal conditions as follows:

Baseline: During this determination, the initial rates of a mother's verbal and smile or other expressive behaviors were assessed so that those of her behaviors with relatively low baseline rates could be selected for conditioning. For Mothers 6 and 8, the red-light sequence denoting infant head-turning was presented randomly on approximately 30% of these baseline trials, and the yellow light denoting the absence of head turning was presented randomly on approximately 70% of the trials. Each such consequence was presented automatically two seconds following the offset of the mother's verbal phrase. During the baseline determination of the rates of full smiles, partial smiles, and nonsmiles for Mother 5, a verbal response class was being consistently reinforced. It was assumed that this condition gave a reasonable estimate of baselevel frequencies of the two smile responses, as it appeared that the head-turn contingency was presented equally often following each of them. There was no initial baselevel assessment of the sustained and clipped oral expressions for Mother 7. During the attempt to condition a verbal class with smiles of Mother 7, these expressive behaviors were noticed. Because they differed from those responses already conditioned successfully in Experiment 1, the earlier conditioning plan was dropped and the oral responses were selected for reinforcement.

Conditionings and reversals: For Mothers 5 and 8, the full smile (Mother 5) and any smile (Mother 8) that had the lower baseline incidences were programmed for initial conditioning. For Mother 7, the sustained oral expression was arbitrarily programmed for initial conditioning because casual observation indicated that it had the lower baseline rate. For Mother 6, the verbal class (B) with smiles that had the lower baseline incidence was programmed for initial reinforcement. For Mothers 5, 7, and 8, in conditioning and reversal phases, the expressive response programmed for reinforcement was followed immediately after onset by the red-light sequence denoting infant head turns. In general, the expressive responses programmed for nonreinforcement were followed two seconds after offset of the mother's verbal phrase by the yellow light denoting infant nonheadturns. However, for Mother 8, when nonsmiles were reinforced during Reversal 1, the nonheadturn light was delayed two seconds after the offset of the verbal component of any verbal class with smiles, as at that time the equipment could not be programmed readily for immediate feedback.

For Mother 6 during Conditioning 1 and Reversals 1 and 2, the response to be reinforced was followed immediately after onset of the smile component by the red-light sequence denoting infant headturns. The yellow light denoting the absence of head turns was presented immediately after the onset of the smile component accompanying the verbal class to be nonreinforced and two seconds following the offset of any verbal phrase not accompanied by a smile. During Conditioning 2 for Mother 6, when nonsmiles with Verbal A were reinforced, the head-turn light was presented immediately following the observer's judgment of nonsmiles with Verbal A and the non-head-turn light was presented immediately following the observer's judgment of nonsmiles with Verbal B. During this condition, the non-head-turn light was delayed two seconds after the offset of the verbal component of any verbal class with smiles.

A conditioning procedure was continued until the conditioning criterion (identical with that of Experiment 1) was attained. Then the treatments were reversed: The previously reinforced response class was followed by the yellow light denoting the absence of infant head turns, and an alternative response class, now programmed for reinforcement, was followed by the red-light sequence denoting head turns. Reversal conditions remained in effect until the criterion increase in the reinforced response was demonstrated. Then the contingencies in effect during the initial Conditioning 1 treatment were reinstituted (except in the case of Mother 6) until the conditioning criterion was met. Mother 5 participated in Conditioning 1 and Reversal 1 treatments. Mother 6 completed two conditioning and two reversal treatments. Mothers 7 and 8 each participated in a sequence of Conditioning 1, Reversal 1, and Conditioning 2 treatments.

Results

Single-Subject Design.   As in Experiment 1, 15-trial blocks were used to determine whether or not a mother's performance attained criterion, but it is convenient to chart the response frequencies for the individual mothers in successive 45-trial blocks. Figure 6 shows that the simulated infant head turning toward Mother 5 functioned to reinforce first her partial smiles, and then her full smiles.

For Mother 6, Figure 7 shows that the infant-head-turn contingency controlled her smiles with Verbal B (during Conditioning 1), her smiles with Verbal A (during Reversals 1 and 2), and her nonsmiles with Verbal A (during Conditioning 2).

For Mother 7, Figure 8 shows that simulated infant head turns functioned as a reinforcer to condition first her sustained oral expression and then her clipped

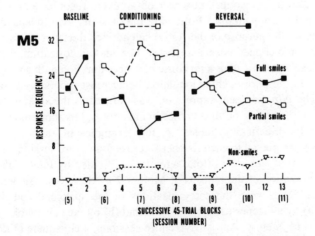

Fig. 6. Frequencies of full smiles, partial smiles, and nonsmiles for Mother 5 under baseline, conditioning, and reversal treatments with incidental infant-head-turn reinforcement.

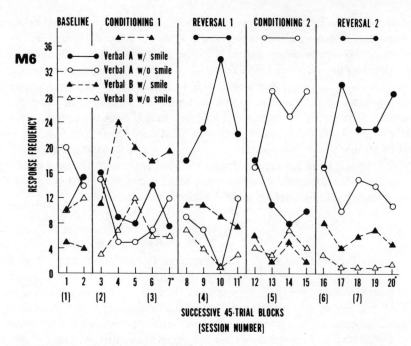

Fig. 7. Frequencies of four verbal response classes, with and without smiles, for Mother 6 under baseline and four successive conditioning and reversal treatments with incidental infant-head-turn reinforcement.

oral expression. These responses were scored on the basis of facial cues alone. Of interest, the listener who monitored through earphones the verbal phrases of Mother 7 during the experiment noticed a relationship between the facial expressions registered by the control observer on an event recorder and certain vocal intonation and stress patterns.[2] Following the sessions, two independent listeners, naive about the purpose of the study, categorized the taped *verbal* responses into sustained and clipped vocal categories. For this categorization, the *sustained* vocal response was defined as a response of longer duration with an elongation of all syllables in the phrase, this elongation being most pronounced for the final syllables. The *clipped* vocal expression was defined as the shorter-duration response with a shortening of all syllables in the phrase, this shortening being most pronounced for the final syllables. A few examples of each of these vocal expressions were played to each listener. Across four entire sessions, the median session proportion agreement (total agreements divided by total trials sampled) of the categorization of the phrases of Mother 7 by these two listeners was .79. The association between the categorizations of the sustained and the clipped responses (a) by a listener using vocal cues and (b) by the control observer using facial cues is of interest. Across five entire sessions, a chi square (1 *df*) value of

---

[2]The authors are indebted to S. Lawson Sebris for this observation.

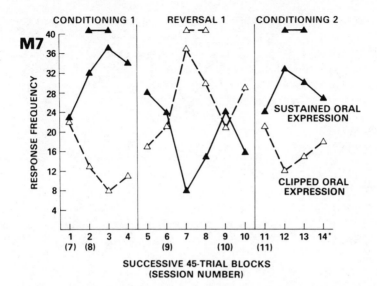

Fig. 8. Frequencies of viewer-judged sustained and clipped oral expressions for Mother 7 and two conditioning and one reversal treatment with incidental infant-head-turn reinforcement.

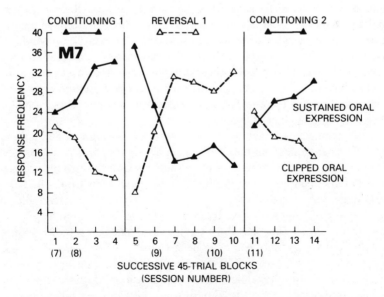

Fig. 9. Frequencies of listener-judged sustained and clipped vocal expressions for Mother 7 corresponding to the viewer-judged curves of Figure 8.

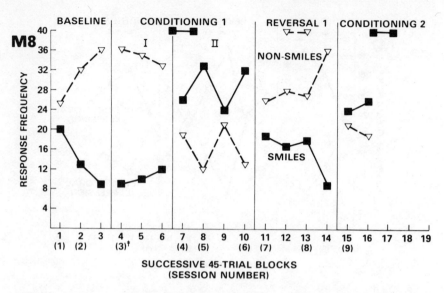

Fig. 10. Frequencies of smiles and nonsmiles for Mother 8 under baseline, two conditioning, and one reversal treatments with incidental infant-head-turn reinforcement.

75.4 ($p < .0001$) indicated that these vocal and facial categorizations were not independent. The strength of association between vocal and facial judgments can be denoted in two ways: the proportion agreement between the categories was .68; and a phi coefficient of association of .36 was obtained between them.

The graph of these listener-categorized vocal responses of Mother 7 is presented in Figure 9. The infant-head-turn contingencies were in effect only for the facial expressions, not for these vocal expressions. However, the similarity in response patterns of the facial and the vocal expressive components apparent in Figures 8 and 9 and the association reported between them suggest that these response classes are linked functionally.

Figure 10 indicates that simulated head turns toward Mother 8 functioned to reinforce first her smiles and then her nonsmiles. Inadvertently, smiles accompanying only one of the two components comprising a verbal response class were reinforced in the first three Conditioning 1(I) trial blocks for Mother 8. This was remedied in the fourth trial block of Conditioning 1(II) and, as is seen, thereafter the conditioning of smiles was readily effected and reversed.

Group Design.   The rates of the reinforced and nonreinforced responses of each of the four subject mothers have been charted in Figures 6, 7, 8, and 10 under a single-subject design. These individual-subject data have provided a sufficient basis for the generalization of the conditioning effects: seemingly-responsive but incidental infant head turns toward the mother, when contingent, conditioned expressive facial responses of Mothers 5, 7, and 8 and the verbal response with and without smiles of Mother 6. The individual-subject data were analyzed also under a more conventional group design, using a routine procedure of statistical inference. The group analysis treats the scores that the largest number of the four mothers have in common.

The first analysis compared Conditioning 1 and Reversal 1 treatments, using the final four 45-trial block scores of Mothers 5, 6, 7, and 8 under the two conditions. The second analysis compared the Conditioning 1, Reversal 1, and Conditioning 2 treatments for the three mothers observed under those three conditions. The final two-block scores were used under each of the three treatments for Mothers 6 and 7. For Mother 8, the final two-block scores for Conditioning 1 and Reversal 1, and her first, and only, two-block scores for Conditioning 2 were used. (Mother 5 was excluded from the second analysis as she participated only in the first two treatment conditions.) For these comparisons, the frequency data of the response reinforced under Conditioning 1 were used for all subjects except Mother 6. Figure 7 shows that the response reinforced for Mother 6 in Conditioning 1 was not again reinforced. Therefore, scores for the response reinforced in Reversal 1 were used for Mother 6 in both analyses to compare Reversal 1, Conditioning 2, and Reversal 2 treatments. In the two group analyses, scores were subjected to an analysis of variance with repeated measures on the treatment and trial-block factors.

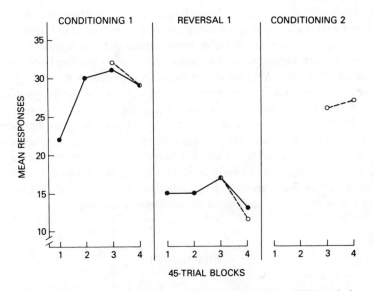

Fig. 11. Closed circles, solid lines represent mean frequencies (Mothers 5, 6, 7, and 8) of the expressive (and verbal) response first reinforced under Conditioning 1, for the final four blocks in two treatments. Open circles, broken lines represent mean frequencies (Mothers 6, 7, and 8) of the final two blocks in three treatments.

A reliable treatment main effect was detected in both analyses, in the absence of a reliable treatment by trial-block interaction effect. Figure 11 shows the final trial-block means involved in the two analyses. Over the *four* trial-block scores for all four mothers (solid circles and lines), the mean of the Conditioning 1 four-block sums (112.3) was found to be reliably higher than the mean of the Reversal 1 four-block sums (60.5)—$F(1,3) = 142.99, p < .002$. And over the *two* final trial blocks for Mothers 5, 7, and 8 (open circles and broken lines), the reliable treatment main effect—$F(2,4) = 41.49, p < .003$—appears due to the mean of the Conditioning 1 two-block sums (61.0) and the mean of the Conditioning 2 two-block sums (52.7) being higher than the mean of the Reversal 1 two-block sums (28.3). As in Experiment 1, these results were not unexpected, given that the training of each mother continued until the reinforced response had reached the criterion of conditioning. Therefore, the individual curves were all in the appropriate direction under the successive conditioning and reversal treatments. On these bases, the same general conclusion is drawn from the group means of the two overlapping analyses under Conditioning 1, Reversal 1, and Conditioning 2 treatments as was drawn from the individual curves charted in Figures 6, 7, 8, and 10. That conclusion is that incidental infant head turns to the mother, when contingent, functioned as reinforcers to condition the facial expressions of three mothers and the smiles and nonsmiles accompanied by particular verbal responses of Mother 6.

Contingency Awareness.   As in Experiment 1, mothers' spontaneous remarks and systematic postexperimental interviews indicated that they appeared unaware that their responses had been conditioned, of the contingencies in effect for the reinforced responses, or that their infants' behaviors had been simulated. In the interview, Mother 6, for whom the final reinforcement contingency was for Verbal A with smile, mentioned that her infant was more responsive to Verbal A during the final sessions but was not differentially responsive to her smiles. Mother 5, whose full smiles were conditioned prior to the interview, stated that her infant responded more when there was enthusiasm in her voice and when she smiled definitively. Also, following sessions that involved a contingency change, mothers commonly remarked that their infants did not attend to them as much as they had earlier. Another mother mentioned that during the session her infant used a new sound he had learned at home.

Discussion

Overall, the results in these two experiments are consistent: Incidental vocalizations or head turns of infants to their mothers functioned as reinforcers to condition the verbal and/or expressive responses of the mothers to their infants. In an interactive context having many features in common with what is known of mother–infant interaction in life situations, these mothers' social responses came freely under the control of what, in the situation, appeared to be the responsive social behaviors of their own infants. Specifically, in Experiment 1, mothers' verbal responses accompanied by smiles, and in Experiment 2, mothers' partial smiles, full smiles, and nonsmiles, clipped and sustained oral expressions, and all smiles and nonsmiles accompanied by particular verbal classes, were conditioned by contingent infant behaviors—vocalizations in Experiment 1 and head turns toward the mother in Experiment 2.

Systematic postexperimental interviews and unsolicited maternal comments during the course of the experiments suggest that this learning may have occurred without the mothers being aware either that (a) there were infant-behavior contingencies in effect for their verbal and/or expressive responses, (b) their responses had been conditioned, or (c) the behaviors of their infants had been simulated. These conclusions receive support also from the fact that, in Experiment 2, smiles and other expressive responses were conditioned even though mothers had not been asked to make these responses.

The design of the experiments presented in this report differed in a critical respect from the Rosenfield and Baer (1970) "double-agent" design, and from the design of a study reported by Berberich (1971) of the reinforcing effects of nominal children's behaviors on adult responses. In both those studies, subjects were instructed to condition the very behaviors that were to be presented contingent on their own responses. Hence, those subjects were instructed to achieve the outcome indicative of the successful conditioning of their own responses. In the present studies, increases in infant vocalizations (Experiment 1) or in infant head turns (Experiment 2) indexed the successful conditioning of the mothers' responses. However, the researchers explicitly avoided giving an instructional set to mothers to condition infant vocalizations or infant head turns, the incidental infant behaviors that were presented contingent on the mothers' responses. Indication of the outcomes actually sought, the systematic rise of each of those contingent infant behaviors, was avoided because it could function as an instructional set to the mothers to increase the rates of the contingent infant behaviors. Mothers' spontaneous remarks during the experimental series and the postexperimental interviews with them suggested that, in fact, the experimenter did not give mothers, inadvertently, an implicit set to foster increases in these infant behaviors. Further, Berberich (1971) gave subjects a fixed set of response alternatives with conditioned responses drawn from this set. A fixed set of verbal response alternatives was also provided in the two studies reported here, but the verbal categories conditioned were formed by grouping these alternatives. Moreover, in Experiment 2 conditioned control was demonstrated definitively for maternal expressions emitted without instruction from the experimenter. Instructions to mothers to foster increases in the infant behaviors that were contingent on their own responses would have impeached the demonstration that maternal social responses can come freely under the direct reinforcer control of what the mothers had been led to believe were the responsive behaviors of their own infants. The demonstration then would have been little more than of an instance of generic problem solving in adults.

In the two experiments reported, instructional and experimental procedures were employed to control for inadvertent reinforcement of the maternal verbal and expressive responses by the infant behaviors that mothers were asked to condition, when those infant behaviors cued the next maternal verbal response. If such inadvertent reinforcement had operated, the results of these studies would have been due not to the mother's verbal and/or expressive responses coming freely under the control of the contingent but incidental behavior of her infant toward her, but rather to the instructional set to the mother to condition that behavior of her infant. Each mother was told that the experimenters would adjust routinely the durations and amplitudes of the infant behavior she was asked to condition and, therefore, that changes in the rate of infant behavior cues should not be taken to index her infant's learning rate. Those infant behavior cues were actually presented at a stable rate across the experimental treatments. Further, there was an automatic delay of at least 6 seconds from the offset of each mother's verbal responses (Experiment 1) and/or expressive responses (Experiment 2) to the onset of the infant-behavior cue for her next verbal response. This delay was assumed sufficient to preclude the functioning of the infant behavior cue as a reinforcer for the mother's verbal response (Experiment 1) or expressive response (Experiment 2) that it followed. However, while there was this automatic 6-second delay between the mother's verbal response and the subsequent infant behavior cue in Experiment 1, there was no such systematic delay there between the offset of a mother's smiles and the onset of that infant (head turn) behavior cue[3] for the next maternal verbal response. Therefore, it was demonstrated definitively in Experiment 1 that the verbal component that accompanied smiles (but not necessarily the smile component itself) of the responses of all four mothers was conditioned successfully by incidental infant vocalizations provided contingent on them.

In Experiment 2, a systematic delay of at least 6 seconds was imposed between the offset of both the verbal and smile or oral expressive responses of the mothers and the onset of the infant vocal cue for their subsequent verbal

[3]The available Experiment 1 latency data, from offset of smile to onset of infant head turn cue, for the four mothers were inspected to provide a basis for evaluating the import of the absence of a systematic delay between them. These latency data indicated that, in but a single treatment for each of two mothers (Reversal 1 of three treatments for Mother 3, Conditioning 3 of eight treatments for Mother 4), latencies of three seconds or less were more likely to follow reinforced than nonreinforced responses. Such short intertrial intervals occurred on only .17 of the total trials sampled during both of the treatments involved. Nevertheless, on this basis the possibility cannot be ruled out entirely for Experiment 1 that the infant head turn cue for the next maternal verbal response may have functioned inadvertently to reinforce the smile component of the response of Mothers 3 and 4 that they followed, diluting further the suggestion of control of the smile component of the responses of those mothers.

responses. With this delay, it is assumed unlikely that the infant vocal cue functioned as a reinforcer for these maternal responses. Therefore, the results of Experiment 2 are taken to demonstrate definitively that the maternal responses of smile amplitude (Mother 5), smiles and nonsmiles with verbal classes (Mother 6), smiles and nonsmiles (Mother 8), and sustained and clipped oral expressions (Mother 7) all came under the control of the contingency provided by an incidental infant behavior, head turns toward the mother. Moreover, the successful conditioning of smiles and nonsmiles with verbal classes in Experiment 2 provides the definitive demonstrations lacking in Experiment 1 that a compound of the two responses, or a verbal response alone, can be conditioned by a contingent infant behavior. The conditioning of these maternal social responses occurred in the apparent absence of an instructional set that the experimenter sought increases in those infant head-turn behavior consequences indicative of the successful conditioning of the mothers' social responses. Further, in Experiment 1, the verbal responses conditioned derived from the phrases mothers were asked to say. However, in Experiment 2, mothers were *not* instructed to be expressive or nonexpressive, and these responses, spontaneously generated, came under the control of the simulated, contingent infant head turns toward the mothers.

A formal control was not included in either experiment for the possible evocative or eliciting effect of the infant behavior cue for the mothers' responses. It has been noted that there was a systematic delay between the offset of the mother's verbal response and the onset of the infant behavior that cued her next verbal response. It is assumed that this trial procedure mitigated against the evocative or eliciting function of the contingent infant vocalizations or head turns for the mother's responses.

There very likely exist nonaversive, nonsocial events within a wide range that could function as reinforcers when made systematically contingent upon the maternal responses studied in this experimental context. However, a reinforcer function of such nonsocial stimuli would not detract from the significance of the positive results obtained: in a social context, incidental vocal behaviors and head turns appearing to the mother to have been emitted by her infant reinforced the mother's responses on which they were contingent.

In the present studies, mother–infant interactions were contrived experimentally to facilitate investigation of the interaction process by demonstrating selective functional relations among the behaviors of mother and infant. It is most difficult to study, or even only to record the details of the flow of interaction in unrestricted life situations. There are many actor turns, involving behaviors that can occur concurrently or in rapid sequence with overlapping durations. Without a theory to limit observations, a few minutes of observation of the behavior flow between a mother and her infant can require the scoring of myriad different sequences. Our procedure reduces markedly the rich and complex detail of natural mother–infant interaction. This has been done on the assumption that it is not necessary to capture all or even many possible features of life interchanges to demonstrate the plausibility and utility of a theoretical conception. Therefore, our initial approach has been to delineate a context for interchange that involves very few actor turns and a single imposed sequence. With this experimental tactic, functional relationships between the behaviors of mother and infant can be determined definitively. This tactic also facilitates a demonstration of the relevance and utility of an instrumental-conditioning model to account for the influence of the behavior of one actor, the infant, upon the behavior of the other actor, the mother.

Because interaction phenomena in natural settings have many overlapping facets and can occur in rapid sequence, it is difficult to analyze them in the detail required to demonstrate their relevance or irrelevance to a particular model like that of operant conditioning. This is not to conclude that such conditioning principles operate only under highly restrictive conditions. Rather, they can be shown to operate definitively only under highly specified conditions. At the same time, the simplified interaction context contrived in the present studies shares many salient features with commonly occurring natural mother-infant interactions. The sequence of maternal verbal and/or expressive behaviors followed by infant vocalizations or turning toward the mother, although simplified and in part simulated, are like behavior sequences that routinely occur in mother–infant interaction in life settings. Therefore, it is proposed that the reported results have validity for much of mother–infant interchange in natural settings and that mutual-conditioning processes may underlie many of these interchanges.

At present, the usual descriptive approaches to mother–infant interaction in life settings sample and summarize interaction instances that are relatively simple, involving few response elements in discrete or otherwise convenient temporal relations. In restricting focus on a small sample of interaction in a contrived setting, the experimental tactic employed in the present studies is not unlike those descriptive tactics used to sample interactions in order to extract regularities within and between actor positions in the natural setting. Indeed, we know no observation tactic that is capable of organizing efficiently the complexities of mother–infant interaction in life settings, except when (a) only a limited segment of the interaction instances is sampled, (b) those instances are relatively simple, involving few response elements that occur in discrete or otherwise convenient temporal relations, or (c) features of interaction sequences are abstracted. Admittedly, it is important to map mutual behavioral regularities as they occur in the natural environment. However, the functional implications of these regularities must often be presumptive in the absence of experimental manipulations. Because it facilitates the determination of functional relations between interactor behaviors, the experimental tactic employed in the studies reported offers a promising alternative to the routine descriptive approach of observing natural interaction in its own terms.

It is planned subsequently to extend the results of these studies to a demonstration of the simultaneous conditioning of the actual behaviors of both the infant and the mother. Initially, it is planned to demonstrate simultaneously a discriminative-cue function of an actual infant's behavior for a mother's behavior and reinforcement control of this actual infant behavior by another of the mother's behaviors. In these contemplated studies, the simulated mother–infant interaction will more closely approximate natural-setting interactions than was the case in the studies reported. As our experimental simulations of mutual conditioning in mother–infant interactions more closely come to approximate naturally-occurring interactions, a conditioning account of the development of a substantial portion of these interactions will become increasingly plausible.

Because the mothers came from the same sources and it was critical to avoid giving them the set to foster the incidental infant behavior that was to reinforce their responses, it was not feasible to debrief each mother completely after she had participated in the experiment. When this series of studies on the mutual-conditioning process is completed, copies of the reports will be sent to the cooperating organizations from which most of the participating mothers came so that they may publicize the results to all members.

Summary and Conclusion

In an interactive context having much in common with mother–infant interaction in life settings, two experiments were carried out. In both studies, each of eight mothers was asked to serve as "experimenter" in an investigation of whether infant "subjects" could learn that their behaviors can have social consequences. Each mother was asked to provide these consequences by saying a short phrase immediately following representations of one of her infant's behaviors. Mother and infant were on opposite sides of a one-way mirror, the mother facing the mirror side. All infant behaviors were simulated. A seemingly responsive but incidental behavior, attributed to the mother's own infant, was identified for her as merely occurring in the situation. An explicit attempt was made to give her no indication to attend to that incidental infant behavior, much less to foster it. That infant behavior was then presented contingent on one of the mother's verbal and/or expressive responses. The actual purpose of the experiments was to determine the reinforcing efficacy for everyday maternal social responses (verbalizations, facial expressions) of those seemingly responsive but incidental infant behaviors (vocalizations, head turns).

Specifically, in Experiment 1, each mother was asked to say a phrase immediately following her infant's head turns toward her. Incidental vocalizations attributed to her child were then presented contingent on the mother's verbal phrases accompanied by her smiles, to determine the reinforcing effectiveness of the infant vocalizations for those maternal social responses. In Experiment 2, this paradigm of instrumental conditioning was reversed and extended to a study of a different infant behavior, the head turn, as a potential reinforcer for different maternal expressive responses. Each mother was asked to say a short phrase immediately following her infant's vocalizations. To determine the reinforcing effectiveness of those infant head turns to the mother for her expressive responses, they were then presented contingent on her facial expressions (in one case crossed with her verbal responses). The maternal expressive responses reinforced were full smiles, partial smiles, and nonsmiles, clipped and sustained oral expressions, and smiles and nonsmiles accompanying particular verbal classes. Control was also effected in Experiment 2 for the possible inadvertent reinforcement of a mother's expressive responses by the infant behavior that cued her subsequent verbal response. This control had been implemented only partially in Experiment 1, where the conditioning results for several mothers raised the possibility that the infant-behavior cue may have functioned to reinforce the smiles that preceded it.

The simulated infant vocalizations (in Experiment 1) and head turns to mother (in Experiment 2) functioned as reinforcers to condition the mothers' verbal phrases and/or expressive responses. Hence, these maternal social responses came readily under the control of what, in the interactive context, appeared to be the responsive vocal and head turn behaviors of their own infants. Systematic postexperimental interviews and unsolicited comments during the course of the studies suggested that this learning occurred without the mothers being aware either that (a) there were infant vocal or head turn behavior contingencies in effect for their verbal and/or expressive responses, (b) their responses had been conditioned, or (c) the behaviors of their infants had been simulated. These conclusions received support also from the fact that, in Experiment 2, expressive responses were conditioned even though mothers were not asked to make them. The reported experimental approach to mother–infant interaction in a contrived setting that emphasizes particular interaction modes is proposed as an alternative tactic to that of investigating the intensive flow of such interchange in unrestricted life situations.

ACKNOWLEDGMENTS

The authors appreciate the discriminating assistance of Patricia Bielke and S. Lawson Sebris in the research reported. This work was sponsored by The Intramural Research Program of The National Institute of Mental Health and is therefore not subject to copyright.

References

Ainsworth, M. D. S. Attachment and dependency: A comparison. In J. L. Gewirtz (Ed.), *Attachment and dependency*. Washington, D.C.: Winston, 1972, 97–137.

Ainsworth, M. D. S. The development of infant–mother attachment. In B. M. Caldwell and H. N. Ricciuti (Eds.), *Review of child development research*. Vol. 3. Chicago: University of Chicago Press, 1973, 1–94.

Beckwith, L. Relationships between attributes of mothers and their infants' IQ scores. *Child Development*, 1971, **42**, 1083–1097.

Bell, R. Q. The effect on the family of a limitation in coping ability in the child: A research approach and a finding. *Merrill–Palmer Quarterly*, 1964, **10**, 129–142.

Bell, R. Q. A reinterpretation of the direction of effects in studies of socialization. *Psychological Review*, 1968, **75**, 81–95.

Bell, R. Q. Stimulus control of parent or caretaker behavior by offspring. *Developmental Psychology*, 1971, **4**, 63–72.

Berberich, L. P. Do the child's responses shape the teaching behavior of adults? *Journal of Experimental Research in Personality*, 1971, **5**, 92–97.

Bowlby, J. The nature of the child's tie to his mother. *International Journal of Psychoanalysis*, 1958, **39**, 350–373.

Bowlby, J. *Attachment and loss*. Vol. 1. *Attachment*. New York: Basic Books, 1969.

Bowlby, J. *Attachment and loss*. Vol. 2. *Separation*. New York: Basic Books, 1973.

Boyd, E. F., & Gewirtz, J. L. An infant's head turns to mother condition her facial expressions, 1976.

Brackbill, Y. Extinction of the smiling response in infants as a function of reinforcement schedule. *Child Development*, 1958, **29**, 115–124.

Cairns, R. B. Attachment and dependency: A psychobiological and social–learning synthesis. In J. L. Gewirtz (Ed.), *Attachment and dependency*. Washington, D.C.: Winston, 1972, 29–80.

Connerly, R. J. A comparison of personality characteristics of parents of brain-injured and normal children. *Dissertation Abstracts*, 1968, **28**, 1291–1292.

Etzel, B. C., & Gewirtz, J. L. Experimental modification of caretaker–maintained high rate operant crying in a 6– and a 20–week old infant (*Infans tyrannotearus*): Extinction of crying with reinforcement of eye contact and smiling. *Journal of Experimental Child Psychology*, 1967, **5**, 303–317.

Ferguson, C. A. Baby talk in six languages. In J. Gumperz & D. Hymes (Eds.), The ethnography of communication. *American Anthropologist*, 1964, **66** (Pt. 2), 103–114.

Gewirtz, H. B., & Gewirtz, J. L. Caretaker settings, background events, and behavior differences in four Israeli child–rearing environments: Some preliminary trends. In B. M. Foss (Ed.), *Determinants of infant behaviour IV*. London: Methuen, 1969, 229–252.

Gewirtz, J. L. A learning analysis of the effects of normal stimulation, privation, and deprivation on the acquisition of social motivation and attachment. In B. M. Foss (Ed.), *Determinants of infant behaviour*. London: Methuen (New York: Wiley), 1961, 213–299.

Gewirtz, J. L. Mechanisms of social learning: Some roles of stimulation and behavior in early human development. In D. A. Goslin (Ed.), *Handbook of socialization theory and research*. Chicago: Rand McNally, 1969, 57–212.

Gewirtz, J. L. (Ed.), *Attachment and dependency*. Washington, D.C.: Winston, 1972. (Distributed by Halsted Press Division of J. Wiley Sons, New York.) (*a*)

Gewirtz, J. L. Attachment, dependency, and a distinction in terms of stimulus control. In J. L. Gewirtz (Ed.), *Attachment and dependency*. Washington, D.C.: Winston, 1972, 139–177. (*b*)

Gewirtz, J. L. On the selection and use of attachment and dependence indices. In J. L. Gewirtz (Ed.), *Attachment and dependency*. Washington, D.C.: Winston, 1972, 179–215. (*c*)

Gewirtz, J. L. The attachment acquisition process as evidenced in the maternal conditioning of cued infant responding (particularly crying). *Human Development*, 1976.

Gewirtz, J. L. Maternal responding and the conditioning of infant crying: Directions of influence within the attachment–acquisition process. In B. C. Etzel, J. M. LeBlanc, & D. M. Baer (Eds.), *New developments in behavioral research: Theories, methods, and applications*. Hillsdale, New Jersey: L. Erlbaum Associates, in press.

Gewirtz, J. L., & Boyd, E. F. Infant vocalizations condition maternal verbalizations, *Child Development*, in press.

Gewirtz, J. L., & Gewirtz, H. B. Stimulus conditions, infant behaviors, and social learning in four Israeli child–rearing environment: A preliminary report illustrating differences in environment and behavior between the "only" and the "youngest" child. In B. M. Foss (Ed.), *Determinants of infant behaviour III*. London: Methuen (New York: Wiley), 1965, 161–184.

Halverson, C. F., & Waldrop, M. F. Maternal behavior toward own and other preschool children: The problem of "ownness." *Child Development*, 1970, **41**, 839–845.

Harper, L. V. The young as a source of stimuli controlling caretaker behavior. *Developmental Psychology*, 1971, **4**, 73–88.

Haugan, G. M., & McIntire, R. W. Comparisons of vocal imitation, tactile stimulation, and food as reinforcers for infant vocalizations. *Developmental Psychology*, 1972, **6**, 201–209.

Kessen, W. Research in psychological development of infants: An overview. *Merrill-Palmer Quarterly*, 1963, **9**, 83–94.

Klaus, M. H., Jerauld, R., Kreger, N. C., McAlpine, W., Steffa, M., & Kennell, J. H. Maternal attachment: Importance of the first postpartum days. *New England Journal of Medicine*, 1972, **286**, 460–463.

Klebanoff, L. B. Parents of schizophrenic children: Parental attitudes of mothers of schizophrenic, brain-injured and retarded, and normal children. *American Journal of Orthopsychiatry*, 1959, **29**, 445–454.

Korner, A. F. Mother-child interaction: One- or two-way street? *Social Work*, 1965, **10**, 47–51.

Lamb, M. E. A defense of the concept of attachment. *Human Development*, 1974, **17**, 376–385.

Leifer, A. D., Leiderman, P. H., Barnett, C. R., & Williams, J. A. Effects of mother-infant separation on maternal attachment behavior. *Child Development*, 1972, **43**, 1203–1218.

Lewis, M. State as an infant–environment interaction: An analysis of mother-infant interaction as a function of sex. *Merrill-Palmer Quarterly*, 1972, **18**, 95–121.

Lewis, M., & Lee-Painter, S. An interactional approach to the mother–infant dyad. In M. Lewis & L. A. Rosenblum (Eds.), *The effect of the infant on its caregiver*. New York: Wiley, 1974, 21–48.

McKenzie, B., & Day, R. H. Operant learning of visual pattern discrimination in young infants. *Journal of Experimental Child Psychology*, 1971, **11**, 45–53.

Moss, H. A. Sex, age, and state as determinants of mother–infant interaction. *Merrill-Palmer Quarterly*, 1967, **13**, 19–36.

Osofsky, J. D., & Danzger, B. Relationships between neonatal characteristics and mother–infant interaction. *Developmental Psychology*, 1974, **10**, 124–130.

Osofsky, J. D., & O'Connell, E. J. Parent–child interaction: Daughters' effects upon mothers' and fathers' behaviors. *Developmental Psychology*, 1972, **7**, 157–168.

Prechtl, H. F. R. The mother–child interaction in babies with minimal brain damage. In B. M. Foss (Ed.), *Determinants of infant behaviour II*. London: Methuen (New York: Wiley), 1963, 53–59.

Ramey, C. T., & Ourth, L. L. Delayed reinforcement and vocalization rates of infants. *Child Development*, 1971, **42**, 291–297.

Rheingold, H. L. The social and socializing infant. In D. A. Goslin (Ed.), *Handbook of socialization theory and research*. Chicago: Rand McNally, 1969, 779–790.

Rheingold, H. L., Gewirtz, J. L., & Ross, H. W. Social conditioning of vocalizations in the infant. *Journal of Comparative and Physiological Psychology*, 1959, **52**, 68–73.

Richards, M. P. M. Social interaction in the first weeks of human life. *Psychiatria, Neurologia, Neurochirurgia*, 1971, **14**, 35–42.

Robson, K. S., & Moss, H. A. Patterns and determinants of maternal attachment. *Journal of Pediatrics*, 1970, **77**, 976–985.

Rosenfeld, H. M., & Baer, D. M. Unbiased and unnoticed conditioning: The double agent robot procedure. *Journal of the Experimental Analysis of Behavior*, 1970, **14**, 99–105.

Rosenthal, R., & Jacobsen, L. Teachers' expectancies: Determiners of pupils' I.Q. gains. *Psychological Reports*, 1966, **19**, 115–118.

Routh, D. K. Conditioning of vocal response differentiation in infants. *Developmental Psychology*, 1969, **1**, 219–226.

Sears, R. R. A theoretical framework for personality and social behavior. *American Psychologist*, 1951, **6**, 476–483.

Sears, R. R. Attachment, dependency, and frustration. In J. L. Gewirtz (Ed.), *Attachment and dependency*. Washington, D.C.: Winston, 1972, 1–27.

Sears, R. R., Maccoby, E. E., & Levin, H. *Patterns of child rearing*. Evanston, Illinois: Row, Peterson, 1957.

Siegel, G. M. Adult verbal behavior with retarded children labeled as "high" or "low" in verbal ability. *American Journal of Mental Deficiency*, 1963, **68**, 417–424.

Siegel, S. *Nonparametric statistics for the behavioral sciences*. New York: McGraw–Hill, 1956.

Snow, C. Mothers' speech to children learning language. *Child Development*, 1972, **43**, 549–565.

Stern, D. N. Mother and infant at play: The dyadic interaction involving facial, vocal, and gaze behaviors. In M. Lewis & L. A. Rosenblum (Eds.), *The effect of the infant on its caregiver*. New York: Wiley, 1974, 187–213.

Thoman, E. B., Leiderman, P. H., & Olson, J. P. Neonate-mother interaction during breast-feeding. *Developmental Psychology*, 1972, **6**, 110–118.

Vuorenkoski, V., Wasz-Höckert, O., Koivisto, E., & Lind, J. The effect of cry stimulus on temperature of the lactating breast of primipara: A thermographic study. *Experientia*, 1969, **25**, 1286–1287.

Wahler, R. G. Infant social attachments: A reinforcement theory interpretation and investigation. *Child Development*, 1967, **38**, 1079–1088.

Weisberg, P. Social and nonsocial conditioning of infant vocalizations. *Child Development*, 1963, **34**, 377–388.

Wenar, C., & Wenar, S. C. The short-term prospective model, the illusion of time, and the tabula rasa child. *Child Development*, 1963, **34**, 697–708.

Wolff, P. The natural history of crying and other vocalizations in early infancy. In B. M. Foss (Ed.), *Determinants of infant behaviour IV*. London: Methuen, 1969, 81–109.

Yarrow, L. J. Dimensions of maternal care. *Merrill-Palmer Quarterly*, 1963, **9**, 101–114.

Yarrow, L. J. Attachment and dependency: A developmental perspective. In J. L. Gewirtz (Ed.), *Attachment and dependency*. Washington, D.C.: Winston, 1972, 81–95.

Yarrow, M. R., Waxler, C. Z., & Scott, P. M. Child effects on adult behavior. *Developmental Psychology*, 1971, **5**, 300–311.

CHAPTER 6

Peers, Parents, and Primates: The Developing Network of Attachments

Paul E. Simonds

Department of Anthropology
University of Oregon
Eugene, Oregon

Anthropologists, psychologists, and sociologists study socialization from different points of view. As Thomas Rhys Williams (1972) has pointed out, anthropologists use the term "socialization" to refer to "the inter-generational transmission of culture"; psychologists, to denote the "acquisition of controls by infants and children for their basic impulses"; and sociologists, to refer to "the training of infants and children for future social performances." The difference in viewpoint can be explained by the difference in approach to the phenomenon of socialization: anthropology regards it as part of the process of cultural transmission; psychology, as a phase in the development of individual behavior; and sociology, as one of the dynamics of social institutions.

These varied approaches have developed in specifically human situations and in many cases are particularly tailored to problems of socialization involving human language and culture. Whereas socialization as it refers to nonhuman primates does not involve language or culture in the strict sense, it is concerned with the communication and transmission of learned behavior patterns. Both processes are surprisingly similar in both human and nonhuman primate socialization. For many years now, psychologists have acquired some of these data from nonhuman primates and more recently anthropologists have established a broad enough base in their field studies to include subhuman primate data in their results.

Even if the conservative is not yet prepared to concede that nonhuman primates transmit a culture from one generation to the next, recent findings may convince him that we ought to investigate how they transmit traditional learned behavior patterns to their offspring. The innovative act of washing sweet potatoes and the transmission of this act to the younger members of the Koshima troop of Japanese macaques have already shown that primates can introduce and transmit new habits from one generation to the next. This example also shows that new habits are acquired far more readily by the young than by the mature members of the group, who in the example cited did not adopt the behavior even when it had spread among the younger members. Other social and behavioral traditions are known to be handed down from one generation of nonhuman primate to the next, one group of a species often differing significantly from another of the same species in the kind and degree of social structure and interaction.

For example, the common forms of tactile contact among bonnet macaques, whether male or female, young or old, are, first, grooming, and then sitting together, playing, and such various greeting behaviors as mounting and embracing. This rather well-established order of contact is not observed, however, by a troop of bonnet macaques in the temple town of Tiruchengode, Tamilnadu, whose young males substitute joint masturbation for grooming. Apparently, older subadult males introduced infant and juvenile males to the practice and the tradition has been maintained. Both the substitution and the continued practice are evidence of the pliability of young macaques and of their readiness to experiment with new patterns of behavior.

The history of how the infant primate acquires control over his basic impulses is another fascinating aspect of socialization as it is exemplified among nonhuman primates. Once the young primate loses the protective infant coloration that exempts it from adult social control, it must respond correctly to the social situation in which it finds itself if it is to avoid repeated aggression on the part of the older members of the group. It cannot, for example, respond to a choice piece of food by eating it if a more dominant individual is making for it at the same time. It cannot, without risking aggression, respond sexually to an estrous female if she is being approached by a more dominant male. In similar circumstances, the young primate must exercise control over basic impulses of sex, hunger, and the like to live successfully within a social group. One way to describe this process is to show how an individual acquires the ability to communicate by gestures as Jay (1965) did for hanuman langurs. The appearance of subordination gestures in the communication repertoire of the infant primate coincides with its developing control of impulses in the social situation.

The infant's developing social expertise can be viewed as the result of training by the older members of the group. Those negative and positive rewards are applied by the adults which tend to reinforce the appropriate behavior in the young.

Network Analysis

Network analysis is a method that can be used to extract information about socialization in all the above senses from field data. While it does not focus specifically on the internal states of the animal, it does involve an analysis of the developing network of social relationships as the individual grows from one life stage to another. As in man, the individual's success in developing a network of social relationships determines his success as an adult in the society. Those who develop a strong and complete network within the society are those who remain in the society and act as the agents of social control and socialization for future generations. Those whose networks are deficient in the percentage of possible links that are actually developed tend to be forced to the periphery of the society; some of these may even become isolated and thus more subject to predation than those remaining in the society. Individuals who develop dense networks (that is, those in which the members of the personal network are in touch with one another independently of the person) and central networks (that is, those in which the individual is near the center of a network for a particular activity) are the ones that will survive and reproduce. It is, therefore, highly advantageous both for the individual and for genetic selection for the growing infant to develop strong networks.

I approach the study of primate socialization by analyzing the nature of network formation in different groups and species of primates. Present evidence indicates that the structure of society into which the infant is born influences his socialization process and that, in turn, the nature of the adult network strongly affects the structure of society. How much each contributes to the other or which is the prior factor cannot, like the old chicken-or-the-egg conundrum, be determined yet.

To do so, one would need a set of behavioral patterns that would be suitable for network analysis and should be closely related to the physiological processes underlying bond formation in the species. Whereas we are not yet ready to relate grooming to a protein base in the individual's physiology, there are strong indications that tactile contact is exceedingly important for the proper development of the social animal. Harlow and his associates are among several groups of workers who show that early tactile contact is of enormous importance to the growing infant primate and that the contact between mother and infant and between peers is reciprocal. Moreover, it is not only initial bond-building that depends on tactile contact. Observation of a wide variety of primate species, including man, demonstrates how a potentially disruptive social interaction which has escalated to the threat level is resolved when the participants come into tactile contact; once flesh touches flesh there is a visible lowering of the level of arousal. One need only watch a film such as Peter Marler and Hugo Van-Lawick's *Vocalizations of Wild Chimpanzees* to see how repeatedly agonistic encounters are resolved by a simple pressing of flesh by flesh. The major function of the other channels of communication in social interaction (visual, auditory, and olfactory) is to facilitate a return to tactile communication and to speed the resumption of stable, friendly social relationships. Any investigation of the social bonds of primates reveals that the tactile contacts between individuals are directly related to the strong bonds within the society. For example, in one-male harem units of hamadryas baboons, whose perpetuation depends upon the early severance of the mother–infant bond and the forging of strong ties between the harem leader and his females, the weak bond between mother and infant is characterized by very little grooming, and the strong bond between male and females is characterized by lavish grooming of the male by the females. The future leader of a harem begins early to mother a young juvenile or infant female by carrying and grooming her so that ultimately by the time she has become a full harem member at adulthood a strong bond has developed between them.

The tactile contacts of grooming, play, and mounting will be the major source of information about socialization reported here. They are the principal means of forging bonds that facilitate the transmission of traditional information, the acquisition of control over the appropriate impulses, and the training of the young for adult roles. Typically, tactile contact for the young female consists of grooming, whereas play and mounting are the forms favored by males who as they mature either substitute them for grooming or use them as supplements.

My method of examining socialization in different species of primates is based on several premises which in turn are based on data derived from laboratory and field studies of various species but not yet conclusively proven. They are working hypotheses that to become valid generalizations about primate behavior must be supported by further research and evidential data.

The first of these premises is that during the socialization process in primate societies, tactile communication underlies the development of attachments between individuals. Thus, every form of tactile behavior—from the newborn primate clinging to the mother's fur and her fondling of the neonate, to the handling of the infant by other animals during the early weeks and months of its life, and ultimately to the grooming, play, greeting, and sexual relationships—is designed to develop and strengthen these attachments. Harlow, Mason, and others have even shown that tactile contact of the newborn infant with another member of its own species is a prerequisite for effective functioning in a social context in adulthood. Harlow and his associates' studies with rhesus macaques clearly demonstrate that for that species the tactile interaction between an infant and its mother and an infant and its peers is crucial to the development of normal social bonds. Similarly, other studies (Soumi, 1974) indicate that the growing infant, especially the male infant, must have an adult male to relate to. It has been assumed that these bonds, much like imprinting among birds and some other animals, are formed at a crucial stage in the infant's development and become permanent and that without their formation the infant's future social life is deficient. Recently, however, Mason and Kenney (1974) through their experiments with rhesus infants taken from peers or parents and placed with spayed female dogs have shown that these bonds can weaken and be replaced by new bonds. Not only were these infants capable of developing new bonds with their surrogate mothers, but two of them later, given a choice between their earlier peers and the dog to whom they were now attached, preferred the dog.

My second premise, therefore, is that primate bond formation is not an imprinting process in the sense that it determines the social bond of the individual for life, but a learning process in which the techniques for developing social bonds are learned during a crucial period in the infant's life in such a way that he can apply them to later situations to form strong and lasting attachments as an adult. This implies, of course, that to be permanent these bonds must be continually reinforced by regular tactile contact. No bond, even that between mother and daughter or mother and son, can be maintained throughout the lifetime of the individuals concerned without such physical contact.

My third premise is based on the work of Jensen, Bobbitt, and Gordon (1967), who have shown how the socialization process of infant male pig-tailed macaques differs from that of infant females. Treated more roughly by his mother than his infant sister is, the infant male not only is more aggressive than she but also tends to sever the close bond between himself and his mother at an earlier age. This thrusts him into a play situation in which the rough wrestling and chasing of his male playmates reinforce the aggressiveness which developed in response to his mother's earlier treatment. I assume that, as a result, play behavior is mainly a male socializing agent and that females reject the play pattern as it becomes rougher, partly because they have not acquired the greater aggressiveness of the immature male and partly because they are focusing their attention on grooming and the other close tactile relationships with females instead.

My fourth and last premise is that any repetitive and relatively intense tactile behavior between social fellows in a primate group is oriented around the areas of greatest social interaction, bonding, and attachment. As a result, the kinds, intensity, and direction of tactile contact differ not only among males and females that are growing and developing into their adult roles in society but also among the various kinds of primate societies—troops, harem organizations, one-male units, and mated pairs.

Let us briefly investigate these premises, first in bonnet macaques and then in several other primate species, and in the process recognize some similarities. I have original data only for the bonnet macaques and must rely on secondary sources for these other species. Many of these published reports are detailed enough, however, to give a relatively clear picture of social interaction among these other species and to show interesting aspects of their behavior that tend to support my generalizations.

Bonnet Macaques

I have limited this report to a discussion of grooming, playing, and mounting (a form of greeting behavior) as the agents of bond formation among bonnet macaques, but do not intend by doing so to exclude other greeting behavior patterns and other forms of tactile communication, some of which may be highly important. For example, Rosenblum and his co-workers (1964) have shown that bonnet macaques sit closer to each other and maintain more actual tactile contact than pig-tailed macaques. But the best data I have is on grooming and mounting; my play data will also be useful even though for most older infants and juveniles the mother–infant relationship was not known to me.

Grooming

I have discussed elsewhere (Simonds, 1974a) the developing network of grooming, which expands as the individual grows and, in many bonnet macaque troops, includes a significant proportion of all possible links between individuals. Basically, the newborn infant starts out with tactile contact with its own mother, but within hours of its birth other individuals come and attempt to touch it. At this point, the only difference between males and females is that the adult females and the mother are far more interested in the genitalia of the newborn male than of the newborn female. The male is subjected to the indignity of having his penis pulled and his scrotum manipulated by the adult females who examine him meticulously. During the first week or so, this process is repeated several dozen times for the benefit of most of the females in the group. This kind of treatment probably helps explain the more aggressive behavior of males, which later on is reinforced by differences in play and hormonal balance. The infant female, on the other hand, is not handled the same way, her contacts with her mother and associated females being characterized by gentler grooming and touching.

The contacts of the newborn bonnet macaque are principally with the females and the younger members of the group. Adult males are conspicuously absent from the vicinity of dark-haired neonates, whom they assiduously avoid, almost with fear. But once the color change becomes obvious, from about 6 weeks on, the adult males no longer avoid the infants, whose presence they then more or less take for granted. The tactile network of the 6-week-old infant, then, includes the mother, her close female associates, and in the larger troops where females with newborn infants tend to cluster in a temporary subdivision regardless of their associations during the rest of the year, those females who would not otherwise be a regular part of their social milieu. In other words, a young infant probably has some visual and tactile contact with most of the females of the troop, assuming, as is often the case, that each has a new infant every year. Juvenile and subadult males, as well as young nulliparous females, show some interest in newborn infants, but it is mainly the females who maintain close and continual tactile contact with them through grooming, holding, and allowing them to climb over the cluster of females.

Aside from sitting together, the major tactile contact for growing females is grooming. It is the infant male, not female, who ventures farther and earlier from his mother and joins play sessions with other young monkeys for longer and more intense wrestling and chasing bouts. The female plays, but her play is milder, and as the play groups become rougher she drops out of them earlier. She follows her mother more closely, feeding with her and grooming her when they rest; by her third year, she is settled into a pattern that is mainly oriented to the female segment of society.

Play

Bonnet macaque play is quite similar to that of other species of macaques. For the young infants, the first attempts are locomotion. They hop about disjointedly on the ground without orientation to other monkeys, or drop through small branches and climb unsteadily up again. As they grow older, they begin to orient toward other young infants; it is not uncommon to see them climbing all over a cluster of females who are sitting with their newborn infants or jumping to the ground and hopping around each other within a few feet of the females. As the weeks and months go by, the play becomes rougher, changing first to chasing and later to more and more wrestling. Wrestling involves these youngsters in extensive tactile contact with one another, more extensive than any other behavior pattern. Regardless of the substratum—whether ground, branches, or water—the patterns of play are the same, wrestling and chasing, and are modified only by the exigencies of the surroundings; after all, one cannot grapple with all four feet while hanging from a branch.

With some individual variations, male bonnet macaques indulge in play from the time they can move about unaided until they die. Females, on the other hand, seem to stop playing by the time of their first parturition and never resume it, even with their own infants. At the beginning, young female infants who are part of the female cluster participate almost equally in a mild kind of chasing because such clusters may include more females than males as often as the reverse. But if older infants and juveniles join a group of playing young infants and the play then switches more and more to wrestling, the females drop out and sit on the sidelines. As they grow older, they respond to the rougher wrestling bouts as though they were a threat rather than play. In fact, if play is defined as behavior of the young during moderate arousal, then the male bonnet macaque's upper limits of play seem to be at a higher level of arousal than those of females, who seem to have a lower threshold of arousal marking the boundary between play and aggression. As a result, play behavior is mainly a male behavior, and the large, boisterous play groups of wrestling and chasing males rarely contain more than an occasional juvenile female.

During the mating season, adult males do not play with younger males. The tension caused by the presence of cycling females may be enough to prevent males from approaching each other or the younger males in the relaxed manner necessary for play. On the other hand, it may be that sexual behavior takes precedence over play.

During the birth season, however, when copulations are rare, adult males are fairly often found in play groups with subadult and juvenile males. They even play with one another during this time, although it can hardly be called a common everyday occurrence. The result is that infants who have just been displaced by their mothers' newborn and are about to become juveniles are in a position to form new tactile bonds with the fully adult males, some of whom even carry such infants for a time. These one-year-olds have, of course, already had an opportunity to come into occasional tactile contact with the adult males, partly because of mild aggression on the male's part and partly because of occasional greeting and grooming contacts. But during these first months of their second year, their play pattern changes subtly and gradually into a rough, intense tactile contact, which involves wrestling with subadult and adult males. This tactile experience is longer and more intense than any other they have yet experienced and facilitates the formation of attachment bonds. Females ordinarily do not experience such contact with the adult males, which is similar to the differentially rough treatment formerly accorded the male infant by his mother and which reinforces and develops the young male's aggressiveness as he grows older.

Each year as he matures, the growing juvenile experiences this play contact during the birth season, but in the intervening months he has, of course, joined the rougher play groups composed mostly of his peers and stays in them until he is one of those hardy stalwarts who remain to the frantic end of the play sequence.

Mounting

Mounting as a nonsexual communicative act has often been considered a sign of dominance among primates. The animal that presents to another is considered to be the subordinate, and the animal that mounts often is, and among some species exclusively is, the more dominant of the two. As a result, mounting is often regarded as a gesture of threat or hierarchical communication rather than as a bond-reinforcing phenomenon.

If, however, mounting is viewed as a pattern of social interaction that involves tactile communication, the consequent interaction between the two partners should be examined in a new light. In this light, mounting is seen as an attachment behavior, a tactile gesture carrying the message ''I am reaffirming or reestablishing normal social interaction.'' When analyzed as such, mounting behavior can indicate the direction of social attachments and elucidate the process of socialization.

According to my data, threat and conciliation behavior in bonnet macaques follows the pattern in which, with very few exceptions, only the dominant animals threaten their subordinates, who always respond with a gesture of subordination or conciliation. But a plot of who mounted whom showed clearly that there were many more exceptions during mounting than during any of the other supposedly dominance or hierarchical communication gestures. A very mixed picture emerged: dominant macaques mounted subordinates, subordinates mounted dominants, dominant animals forced subordinates to mount, subordinates took the initiative and quickly mounted dominants, all of which led me to hypothesize that as a rule mounting is not an expression of hierarchical status among bonnet macaques.

When I further analyzed the context in which these various mounting incidents took place, however, the pattern that emerged could be usefully interpreted in terms of both hierarchical interactions and social attachments. The mountings that occurred during social interaction involving tension and hierarchical disputes conformed strictly with the lines of dominance whereas those that occurred during relaxed social intercourse were performed about equally by dominants and subordinates and were similar to other forms of greeting behavior. Let me cite two typical examples taken from my notes on the Somanathapur troop in November, 1961.

> Sanna (lambda male) screech-threatens Kink (eta male) from banyon tree 51 west. Kink, who is sitting with Zeb (beta male) and Pim (gamma male) on the road, growl-threatens back while Zeb and Pim growl and jaw. As Sanna continues his screech-threatening, Pim tries to mount Kink, who jumps away. Andy (zeta male) goes up to Sanna, who presents to him while continuing to screech-threaten Kink. Zeb and Pim now growl-threaten Kink, who moves away a bit and continues to growl-threaten Sanna. One-eye (epsilon male) comes down to join Zeb and Pim. Sanna moves into tree 39 east and starts to descend, still screech-threatening Kink. Finally Kink chases Sanna up the tree to the top. When he descends, he is growl- and screech-threatened by Zeb, Pim, One-eye, Andy, Hala (delta male), and several young adult males. Finally, Pim attacks, then mounts Kink. In the meantime, Sanna continues screech-threatening from the tree top, and Kink moves toward him several times and then begins to screech-threaten Sanna. Undaunted, Sanna continues his screeching and there are several fights in the top of the tree. Then things quiet down.

In this rather lengthy sequence, the mounting occurred as part of an intense hierarchical altercation. Kink was the object of threats from a lower ranking male, who was joined by high-ranking males, until one of them (Pim) finally succeeded in mounting Kink toward the end of their involvement. The early unsuccessful attempt at mounting is an indication of the tension between these males.

The following is an example of a more relaxed social context in which a subordinate mounts a dominant male.

> As Dan (alpha male) moves across the field toward the trees, Hala (delta male) runs over to him and mounts, lip smacking as he does so. Dan reaches back with both

hands and grabs Hala's legs. This sequence ends and Dan moves toward Chira, a
female, and lifts her tail. When Chira jumps away, Dan moves on.

In this example, no tense hierarchical altercation had preceded the mount.
The subordinate male simply approached and mounted the dominant male without incident. In this situation and in many similar cases, the mounting gesture
could only be interpreted as a simple greeting or a reaffirmation of a social bond,
not a reaffirmation of a particular dominance relationship.

A change occurred in the hierarchical structure of the troop, which might
have complicated matters, but which fortunately strengthened the analysis. During the study, the dominance relationships of the high-ranking males shifted and,
whereas that shift made no appreciable difference in the relaxed mounting, it did
change the relationships between the males in the dominance mounting. Plots of
the relaxed or greeting mounting before and after the hierarchical change showed
the same scattering of mountings by subordinate and by dominant males. (See
Figures 1, 2, and 3 in which the mounting animals are listed on the left and the
mounted animals are listed across the top.)

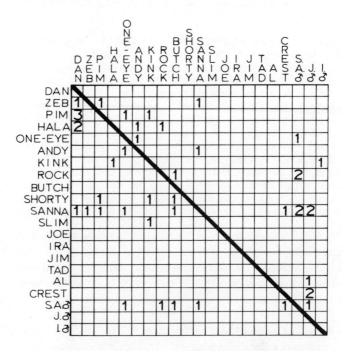

Fig. 1: Greeting mounting before a change in the dominance hierarchy.
Individuals listed by rank from alpha male at top left; mounter listed in
the column, mountee across the top.

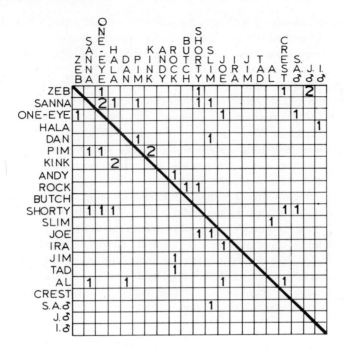

Fig. 2. Greeting mounting after a change in the dominance hierarchy.

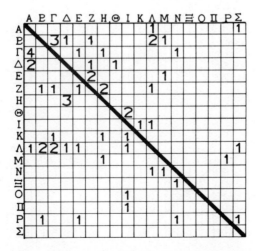

Fig. 3: Greeting mounting by rank rather than individual through both periods of hierarchical stability.

When the mounting incidents during or immediately after hierarchical interactions were plotted before and after the hierarchical change, we found that all dominance mounting consisted of a subordinate animal being mounted but never mounting during one of these situations. The pattern was fully consistent with the change in dominance and is shown in Figures 4, 5, and 6.

While the highest proportion of mounting occurred between subadult and adult males, occasional nonsexual mountings were observed between infants, juveniles and females. The few female mountings conformed to the pattern of a dominant female mounting a subordinate female after a tension-ridden social interaction. But the infant and juvenile mountings were mostly greeting behaviors which developed and reinforced attachments.

The greeting mounting, along with the grooming data previously mentioned, is useful in evaluating the strength of social bonds. Figure 7 is a sociogram showing the mounting contacts of immature males from 1 to 4 years of age, which reach all levels of male society. Central males, like subadult males, tend to interact with immature males whereas low-ranking males, who are peripheral to the main social interaction of the troop, tend to have less to do with immature males. In grooming interactions, the high-ranking central males and females groom the immature animals.

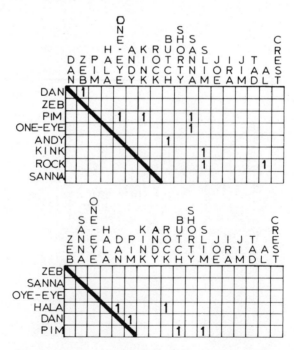

Figs. 4 and 5: Dominance mounting before and after a change in hierarchy.

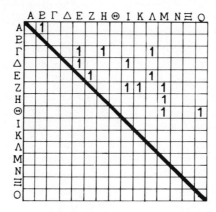

Fig. 6: Dominance mounting by rank rather than individual through both periods of hierarchical stability.

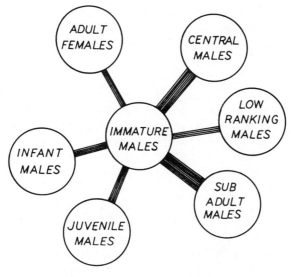

Fig. 7: Mounting contacts between immature (infant and juvenile) males and other classes of animals in the Somanathapur troop.

Thus, relatively early in his life, the growing bonnet macaque male begins to be included not only in play situations with high-ranking adult males but in a regular pattern of relaxed greetings involving tactile contact. Female infants and juveniles are not a regular part of this greeting network, another indication of the separation between female and male socialization.

In the Moyar River troop, the deficient grooming network among adults and young males is duplicated in the weak network of mounting. In fact, the alpha male rarely succeeded in mounting the beta male under any conditions and the latter never even attempted to mount the former. The subadult and juvenile males were not involved in any form of tactile contact with the two high-ranking males, and one subadult male left the troop to join two already isolated males. Thus, the young males had no opportunity to develop the necessary attachments to an adult male which would enable them to function successfully in the adult social relationships of the troop. On the other hand, Sugiyama and others have seen males change quickly from one troop to another and become integrated into their new troop with little difficulty. They probably developed the techniques of bond formation at the crucial times in their development and were therefore able to move into a new troop, practice their techniques of developing attachments, and become successful participants in their new troop.

In summary, among bonnet macaques the development of attachments proceeds differently for males and females. Among the females, grooming and sitting together are the major factors in developing tactile contacts and forming and maintaining attachments; neither mounting nor play forms a significant percentage of the everyday behavior of the females. The males, on the other hand, maintain an interest in grooming throughout their juvenile and subadult years and, as adults, perform many grooming bouts with other adult males and with females. But to initiate tactile contact with other males of all ages and to reinforce those attachments which develop, they turn primarily to a series of play encounters and greeting behaviors. In a relatively stable bonnet macaque troop, the young male has ample opportunity to develop attachments with virtually all other individuals in the group: he is groomed by his mother and associated females even in his juvenile and subadult years and through his play contacts he develops close attachments to his peers and initiates attachments to the adult central males of the troop.

Some groups of bonnet macaques, such as the Moyar River troop, are deficient in these contacts (Simonds, 1974a). Grooming does not occur between the adult males, greeting behavior is heavily restricted, and the young males growing up have very little contact through grooming, mounting, or play with the alpha male. As a result, these young males leave the group, probably, as Mason and Kenney's work supported, because they lack the ability to generalize bond-forming to other individuals. Even when they join another troop later, as sometimes happens, they never learn to form attachments.

Interspecific Comparisons

To determine whether the relationships between the tactile networks and social structure of bonnet macaques have any validity for other species, I will compare them briefly with those of baboons, hanuman langurs, and orangutans.

They can be ranked to some extent by the degree of tactile contact between the various members of the group. As we have seen, the common troops of bonnet macaques have a very high degree of tactile contact among almost all individuals and categories of animals. Grooming, play, and mounting behaviors add up to a picture of repetitive tactile contact among group members which is augmented and strengthened by their tendency to sleep and sit huddled together in contrast to other macaques (Rosenblum, Kaufman, & Stynes, 1964). In general, baboons rank somewhat lower than bonnet macaques in contact behavior since they groom less frequently and for shorter periods of time, but they still devote a very impressive amount of time to this activity. The social distance between individual animals is higher among baboons, however, so they spend less time in actual contact. Baboons should probably be ranked medium-high on a scale of tactility.

Among hanuman langurs, the tactile contact has a rather different character. Among the adult females and between them and the younger members of the group, tactile contact is relatively high, but between males and other members of the group it tends to be relatively low because infants do not groom and are not groomed by adult males and play between the two groups is rare. The males generally make very little attempt to contact infants and tend to ignore them.

Orangutans live in very small social groups, rarely consisting of more than a female and her most recent offspring. The network of social relationships, however, may extend far beyond the immediate cluster of two or three animals to include many females, males, and young, but these attachments do not result in a permanent group that moves together day after day. The intensity of orang social bonds must be relatively weak because only the young seem to make any attempt to get close to one another to play or touch. The occasional sexual contacts between males and females are a relatively minor exception. The result is a society with a minimum of social tactile contact and comparatively weak bonds, in strong contrast with the relatively impermeable immediate social groups of baboons, macaques, and langurs in which the members are in visual contact day after day for the whole lives of many members.

Although the baboon genus *Papio* and the species of langurs (*Presbytis entellus*) and orangutans (*Pongo pygmaeus*) contrast with bonnet macaques in social interaction and socialization, the tentative application of network analysis to them indicates that the same principle of socialization through tactile contact prevails. Thus, it will be profitable to examine who grooms whom, who plays with whom, and who mounts whom in baboon, langur, and orang society and to trace briefly the developing network of such relations in growing individuals.

Baboons

The classic descriptions of open-country or savanna baboons and the desert or hamadryas baboons give a picture of two very different social organizations.

Savannah baboons live in a tightly knit social organization that focuses on a cluster of central males whose major role is to protect the whole troop from the large predators in the open grasslands. No permanent subdivisions can be recognized within the group, which moves as a unit from sleeping place to feeding areas and back. Hamadryas social organization, on the other hand, is based on clearly-definable, small, one-male units within the larger troop, and the main focus of social relations is between the male and his females. There is a central core of males similar to that among the savannah baboons, but it is a much weaker organization than the harem unit. These groups sleep together as a troop, but forage during the day as independent one-male units. The usual interpretation is that hamadryas organization has evolved out of the savannah organization and is based on the fact that hamadryas food sources are scattered and sparse and that their sleeping areas are often restricted to a few suitable cliffs, which are in sharp contrast with the more plentiful sleeping trees available to the savannah baboons.

More recent studies by Rowell (1966) and by Ransom and Ransom (1971) show that these are not the only forms of baboon social organization and suggest the distinct possibility that the military form of organization has been developed out of the more relaxed forest and woodland form that has been described by the above authors on the one hand by savannah baboons as a protection against severe predation on the open grasslands and, on the other hand, that the harem system has been adopted by the hamadryas in response to sparse foraging in the desert.

We will first examine the two extreme forms of baboon social organization to see how they differ and then consider the forest-dwelling baboons in order to link the other two. Taxonomically, the forest baboon and the savannah baboon of east Africa are generally considered one species, the hamadryas another. However, hamadryas and savannah baboons can interbreed and produce offspring, so it may well be that they should all be listed as a single species. Better authorities than I have wrestled with baboon taxonomy to little avail, so I will arbitrarily consider them as members of a single genus and disregard the arguments over specific identity.

Savannah Baboons

According to Hall and DeVore (1965), the savannah baboon troop is made up of a permanent complement of adult males, adult females, and their young. Among themselves, the males have strong attachments, which bind them in a cooperative association that forms the central core of the group. They are the protectors, the peace-keepers, and the inseminators of the group. Individual males do not horde females, and no particular or permanent bond appears to develop between individual males and females. Temporary consortships last only a few days. When the female first comes into estrus, she copulates with low-ranking and subadult males; only when she is at the peak of estrus and most likely to ovulate do the dominant males become interested in her. The result is that many males have access to each estrous female even though the high-ranking males are more likely to be the inseminators.

Whereas the young are in closest contact with their mothers, they have a rich network of relationships, including virtually all individuals in the troop. The troop itself is a complete, self-perpetuating social organization that does not need any input from the outside, even though genetic exchange between groups is desirable and is facilitated by the occasional exchange of males. The troop is a self-contained reproductive, socializing, and economic unit, so self-sufficient that it has no need to share its sleeping places, its food resources, or any other aspects of its behavior and adaptation with other troops nor to maintain friendly social relations with other groups to ensure these resources. In fact, of course, neighboring troops do meet from time to time and overlap in their use of space.

The infant savannah baboon initially develops an intense relationship with its mother, which includes the close contact of being carried and cuddled, groomed, and lip smacked by her. Lip-smacking is a greeting gesture with tranquilizing qualities, infants and adults alike being calmed by it. Anthoney's (1968) description of lip-smacking as a complex gesture which develops from a tranquilizing agent at birth to a means of introducing young males to sexual approaches and mounting, and finally to an element in the greeting embrace of adults, suggests that lip-smacking is as important a socializing agent among savannah baboons as mounting is in bonnet macaques.

Somewhat like infant bonnet macaques, newborn savannah baboons are brought together in clusters of mothers and other females near the center of the troop where they can associate with other infants of their own age and with other females, some of whom are related to them through their common ancestress (a mother-lineage). Savannah baboon infants have an opportunity to maintain the close bond with their mothers until they are weaned at about 15 months. In the meantime, they move into a play group that consists of individuals drawn from peers that cuts across vertical mother-lineage lines in the troop. This is particularly effective among savannah baboons because the female spaces her births up to two years apart; thus a cluster of females consisting of a mother and her adult daughters would rarely have more than one or two infant males of the same age at the same time (Simonds, 1974b). The infant males begin playing in the context of the troop, which includes infants of other mother lineages than their own.

In a sense, the infant baboon, growing up in the cocoon of females with newborn infants, faces two rejections. First, at about the age of six months when the infant's coat has just changed from the early black to the adult olive gray, he begins to be rebuffed by the other females. Then, at the end of 15 months, he is rejected by his own mother, who begins to wean him. In these circumstances, the infant has two growing sets of relationships to which he can turn: first, to the play group, which has already become a major focus of male play, and second, to the adult males who have shown protective behavior to the infants throughout their early months and continue to do so now.

Hall and DeVore's (1965) description of presenting and mounting patterns among savannah baboons shows that a higher percentage of dominant animals mount subordinates than among bonnet macaques. However, the higher tension factor of having large predator-chasing males as part of the troop probably precludes their experiencing the more relaxed form of mounting most bonnet macaques enjoy. The end result, however, is very similar since the tactile contact between the dominant mounting animal and the subordinate that is mounted provides the opportunity for the two individuals to reestablish friendly relations. Thus, the savannah baboon infant male has an opportunity, in its first year or two, to develop strong bonds with many members and all classes of its society, first through tactile contact with its mother and other females in its early months, then through rough play with its peers during later infancy, and finally through its tactile association with adult males throughout this whole period. The result is a strong social network that binds the growing baboon to the society at all levels.

The female infant savannah baboon, on the other hand, remains close to the adult females, but comes into contact with the males as the females groom them. She does not spend long hours playing, but her social network is nonetheless completed through her grooming associations with most males and females in the group. If the group is regarded as a total network of relationships, the links between its members form a rich interconnection of the social whole, all of whom use one or another form of tactile contact in their relations with one another.

Hamadryas Baboons

The hamadryas baboon troop, too, is probably a self-perpetuating unit, but in the interests of adaptation the troop itself has been subordinated strongly to the one-male unit as the main functioning element of hamadryas society (Kummer, 1968). The troop also consists of several males, females, and their offspring. But here the resemblance to savannah baboons ends because the hamadryas male collects his females, who become permanently attached to him and, for the most part, focus their social relations on him alone. The male, who also forms permanent attachments to his females, begins his harem by kidnapping an infant or juvenile female, mothering her, and aggressively herding her. Grooming centers on the male, and Kummer (1967) suggests that the heavy mane of hair that hangs about the male's shoulders is a supernormal stimulus designed to reinforce the tendency of the females to groom him. Once the male begins his harem he never copulates with other females, but young males who have not yet established a harem attach themselves temporarily to a harem and occasionally manage to copulate with its females.

Formed as it is by a male who is collecting females from other sources, the harem unit is not a self-perpetuating group. As the male grows older and ceases to herd his females effectively, he eventually loses them all, even though he still functions as one of the males in the troop, often commanding a higher rank among other males than when he was in his prime. The young male, who cannot simply grow up in the harem of his birth and take over from his aging father, leaves it and builds a new harem. Thus, whereas the harem is the primary economic unit, it is not the major socializing unit. Hamadryas socialization is a complex arrangement that forces the infants to break the bonds between them and their parents and to reestablish new bonds with individuals that come from outside the harem but not necessarily outside the troop: the female with her future harem leader and the male with his future harem followers. Thus, the troop appears to be the context in which socialization takes place, whereas the harem is the main economic and breeding unit. For hamadryas, there is a selective development of networks within the harem of reproduction and a selective weakening of the networks within the harem of birth.

Among hamadryas baboons, tactile contact is limited principally to the male and his females. Thus, grooming, sex, and mounting are performed mostly to maintain an attachment relationships between a male and his females or to establish and strengthen the relationships in a new harem. The relationship between a mother and her black infant is similar to that between savannah mother and infant. In both species, the mother cares for her black infant by nursing, grooming, carrying, and retrieving it; and for the first four to six months of its life, the black infant is allowed to climb with impunity over the adult male, its social father.

Once the coat color has changed, however, the hamadryas infant's social relationships take a markedly different turn from those of the savannah baboon. The hamadryas mother no longer retrieves the infant when it leaves the area of the harem unit under its own power or is carried by some other baboon, although she continues to carry and nurse it when it is present. In stark contrast to the savannah male's continued protective role, the hamadryas male shows no further tolerance of his offspring. From that time on, any bonds between the growing hamadryas infant and its parents must be initiated by the grey infant, who gets little reciprocal attention from his parents for his pains. Instead of developing an ever-widening network of social relationships, the hamadryas baboon begins to sever even the tenuous early bonds that exist.

Kummer (1968) also reports a sex difference, which is believed to characterize all nonhuman primates, in the speed with which a black infant male begins to move away from its mother as compared with a female: "Obviously, the male infants are nursed and groomed by their mothers nearly as often as female infants, but between these contacts, the black female will remain near the mother, while the black male tends to leave her." As the male infant hamadryas grows older, his activities center around the play group with whom he begins to sleep at night instead of with his parents' harem unit. As the female infant grows older, she begins to be carried about by juvenile and subadult males and after she is one year old is usually adopted by one of the subadult males as the initial step in forming his harem. The subadult male carries his kidnapped infant female, helps her across rough spots as they travel, and grooms her. Although not yet fertile, she is physiologically adapted to come into estrus a year earlier in her life cycle than the savannah baboon; thus, the tactile contact of sex helps to reinforce the developing attachment between the subadult male and his adopted female.

Mounting behavior as a greeting gesture between adult males is very rare among hamadryas. Presenting for mounting is an almost exclusively female trait which is related to the female's seeking the support of her male in altercations with other females (Kummer, 1967). Thus, whereas savannah baboons expand and emphasize a total network of tactile behavior, hamadryas baboons severely restrict theirs.

Forest Baboons

Forest baboons have none of the extreme features and share features of both savannah and hamadryas baboons. Rowell (1966), who observed forest baboons in Uganda, reported that they were far more flexible than those on the open savannah. Many of the males, for example, formed a relatively free-floating population which moved back and forth among neighboring groups. Rowell suggests that such free exchanges take place between members of troops that had split away from a single troop in the past or that the habitat allows a much greater flexibility in social relations than the open savannah. The male baboons do not play the role of protector against predation, though they do give warnings of approaching danger. At such a warning, all animals run directly for the trees, which the males, being larger and swifter, usually reach first! Since their roles in the forest habitat are less rigidly defined, these males may be freer in their attachments, or, conversely, since trees always offer safety, the females do not need to develop strong attachments to and follow a particular set of males.

In the Gombe Stream Reserve, Tanzania, Ransom and Ransom (1971) observed other patterns of social interaction and attachment which are reflected in the troop structure of these baboons. Unlike the savannah baboons, the Gombe Stream troops were divided into subdivisions that were more or less permanent but without the solidarity of the harem units of hamadryas. Instead of a unified adult male association forming the core of the troops, each of the two troops of 55 and 75 animals in the Gombe Stream Reserve ''showed long-term and relatively consistent divisions into two groups, each with its complement of adult males.'' In addition to these major subgroupings, permanent pair bonds tended to form between individual males and females. In both Uganda and Tanzania, birth spacing was not so pronounced, the same mother often conceived and bore an infant each year, and last year's infant was not abruptly ejected by its mother into the mainstream of society. Rather, the mother–infant relationship was reestablished with last year's infant even after the birth of a new infant, some females even allowing both infants to nurse at the same time.

The pair bond formed in the Gombe Stream Reserve troops allowed infants to interact not only with other mothers of newborn infants but also with particular males who spent much of their time with the mothers and their new infants. The mature male in the pair baby-sits with the infant and juvenile of his consort female and grooms, protects, and carries the infant. As the latter matures, it continues to associate with this male, seeking support and comfort from him as it would from its mother. One interesting example shows that this bond is a specific attachment between a male and a particular infant rather than the generalized attachment between savannah baboon males and infants in general. Ringo, a high-ranking male, cared for a primiparous female's infant whose mother had laid it down and failed to respond to its calls of distress. Ringo carried this infant for long periods of time and protected it from some chimpanzees who were trying to catch it. When the infant died at the age of three months, Ringo did not generalize this behavior to other infants.

Young juvenile males pick up and care for infants, often using them to protect themselves from attack by older and more dominant males. Carrying an infant, they dare to pass close to a high-ranking male and even to deflect an attack. This behavior could underlie the genesis of harem structure among hamadryas and certainly is similar to the behavior of subordinate hamadryas males who, if they can find an available infant to carry, escape being attacked by an adult male who is too close for comfort.

An infant in the Gombe Stream Reserve troops undergoes a rather different socialization process than either savannah or hamadryas infants. To begin with, it is not drawn into the relatively complete and uniform network of relationships that characterize the savannah baboons but limits its contacts to the subgroup males who are associated with its mother and particularly to the male who forms the pair bond with its mother. Because of the one-year birth spacing, the male infant's play group consists of a narrower range of peers and is composed chiefly of those who are closely related to him through his mother and his mother's sisters and daughters. According to Ransom and Ransom (1971), unlike the savannah infant, the forest baboon shows definite preferences in his selection of playmates. Contact with many juvenile, subadult, and even adult males, who carry infants not only to protect themselves against attack but also to get the infant's mother to groom them, enables these infants to develop a rather complex network of strong attachments with many adult males.

In addition to the subdivisions that are clearly demarcated within their society, forest baboons extend their network of grooming, play, and other tactile contacts beyond the subdivisions to embrace the whole troop in a wider and stronger network than that of the hamadryas troop. There is some evidence that the highly developed herding and harem-building behavior of the hamadryas male is inherited rather than learned. Thus, selection for that form of social organization must have been strong enough to continue for many hundreds of generations for the pattern to be fixed genetically. Savannah baboons may also have an inherited basis for some of their behavioral modifications. The change in birth spacing, for example, may have resulted from selection for strong social bonds which supersede both the bisexual pair bonds and mother–infant bonds in favor of adult male association through play groups which draw upon unrelated infants and juveniles.

Langurs

Hanuman langurs (*Presbytis entellus*), another species with a diverse social structure, have been studied by several primatologists in north, west, central, and south India and in Sri Lanka. Their social structure includes both one-male groups living close to all-male groups and the classical troop organization like that of macaques and most baboons. At the risk of oversimplification, it is tempting to correlate the troop structure of these langurs with their particular ecology. Food availability, protective cover, and degree of predation undoubtedly influence the size and composition of these groups. However, the history of each of them must also have had a major impact on their composition. Sufficient information is now available to help us reconstruct the processes that led to the formation of the different group compositions which characterize the hanuman langurs.

Groups of 50 or more animals generally include several males as well as many females and their offspring (Jay, 1965). These groups are stable, and young males are probably able to grow up to become an integral part of adult society. Generally, these groups have no contact with neighboring groups since they usually live in temple compounds or in villages with enough vegetation to support a local group but with sufficient open ground between them to effectively isolate one group from another. This isolation, of course, contributes very strongly to their stability. In forested regions, or wherever neighboring troops come into contact with each other on a regular basis, the group size tends to be considerably smaller, often containing no more than one or two adult males. In addition, all-male groups of varying size are often reported in their vicinity. Several observers have reported cases where several males from an all-male group invaded a bisexual group and chased out the resident males. After such an attack, one of the invading males generally makes the troop his exclusive domain by ejecting his supporters in the attack and during the next few days or weeks killing all of the infants and some of the juveniles. The females of the group subsequently come into estrus and within the next few months virtually all are impregnated by the new group male (Sugiyama, 1965). Sarah Hrdy (1974) postulates that the multi-male bisexual groups either have not been invaded or have been able to withstand the invasion sufficiently well to allow the resident males to continue to control the group. Young growing males are tolerated by their father and are socialized into the troop so that a multi-male bisexual group is formed. Under these circumstances, groups that are isolated from contact with other langurs tend to develop this kind of organization over a long period of time and as a result increase fairly considerably in size. Once a large troop of this sort splits into two or more new troops, a new round of aggressive invasions becomes possible, and in fairly short order the remaining troops are reduced to one-male groups and the cycle begins all over again.

Like the bonnet macaque infant, who builds a network of tactile relations with other members of the group during the first few weeks of life, the infant langur develops attachments, but even more rapidly. Within hours of its birth, the mother allows other females to hold and carry the infant several feet from her (Jay, 1963). Thus, during the first few days, the infant has tactile contacts with most or all of the adult females in the group and begins to develop social bonds with them. Later the subadult females also begin to carry and hold the newborn infant and are thereby included in its growing social network. And yet, despite this association with other females, the infant knows its own mother and develops its strongest contacts with her. In fact, for the first five months of its life, the mother–infant relationship is closer than any other in which the infant becomes involved.

Young langur infants have little or no contact with the adult males who are characteristically indifferent to them even to the point of not responding to their distress calls. Female langurs have completely assumed the protective role, and if a male accidentally frightens an infant, its mother, joined by other females, chases him away. Hrdy reports a complicated case of a male who was attempting to maintain control over two neighboring groups of females, one of which was being invaded by another group of males. When the leader of the invading males attempted to kill the infants in the group, two females repeatedly intervened between the attacking male and a mother whose infant was the object of his attack.

Contact with adult males varies with the infant's sex: throughout their infancy, female infants have almost no contact with them since they remain in the protective cluster of females who supply all their social contacts. At the age of about 10 months, the male infant begins to establish contact with the adult males by approaching and ultimately developing a mounting relationship with them. Such infant males are tense and hesitant at first, but as they grow older their tension decreases and they mount more frequently until a relatively stable social bond is developed between them and the adult males. If this relationship is ever to be developed it must begin slowly and develop along with the infant's growth; it cannot be established by older juveniles. Among the captive langurs in Berkeley and San Diego, quite different relationships between the juvenile and adult males characterize each group. In the San Diego group, the young males have grown up in the troop and have had the opportunity to develop a stable relationship with the dominant male from the outset. They approach him readily and touch him frequently. In the Berkeley group, however, the juvenile males were introduced into the unit after their infancy and have never succeeded in establishing any tactile relationship with the resident male (McKenna, 1975).

Thus, like bonnet macaques, juvenile male langurs who are socialized into the group by the gradual development of a full network of tactile contacts tend to remain in the group and become a permanent part of the social organization. Those who cannot develop such contacts with the adult male, like their caged counterparts in Berkeley, are less able to maintain their social bonds with the group and eventually move into all-male groups which later make forays on bisexual groups. On the other hand, the female langur, who is socialized into the female network early in life, makes contact with the adult males only late in her youth. Since the bond between the females and the males is generally rather tenuous, the replacement of one male by another is unlikely to disrupt the social organization very significantly. Even when it results in the death of the present infants, the female cluster and the female network of relationships continue very much as they were before.

Orangutans

In contrast to macaques, baboons, and langurs, orangutans live an almost isolated existence. John MacKinnon (1974) describes orangutan groups, particularly in Borneo, as composed either of isolated females with their most recent offspring (occasionally coming together with each other) or of isolated males who occasionally contact the females for a very short time to form larger groups of bisexual pairs. Many potential encounters between males and between males and females are characterized by avoidance, one animal silently disappearing from the vicinity. Under these circumstances, the social contacts of orangs are far different from the intense and close personal contact between individuals living in a social group that moves together day after day, week after week, and year after year. As a result, the infant orang grows up making only occasional contacts with any individuals other than its mother and immediate sibling. The mother–infant relationship is close, and contact between the mother and her growing juvenile may last for several years. Play groups are virtually nonexistent; what play the growing orang can solicit is confined primarily to its mother and sibling, with only an occasional contact with its peers if they happen to be feeding nearby. As a result, by the time male orangs attain adulthood, they have become virtually isolated. They form only the temporary social bonds needed for mating; it is not surprising then that MacKinnon characterizes many orangutan matings in Borneo as rapes.

The infant orang's network of tactile (and thus social) relationships is severely limited both as to individuals contacted and the duration and intensity of the contacts that are made. It does not play with other adult females or have an opportunity even to sit with them. Grooming contacts are limited to mother-infant grooming and no patterns of greeting behavior comparable to lip-smacking or mounting and embracing are described. The socialization of an infant orang is primarily involved with learning the economic and technological aspects of survival, food sources, and nest-building.

Conclusions

An aggregation is an unstructured collection of individuals whose association is based on external factors that influence each individual but do not require any bond between them to bring them together. Such external factors include the sources of food, optimum conditions of temperature and light, or the accessibility of predation-free havens. No communication and no social bonds are apparent in such an aggregation and, theoretically, at least, the individuals do not relate to one another in any way. In reality, however, such aggregations are probably extremely rare. Most conspecific animals who come together by chance respond to each other in some fashion since even asexual clones tend to have a structure beyond the minimum chance aggregation brought about by common need and behave differently when other conspecifics are present.

The differentiation of the sexes and the necessity for cooperating in sexual reproduction are the basis of one major attachment in social organization (Figure 8). Under some conditions and at some time in their lives, a male and a female must come together and so coordinate their activities that copulation, fertilization, and incubation ensue. With the evolution of internal fertilization, the two individuals had to coordinate their activities even more efficiently. To do so, both sexes had to overcome their tendency to avoid the approach and tactile contact of the other. Thus, signals of conciliation, nonthreat, or friendliness had to be developed to form the temporary social bond needed for copulation. This tenuous relationship, however, has little to do with the socialization of the pair's progeny because the male most often departs long before the infants are born. Phylogenetically, therefore, socialization is first a function of the peer group that hatched together without the presence of either parent (Count, 1973).

In fact, neither the male nor the female is needed to socialize newborn infants into a society. Mating patterns between male and female of a species can be triggered by an innate releasing mechanism if mating is an inherited fixed action pattern. The individual offspring do not need to go through a period of socialization, which is, essentially, a period of acquiring learned patterns of behavior. When parental protection evolved beyond the simple reproduction of offspring, there was no innate need to choose one parent over the other to provide that protection. In fact, many forms of vertebrates rely on the male to care for the

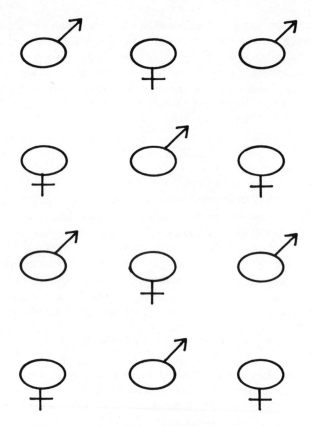

Fig. 8: An aggregation of sexually reproducing organisms
showing no social bonds.

eggs, to hatch them, and to protect the offspring in their early days and weeks. Only when internal fertilization and viviparity evolved did the female become the logical evolutionary choice for caring for the newborn. The phylogenetic addition of nursing among mammals tied the female irrevocably into the parent–infant attachment. Thus, mammalian social organization is based on a strong initial bond between mother and offspring (Figure 9). This attachment is established by imprinting in some species, but is easily and quickly learned in primates. Once learned, the techniques for developing this attachment can be used to develop attachments to other individuals in the society as well. The fact is that males and females exhibit different patterns of behavior, some of which can certainly be attributed to inherent differences in hormonal balance. On the other hand, a mother monkey reacts differently to her male and female offspring, with the result that the male is forced to become independent earlier than the female and to associate with his peer play group. Thus, subgroups, based on the mother–daughter attachment, are found in many mammalian societies. These permanent social attachments, which arise from the lactation complex, continue to be supported by other bond-building and maintaining activities of a tactile nature throughout their lives. Such associations have been clearly demonstrated among rhesus and Japanese macaques through two decades of observations.

Apparently several primate societies are based on just such a cluster of females. The descriptions of monkeys in the rain forests of Africa and the structure of many patas and langur groups in Africa and India fit the pattern of a stable female core to which a male is added (Figure 9). The infant female is socialized into a stable female society and the most significant attachment she forms is with other females. Males are expendable and are relatively free to move from one group to the next. If they are driven out, as among hanuman

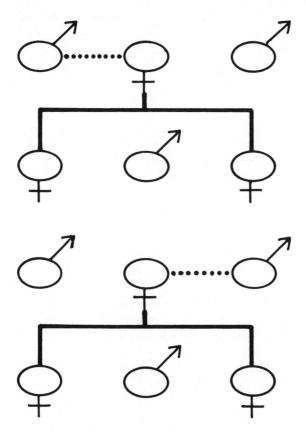

Fig. 9: The aggregation modified by mother–daughter bonds into a structured society. Weak male–female bonds are represented by dotted lines.

langurs, or if a predator manages to catch the decoying male, as among patas, new males are added to the society with relatively little disruption of the stable core of females that continues to form the basis of the society. Infant males are socialized with and by the females and develop attachments with them, but the differential treatment of male and female infants encourages the males to move away from close association with the females and causes them to be deficient in forming stable permanent bonds. Since such males do not develop permanent bonds with other males, stable dominance hierarchies are not found in such societies.

We can describe three modifications of the primate mother-lineage and attached-male groupings: the pair-bond group, the harem system, and the troop. Each of these makes different use of possible social bonds among individuals. Even the mother-lineage-and-attached-male (commonly called the one-male) grouping is selective in the kinds of social bonds it emphasizes, for example, restricting the males. The mated-pair group emphasizes a permanent male–female bond which does not accommodate the addition of other males or other females and is de-emphasized by the one-male groups (Figure 10). For example, as the infant gibbon grows, it is forced by the parent of the same sex to the periphery and, at puberty, out of the group. The appearance of adult characteristics in the offspring is probably the signal that changes the response of the parent to it from protective to aggressive. Thus, in such a society, not even the mother–infant attachment between females is preserved, each offspring ultimately being forced out to form a new attachment with another outcast and to establish a new society. Early socialization in the pair-bond society develops techniques of bond formation, but the bonds themselves are not, as in the case of imprinting, specific for one individual. Instead, the capacity is generalized and the growing primate is able to transfer its bond-forming capabilities to making new associations in a new mated pair.

The harem system is also based on permanent social bonds between a male and a female, but the male–female bond develops differently from that between the mated pair above. The initial bond between a male hamadryas and his female is more akin to that between a mother and her daughter than to a sexual bond. In a very real sense, the hamadryas male begins his social group as a male mother, establishing a pseudo-mother lineage, and later adds the role of male inseminator to his earlier one of protector and socializing agent. Additional friendly bonds are also formed between harems in what is a larger, if more diffuse society, the hamadryas troop (Figure 11). While the young females are being socialized by their "male mother," the young males are socialized by their play group into a series of attachments with other males which later on form the basis for cooperation among harems that are foraging for food and choosing sleeping places at night.

Both the mated pair and harem system must be embedded in a larger matrix with some elements of cooperation; for example, the mated pairs must cooperate

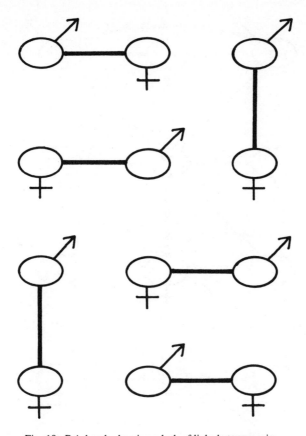

Fig. 10: Pair bonds showing a lack of links between pairs.

in spacing themselves through territorial displays and in providing one of the members of newly forming pairs and thus facilitate the exchange of genes and learned behavior. The harem system involves a similar exchange because the male mother begins collecting his females from the offspring of surrounding harems that are already established.

The third modification of the presumably original mother-lineage-plus-attached-male society is the troop, which adds an association of adult males to form the core of the society. Two kinds of subgroups are bound together by primary attachments in a troop: the mother lineage, which may or may not be weakened by the addition of extra male bonds, and the adult male association, which has strong attachments between adult males who cooperate in protecting the troop from predators and/or maintain stable social relations. When more males are added, a more complex and larger society may form. In addition to these primary bonds, there are attachments between males and females in a

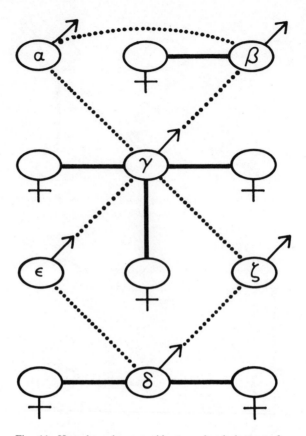

Fig. 11: Hamadryas harems with strong bonds between females and their harem leaders; weaker bonds between males
and a dominance hierarchy of males.

generally diffuse network (Figure 12). In many cases, there is also a differentiation between central males who form the adult male association and peripheral
males whose attachments to other members, both male and female, are so weak
that they sometimes lead to isolation as the only alternative. Central males in
such a society usually form stable dominance hierarchies.

Infant socialization in a troop involves forming attachments with many
more individuals of all categories than in the previous social forms discussed.
Males play a significant role in the tactile contacts with infants and draw them
into the troop network. But even here there are distinctions between male and
female socialization in that females, as in one-male groups, continue to associate
closely with their mothers and other adult females in the gentler tactile interactions of grooming and sitting together while the males move into rough play

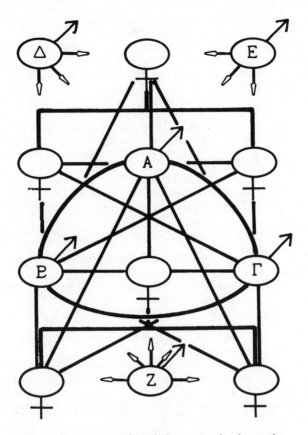

Fig. 12: The network of bonds in a troop showing mother-lineages linked to an adult male association with males ranked in an hierarchical system.

groups. But it is this association in play groups that helps them develop the attachments to adult males whose occasional participation facilitates the process.

Thus, the social structure itself determines the form of socialization and successful socialization perpetuates the social structure.

References

Anthoney, T. R. The ontogeny of greeting, grooming, and sexual motor patterns in captive baboons (superspecies *Papio cynocephalus*). *Behaviour*, 1968, **31**, (1-2), 359–372.

Count, E. W. The biogenesis of human sociality. In Earl W. Count, *Being and Becoming Human, Essays on the Biogram*. New York: Van Nostrand Reinhold, 1973.

Hall, K. R. L., & DeVore, I. Baboon social behavior. In I. DeVore (Ed.), *Primate behavior: field studies of monkeys and apes*. New York: Holt, Rinehart & Winston, 1965.

Hrdy, S. B. Male-male competition and infanticide among the langurs (*Presbytis entellus*) of Abu, Rajasthan. *Folia Primatologica*, 1974, **22**, 19–58.

Jay, P. Mother–infant relations in langurs. In H. L. Rheingold (Ed.), *Maternal behavior in mammals*. New York: Wiley, 1963.

Jay, P. The common langur of north India. In I. DeVore (Ed.), *Primate behavior: Field studies of monkeys and apes*. New York: Holt, Rinehart & Winston, 1965.

Jensen, G. D., Bobbitt, R. A., & Gordon, B. N. Sex differences in social interaction between infant monkeys and their mothers. *Recent Advances in Biological Psychiatry*, 1966, **9**, 293.

Jensen, G. D., Bobbitt, R. A., & Gordon, B. N. Sex differences in the development of independence of infant monkeys. *Behaviour*, 1967, **30**, 1–13.

Kummer, H. Tripartite relations in hamadryas baboons. In S. A. Altmann (Ed.), *Social communication among primates*, edited by Chicago: University of Chicago Press, 1967.

Kummer, H. *Social organization of Hamadryas baboons*, Chicago: University of Chicago Press, 1968.

Mackinnon, J. The behavior and ecology of wild orang-utans (*Pongo pygmaeus*). *Animal Behaviour*, 1974, **22**, 3–74.

Mason, W. A., & Kenney, M. D. Redirection of filial attachments in rhesus monkeys: dogs as mother surrogates. *Science*, 1974, **183**, 1209–1211.

McKenna, J. *An analysis of the social roles and behaviors of seventeen captive Hanuman langurs (Presbytis entellus)*. Unpublished dissertation, University of Oregon, 1975.

Rahaman, H., & Parthasarathy, M. D. The expressive movements of the bonnet macaque. *Primates*, 1968, **9**, 259–272.

Ransom, T. W., & Ransom, B. S. Adult male–infant relations among baboons (*Papio anubis*). *Folia Primatologica*, 1971, **16**, 179–195.

Rosenblum, L. A., & Kaufman, I. C. Laboratory observations of early mother–infant relations in pigtail and bonnet macaques. In S. A. Altmann (Ed.), *Social communication among primates*. Chicago: University of Chicago Press, 1967, 33–42.

Rosenblum, L. A., Kaufman, I. C., & Stynes, A. J. Individual distance in two species of macaque. *Animal Behavior*, 1964, **12**, (2-3), 338–342.

Rowell, T. E. Forest living baboons in Uganda. *Journal of Zoology*, 1966, **149**, 344–364.

Simonds, P. E. Sex differences in bonnet macaque networks and social structure. *Archives of Sexual Behavior*, 1974, **3**, 151–166. (*a*)

Simonds, P. E. *The Social Primates*. New York: Harper & Row, 1974. (*b*)

Soumi, S. J. Social interactions of monkeys reared in a nuclear family environment versus monkeys reared with mothers and peers. *Primates*, 1974, **15**, (4), 311–320.

Sugiyama, Y. On the social change of Hanuman langurs (*Presbytis entellus*) in their natural conditions. *Primates*, 1965, **6**, 213–247.

Williams, T. R. The socialization process: A theoretical perspective. In F. E. Poirier (Ed.), *Primate socialization*. New York: Random House, 1972.

CHAPTER 7

Pheromonal Mediation of Maternal Behavior

Michael Leon

Department of Psychology
McMaster University
Hamilton, Ontario, Canada

The Synchrony of the Mother–Litter Interaction

One critical aspect of the maternal period in rats (*Rattus norvegicus*) is the fine synchrony which characterizes the interactions between the mother and her young for the duration of the nurtural relationship. It is the close timing of the physiological and behavioral responses of the mother with the continually changing behavioral, physiological, and physical characteristics of her developing pups that insures the survival of the young. While the fine adjustments by the mother are essential for the growth of the litter, the developing young must also make adjustments in response to the changing physiological and behavioral patterns expressed by their mother.

During the first two weeks following birth, the young remain in the maternal nest and must rely on their mother for the initiation of the care-taking activities. The mother huddles over the young, keeping the ectothermic pups warm while she nurses her litter (Hahn, Krecek, & Krechova, 1956). In addition to supplying the sole source of nourishment, the mother facilitates elimination by licking the ano-genital area of the developing young. If a pup should be separated from the nest site, the mother will grasp the pup with her mouth and retrieve it back to the nest. Similarly, if the nest is disturbed, the mother will transport the young to a place of safety.

During this period, the young will approach the warmth of the mother (Gustafsson, 1948) and will nuzzle in her ventral fur until a nipple is secured. The pups will then suckle until the mother moves off the nest.

During the second two weeks of the maternal cycle, the pups become able to leave the nest (Rosenblatt, 1965), to consume some solid food (Babicky, Parizek, Ostadalova, Kolar, 1973; Babicky, Ostadalova, Parizek, Kolar, Bibr, 1970), to regulate their body temperatures, and to control their eliminative functions. The young continue to nurse during this time (Rosenblatt, 1965; Moltz & Robbins, 1965) and must be united periodically with the mother until weaning occurs at about 30 days postpartum. During this second two-week period, the young must either remain grouped in the nest area for the return of the mother, or must approach the mother and initiate the nursing bout themselves. The mother spends less and less time with the pups (Grota & Ader, 1969), no longer keeps the maternal nest in good repair, and stops retrieving the mobile pups (Rosenblatt, 1965). Eventually, the mother will no longer approach the young for a nursing bout, nor will she tolerate the initiation of nursing bouts by the weanlings, and the mother–litter interaction is terminated.

What follows is a description of one of several mechanisms that may serve to facilitate the fine synchrony that is observed in this mother–litter interaction. The phenomenon to be discussed is simply that mobile young will approach an odor that is emitted by their mother during the third to fourth postpartum week, at a time when mother and young are periodically reunited, and initiate a nursing bout. We will therefore examine the mechanisms mediating the control of the odor emission in the mother and the control of the approach response by the pups.

The Properties of Maternal Pheromone

We observed that mobile pups in a large enclosure will approach their mother in preference to a virgin female rat. This observation indicated that there was a stimulus emitted by the lactating female that was attractive to the pups, and we sought to examine the possibility that the cue might be olfactory in nature (Leon & Moltz, 1971). To that end, an olfactory discrimination apparatus was designed (Figure 1) in order to present a series of paired stimuli to mobile young. In essence, the apparatus was designed to permit an airflow to move through both goal compartments across a triangular open field to a start compartment. Mobile day 16 pups, previously observed to approach their mother in preference to a virgin rat in a large enclosure, were placed in the start box and allowed 15 minutes to choose between the goal stimuli. A choice was recorded if the young descended the small cliff that led into the goal compartment. After three pups of a six-pup litter were tested for their preference, the position of the goal stimuli

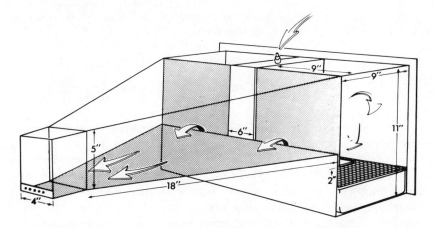

Fig. 1. The olfactory discrimination apparatus was designed to allow paired, unseen comparisons to be made by the pups when they descended a cliff into either goal box.

was reversed, the entire apparatus washed and dried, and the remainder of the litter was tested. Each pup was tested only once, and a clean, ploythene-backed, absorbent pad was used to cover the start box and open field for each pup.

Day 16 pups overwhelmingly preferred the goal compartment occupied by their mother in comparison to either a virgin female or an empty goal box. Little preference was demonstrated for the virgin female if she was paired with an empty goal box, and the pups approached neither goal box if they were both empty. Day 16 pups also demonstrated a strong preference for a day 16 mother with whom they were not familiar and approached the unfamiliar mother as often as their own. These data indicate that the cue that mother rats emit is not specific to each mother for her own litter.

Although the pups were approaching a cue that was being emitted by lactating females, we had not yet established the presumed olfactory nature of this attractant. Two conditions were therefore employed to determine whether or not the attractant was olfactory in nature. In the first condition, we allowed the mother and virgin to remain in the goal compartments during the test but reversed the flow of the air. This procedure left the pups upwind of any airborne chemicals while remaining in the test apparatus with the mother and the virgin. In the second condition, the mother and the virgin were placed in the goal compartments for 3 hours and then removed, leaving only airborne chemical cues to reach the test pups that were introduced into the start compartment. When only olfactory cues were available, the young chose the side previously occupied by the mother, and when only olfactory cues were eliminated by reversal of the airflow, the pups no longer preferred the mother to the virgin. The cue that was attracting the young was clearly an olfactory attractant, and since chemical signals between members of the same species are called pheromones, we have referred to this odor as a maternal pheromone.

The Developmental Course of the Pheromonal Bond

All of the mothers and young were 16 days postpartum in the first group of experiments. The next question to which we addressed ourselves was the tracing of the natural time course of the pheromonal bond in the mother–litter interaction (Leon & Moltz, 1972). To determine the onset and offset of the approach of the pups to the odor of their own mothers, pups were given a choice between their own mother and a virgin female at days 1, 10, 12, 14, 16, 21, 27, and 41 postpartum. Each pup and adult was tested on only one day, and the criteria for an approach response were altered to accommodate the different neuromuscular development of pups of different ages. The pups began to approach the mother at 12 to 14 days and continued to approach the mother until day 21, at which point the attraction began to wane and by day 41 the preference for the mother had ceased (Figure 2).

Here, we have shown the natural development of the pheromonal bond in the mother–litter interaction. This olfactory-mediated interaction, however, consists of both the ability of the mother to emit the odor and the development and

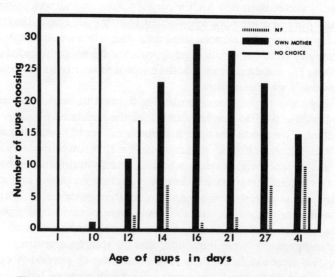

Fig. 2. The number of pups approaching either their own mother or the virgin, nulliparous female (NF) at different postpartum periods is shown.

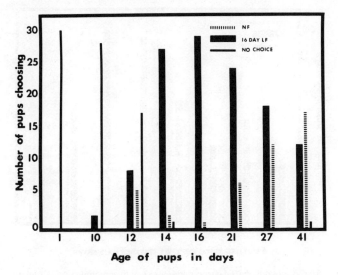

Fig. 3. Pups of different developmental ages were given a choice between a standard day 16 lactating female (16 day LF) and a virgin, nulliparous female (NF) and the number of pups making a choice is shown.

subsequent decline of the approach response by the young pups. In order to determine the separate development of mother odor and pup approach response, we would have to vary the postpartum age of the young or of the mother while keeping the stimulus mother or the test pup at a constant postpartum age.

We first investigated the development of the pup approach response by taking pups of different postpartum ages and allowing them to choose between a virgin female and a standard day 16 mother that previously had been found to be highly attractive to pups. This procedure allowed us to examine the development of the approach response in young rats to a constant pheromone source. The young began to approach the odor at 14 days and continued to approach the odor through day 21; by day 27, the differential approach to the lactating female had declined, and by day 41 it was absent (Figure 3).

The converse of this procedure was then performed with mothers of different postpartum ages compared to virgin female rats and standard day 16 pups, who were previously shown to be highly attracted to day 16 maternal odor and were allowed to choose between them. This procedure allowed us to examine the onset and offset of the maternal attractant by using the day 16 pup as a constant pheromone detector. Mother rats begin to emit an odor that is attractive to day 16 pups at day 14 postpartum and continue to emit the pheromone through day 21. By day 27 their attraction has declined, and at 41 days postpartum they are no longer more attractive than virgin female rats (Figure 4).

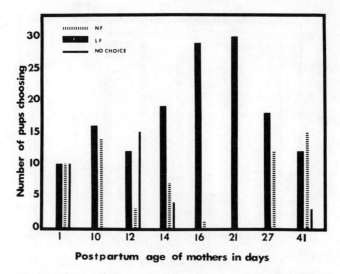

Fig. 4. Standard 16-day test pups choose between mothers of different postpartum ages (LF) and virgin, nulliparous females (NF) and the number of pups choosing either is shown.

These results indicate that a striking synchrony exists between the onset and cessation of pheromone emission in mother rats and the onset and cessation of the approach response in the developing pups. Mothers begin to emit the pheromone at the end of the second postpartum week, a time coincident with the onset of approach behavior by the pups to that odor. Similarly, the offset of pheromone emission and approach behavior occurs at the end of the fourth postpartum week. This close synchrony is particularly interesting because it is during the last two weeks of the maternal episode that the young are able to leave the nest and must be reunited with the mother for the continuing nursing bouts. Perhaps the maternal pheromone is the basis for this critical interaction in the mother–litter relationship.

The Role of Pup Stimulation in the Control of Maternal Pheromone

The onset of maternal pheromone emission is closely correlated with a time in which the pups are rapidly changing their behavioral, physical, and metabolic characteristics. Perhaps there is some cue which these pups emit that triggers maternal pheromone release in lactating female rats. If the pups trigger the emission of the odor in their mothers, then it should be possible to interfere with pheromone release by limiting the experience of mothers to neonatal young.

Also, one should be able to advance the time of onset of maternal pheromone release by allowing parturient females to nurture older pups (Moltz & Leon, 1973).

When mother rats were kept with day 1 pups for 16 days and then compared to a virgin female in the olfactory discrimination apparatus, the mothers did not attract the standard day 16 test pups in preference to the virgins. In contrast, the control mothers that received a foster litter of appropriate developmental age each day were highly attractive to the test pups. In a second experiment, day 1 mothers were given day 10 pups and tested for the onset of maternal pheromone emission 6 days later. At postpartum day 6 the mothers were nurturing day 16 pups, but the pups did not prefer these females to the virgins. Control mothers who raised foster litters of appropriate age also did not attract young when compared to the virgin. These data indicate that the emission of maternal pheromone is under the control of the stimulus characteristics of the pups. But while the appropriate stimuli emitted by the pups are essential for the onset of maternal pheromone emission, we were not able to advance the time of onset of maternal pheromone emission by keeping a parturient female with older pups (Figure 5). Perhaps the older pups were unable to advance maternal emission

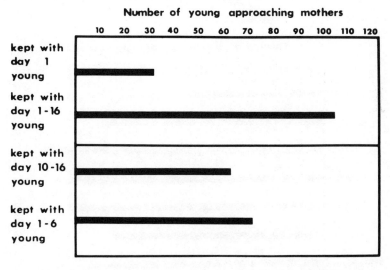

Fig. 5. Parturient mothers, kept with either day 1 pups or pups of advancing age till 16 days postpartum were tested in comparison to virgin females with 120 standard day 16 test pups. The number of test pups approaching the experimental and control mothers in preference to the virgin is shown. Similarly, the approach behavior to parturient mothers given day 10 pups and tested against a virgin at day 6 when the pups were 16 days old is shown as is the approach behavior to the control mothers kept with day 1-6 pups and tested against a virgin female by 120 16-day colony young at day 6 postpartum.

because both constant contact with neonatal pups for day 16 mothers or short-term contact with the older pups for day 6 mothers both constituted inappropriate pup stimulation for the mother rats.

Hormonal Mediation of Pup Stimulation

If the stimulation of the pups is critical for the emission of maternal pheromone, perhaps these stimuli are mediated by the hormones that are known to be released by the young during their contact with the mother (Amenomori, Chen, & Meites, 1970; Zarrow, Schlein, Denenberg, & Cohen, 1972). In order to determine whether the hormones released by developing pups served to control the emission of maternal pheromone, the classic endocrinological procedures of extirpation of endocrine glands were employed. Mothers that had been ovariectomized, adrenalectomized, or subjected to the combined operation on day 1 postpartum remained highly attractive on day 16. However, when ergocornine hydrogen maleate, a substance known to inhibit the release of prolactin from the pituitary gland, was administered (Shaar & Clemens, 1972), maternal pheromone emmission was inhibited in mother rats (Figure 6). When prolactin was administered to ergocornine-treated mothers, the attractive capability of

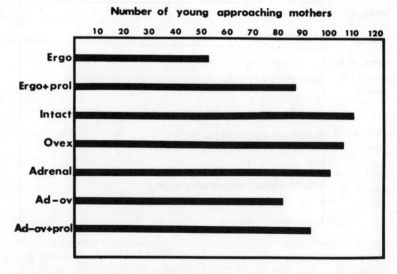

Fig. 6. The number of pups choosing the mother as opposed to the virgin female is recorded here. Mothers were subjected to adrenalectomy (Adrenal), ovariectomy (OVEX), the combined operation (AD-OV), or were injected with ergocornine (ERGO), a prolactin inhibitor. Ergocornine-treated mothers were given replacement therapy with prolactin (60IU/day) as were adrenalectomized, ovarriectomized mothers.

the mothers was restored, demonstrating the specificity of prolactin inhibition on the inhibition of pheromone emission. The pheromone may therefore be dependent on the high levels of prolactin that are released in the mother by the nursing pups during lactation (Amenomori *et al*., 1970) for the attraction of mobile pups.

The Site of Maternal Pheromone Emission

While the maternal odor appeared to be dependent on the high levels of prolactin induced in the mothers by developing young, it remained unclear as to whether the mechanism for this control was at the level of synthesis or at the level of emission. In order to find out if the high titers of prolactin present in lactating females were controlling the synthesis or the release of the maternal odor, it was first necessary to determine the locus of pheromone synthesis and emission, and then to determine the level at which prolactin exerts its control over the maternal pheromone.

The strategy here was to observe whether day 16 pups would approach various excretions of the mother and virgin rats, collected over a 3-hour period. While neither the urine of day 16 mother rats nor that of virgin rats was attractive to pups, the anal excreta of the mothers was highly attractive to the test pups, while the virgin anal excreta was not. These data indicated that the site of odor emission was in the anal excreta of mother rats (Leon, 1974).

If the site of pheromone emission was in the anal excreta of the mothers, it should be possible to observe the same development of attraction seen in intact mother rats when their anal excreta alone is tested against the anal excreta of virgin rats. Figures 7a and b show that the functional capability of the anal excreta of virgin rats to attract standard mobile pups is virtually identical to the development of attraction in intact mother rats. In addition to the functional ability of the anal excreta to attract pups, there also exists a striking change in the quantity and quality of the anal excreta defecated by mother rats at the time that the material is capable of attracting pups. Specifically, the mother rats are emitting large quantities of anal excreta with a high proportion of volatile components at the time during which they are attractive to pups.

This increased volatility of maternal anal excreta is due to the large proportion of a substance called cecotrophe, which emanates from the cecum of all adult rats (Harder, 1949). The cecum is a rather large structure that pouches out at the junction of the small and large intestine. Semidigested food enters the cecum and the material that remains in the proximal portion of the structure becomes the familiar, dark, well-formed boli that are called feces. The material that moves to the distal portion of the cecum is acted on by enteric microorganisms, the structure serving as a fermentation chamber for enteric bacteria. This substance is defecated as cecotrophe which is light colored, unformed, and highly odoriferous. Most of the cecotrophe is reingested directly from the anus of

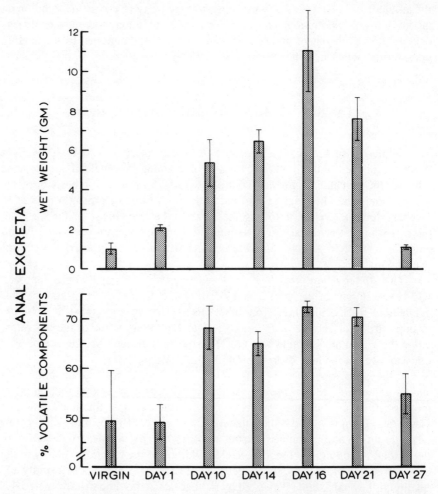

Fig. 7a. The wet and dry weight of that material defecated in a 3-hr period by mothers at the different postpartum days. Percent volatile components of the anal excreta, reflecting an increase in cecotrophe emission is similarly compared to the attractive capability of maternal anal excreta for the young. Standard errors are indicated.

the adult rat, and while the virgin female rats were not emitting excess ceco- trophe in their anal excreta, the mother rats were emitting great amounts of the material that remained uningested. One obvious difference between the attractive anal excreta of mother rats and the relatively unattractive anal excreta of virgin females was the excess cecotrophe defecated by mother rats. In fact, the attrac- tant is emitted in the cecotrophe portion of the anal excreta, for although the cecotrophe of mother rats was highly attractive to the pups, their feces were relatively unattractive to them.

NUMBER OF DAY 16 YOUNG APPROACHING

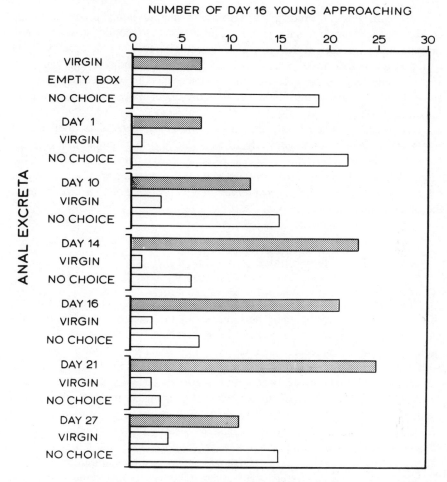

Fig. 7b. The pattern of attraction for maternal anal excreta when opposed to virgin anal excreta for 180 standard day 16 colony young.

The Site of Maternal Pheromone Synthesis

If the cecotrophe was the carrier of the pheromone to the external environment, then it seemed possible that the site of cecotrophe synthesis might also be the site of maternal pheromone synthesis. We first determined that the attractant was not present in the stomach contents or small intestine of the mother rats by presenting this material alone in the olfactory discrimination apparatus. We then took the cecal material directly from the cecum of day 16 mother rats and presented this substance alone in the test situation. The cecal material was highly attractive to the pups, indicating that the cecum was the site of synthesis of the maternal pheromone (Leon, 1974).

Since all adult rats produce and emit cecotrophe, it seemed probable that the cecal material of virgin female rats would be attractive to mobile pups, and when this substance was tested, the pups overwhelmingly preferred the cecal material of the virgin female to an empty goal box. These data indicate that while the virgin female rat synthesizes cecotrophe and the cecal odor, it does not emit large amounts of the material into the external environment. In contrast, the lactating female emits large quantities of the attractive substance.

Interestingly, when equal amounts of the cecal material of mother and virgin are compared simultaneously in the olfactory discrimination apparatus, cecal material taken from the mother is more attractive than that taken from the virgin. While it is possible that mothers and virgins emit different attractants in their cecotrophe, the preference observed here is probably due to differences in the concentration of a single odor.

Maternal Pheromone Synthesis

The cecum is the site of growth for enteric bacteria, and it seemed possible that these microorganisms might be synthesizing the cecal odor and being emitted as the maternal pheromone. In order to test this hypothesis, we sought to inhibit the growth of cecal bacteria with the use of an antibiotic substance administered orally. When neomycin sulfate was placed in the drinking water of mother rats from days 13–16 postpartum, these females were no longer capable of attracting pups, even though they were defecating as much as the control mothers, and their anal excreta had similar proportions of volatile components (Leon, 1974). Importantly, the material taken directly from the cecum, which is the site of odor synthesis, no longer was attractive to pups (Figure 8). Similarly, the odor of the cecal material of virgins was suppressed by antimicrobial action. To be confident that the effects of neomycin administration were not specific to that antibiotic alone, we administered tetracyclene, an antibiotic with a different mode of action, to mothers in a similar manner. Neither the mothers nor their cecal material was preferred by the pups, indicating that the inhibition of cecal odor synthesis was not specific to the administration of a single drug.

Although these drugs are capable of interfering with bacterial growth, they may also have been capable of reacting with the cecal odor and destroying it, not by means of bacterial interference but rather by a direct chemical action on the pheromone itself. To avoid that problem, we sought to eliminate cecal bacteria by means other than by chemical administration. This aim was accomplished by depriving the cecal bacteria of carbohydrate, which is their medium for growth. Mothers were given free access to a diet in which the only carbohydrate was sucrose, a substance that is taken up completely in the digestive tract above the level of the cecum. These mothers produced anal excreta that was not attractive to the test pups, and the contents of the cecum were similarly unattractive. Since

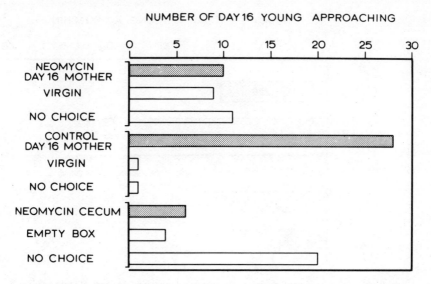

Fig. 8. The number of day 16 test pups that chose either the neomycin-treated or control mother is shown when each lactating female was opposed to a virgin female in the olfactory discrimination apparatus.

we eliminated the maternal pheromone by inhibiting bacterial growth both directly and indirectly, it seemed reasonable to conclude that the cecal odor that attracted mobile pups was synthesized by the action of cecal bacteria.

The Mechanism for Maternal Pheromone Emission

It appeared that mother rats were defecating large quantities of cecotrophe which they were not reingesting, and that the odor synthesized by the cecal bacteria attracted mobile pups. The question then was what is the mechanism for the control of the emission of these large quantities of unconsumed cecotrophe.

One likely explanation is that the mothers are eating large amounts of food, which are being processed and defecated in large amounts. In fact, a 300 g virgin rat might be eating 20-25 g of Purina Laboratory Chow each day, while her day 16 lactating counterpart might be eating in excess of 65 g in a day, though neither female is gaining much weight at that point. If the increased food intake were accounting for the increase in defecation by the mother mother rats, then one should be able to restrict the amount of food eaten by the lactating female to the levels of food consumed by the virgin and thereby reduce the amount of anal excreta containing the attractive cecotrophe that is defecated. Such a procedure should result in an inhibition of pheromone emission.

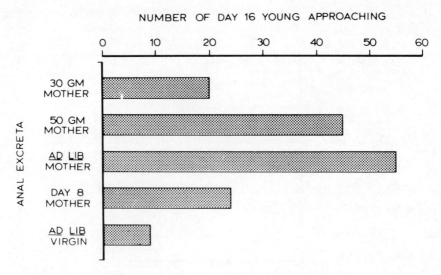

Fig. 9. The number of standard day 16 pups approaching the anal excreta of mothers given a rationed or *ad lib* diet when compared to virgin females is shown.

We rationed the amount of food that mother rats were allowed to eat in graded steps to approach the levels of food eaten by virgin rats without inducing a cessation of lactation in the mother (Leon, 1975). Mothers that were given less food than those that were allowed to eat at liberty lost weight, defecated less, and were less attractive to pups (Figure 9). Those mothers that were restricted to 30 g/day did not produce anal excreta that was attractive to day 16 colony pups, and it was only when food levels reached 50 g/day that the mothers began to defecate sufficient amount of uningested cecotrophe in their anal excreta to attract test pups as did the mothers on *ad lib* food. Moreover, if food levels of lactating females were restricted to the amount of food eaten on day 8 postpartum, a time before the onset of pheromone emission in the rat mothers, the pheromone was not emitted at day 16. These data indicate that the large quantities of food ingested by mother rats is responsible for the large amounts of anal excreta that is defecated which contains the pup attractant. It is perhaps only at the end of the second postpartum week when the weight of the mothers stabilizes while food intake levels continue to increase that the uningested cecotrophe is observed and the pheromone begins to be emitted.

Control of the Increase in Food Intake in Lactating Female Rats

We now know that the synthesis of the maternal pheromone is present in virgin females as well as in mother rats, and that the difference in their attractive capabilities seems to be a difference in the amount of excess cecotrophe that is emitted into the external environment. The increase in excess cecotrophe defecation appears to be induced by the large increase in food consumed by the mother rat during the second postpartum week. The question then becomes the identification of the factors that are responsible for the great increase in food intake that is observed in the mother rats.

Recall that the pheromone was dependent on the high levels of prolactin that are released in the mother by her developing pups. One possibility is that prolactin, previously shown to be essential for pheromone emission (Leon & Moltz, 1973), might induce the rise in food intake that results in the emission of the uningested cecotrophe that carries the pup attractant to the external environment. When prolactin is blocked by ergocornine injections, the mother rats do not demonstrate the increase in weight nor the increase in food and water intake that characterizes the control mothers (Leon, in preparation). They also do not defecate excess cecotrophe, and their anal excreta does not attract pups (Leon, 1974). Mothers receiving both ergocornine and prolactin replacement therapy demonstrated an increase in food intake that was reflected in defecation of anal excreta that increased by sufficient amounts to attract pups. Prolactin therefore appears to be necessary for the increase in food intake that is essential for the emission of the excess cecotrophe that carries the maternal pheromone to the external environment. Importantly, those females that were subjected to prolactin inhibition did not stop synthesizing the cecal odor, for the cecal material of ergocornine-treated mothers was highly attractive to the test pups. The prolactin-blocked mothers were similar to the virgin females that have endogenously low levels of prolactin, in that neither eat great quantities of food nor defecate large enough amounts of unconsumed cecotrophe to attract mobile pups.

Although prolactin is necessary for the large increase in food consumed by mother rats, it is also necessary for the maintenance of lactation, and prolactin inhibition may simply have interfered with the increase in food intake induced by the metabolic needs of lactation rather than with the direct control of food intake. There are at least two lines of evidence that point to the direct control of the increase in food intake by prolactin, rather than by the energy needs of lactation. Cotes and Cross (1954) found that even when they had severed the galactofores of mother rats, stopping lactation while continuing the nursing stimulation by developing pups, which is known to induce the release of high levels of prolactin, the mother rats showed the characteristic increase in food intake. Furthermore, adrenalectomized-ovariectomized mothers, who also do not lactate, but nevertheless receive the nursing stimulation of developing pups, eat a great deal and emit sufficient quantities of anal excreta to attract mobile pups (Leon & Moltz, 1973; Leon, in preparation). Prolactin, therefore, may be capable of inducing the high levels of food intake directly in mother rats.

The difference between mother rats and virgin rats appears to result from a difference in the ability to emit large quantities of anal excreta, which itself may be caused by a prolactin-induced rise in food intake. One should then be able to

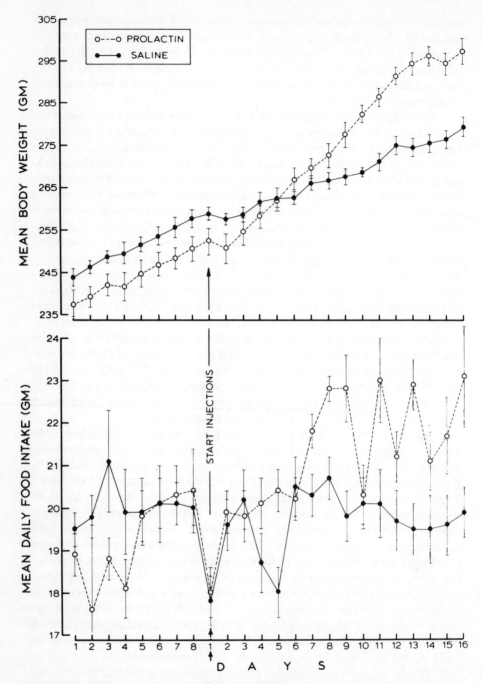

Fig. 10. Body weight food intake of virgins injected with either prolactin (25 IU, 2 ×/day) or with saline.
Standard errors are indicated.

impose high levels of prolactin on virgin rats that have endogenous low levels of the hormone and produce weight gain, increased food and water intake, an increased amount of anal excreta defecated, and then these virgins should attract the test pups. When virgins were injected with prolactin daily for 16 days, they demonstrated an increase in food and water intake, weight gain, and were over-whelmingly preferred by the mobile pups in the test situation when compared to saline-injected control virgin females (Fig. 10, Leon, 1974).

These data suggest a model for the control of maternal pheromone synthesis and release. It appears that the developing pups release high levels of prolactin in their mothers, and these high-hormone levels induce the characteristic increase in the consumption of food which is processed in the cecum and emitted into the external environment. The odor of the emitted cecotrophe attracts mobile pups.

How Do Pups Come to Approach the Odor of Their Mother?

We have discussed the causation of maternal pheromone synthesis and release in the mother but have not yet spoken about the mechanism by which the young approach the maternal pheromone. Originally, the pheromonal bond appeared to be a species-typic odor that released a specific approach behavior on the part of the young. However, recent observations indicate that although the ability to produce the odor is typical of mother rats, and the form of the approach behavior is common to rat pups, the specific pheromonal bond is established by means of experience.

Although unfamiliar mothers had been shown to be as attractive to the young as the pups' own mother, all the mothers in these previous experiments had been kept in the same colony, consuming the same kind of food. If the kind of food that a mother eats is changed, the cecal bacterial pattern and metabolic products are altered (Porter & Rettger, 1940). Since these microorganisms are responsible for the synthesis of the pheromone, it seemed likely that the odors might change as a function of the diet consumed by lactating females. If that were the case, then the individual litters must develop the approach response by means of experience with the specific odor that their mother emits.

When pups were isolated with their mothers who were eating one of two arbitrarily chosen diets, the pups preferred to approach only that odor with which they had experience. That is, they approached the anal excreta of an unfamiliar mother eating the same diet as their own mother in preference to a virgin female (Leon, 1975). The anal excreta of mothers eating a different diet was not approached preferentially. The implications of these data are that the maternal pheromone is an arbitrary odor that may be associated with the positive aspects of maternal presence thereby eliciting an approach response. Perhaps the ceco-trophe odor attains its ability to attract pups because of the salient characteristics of the odor. One would expect less salient or artificial odors to exert a similar effect on the pups in the absence of a cecal odor if the odors are associated with the presence of the mother. These other arbitrary odors may then function as does a naturally occuring maternal pheromone. In fact, Marr & Gardner (1965) and Marr & Lilliston (1969) have found that young rats exposed to an arbitrary artificial odor will demonstrate an extended preference for that odor.

The Function of the Pheromonal Bond in the Mother–Litter Interaction

We have discussed the mechanisms controlling the synthesis and release of maternal pheromone in mother rats and a possible mechanism for the development of responsiveness to the odor by the pups. We will now turn our attention to the possible adaptive function of the pheromonal bond.

The maternal pheromone may serve to reunite mother and young during the last two weeks of the nursing period. If one deprives young rats of the olfactory sense, the young do not approach their mother, even if she has been anesthetized. (Singh, Tucker, & Hofer, in press; Singh & Tobach, 1972; Alberts, 1974). The young seem unable to direct themselves to the nipple and they rapidly lose weight and many die.

The pups are marked by the cecotrophe odor of their mother (Leon, 1974), and can attract other pups by means of olfactory cues, and the common odor of the litter may serve to facilitate litter cohesion. Alberts (1974) has found that anosmic pups will not congregate as do pups that are able to utilize their sense of smell. Moreover, the nest material also appears to be marked by the maternal odor, for pups will approach that nest material alone (Gregory & Pfaff, 1971). The combination of a familiar odor in the nest and on the pups that have been marked with the maternal odor might serve to keep the young together in the nest area until they are weaned. The congregation of the litter in a specific place might facilitate the reunion of the mother with her pups.

Rat pups also prefer to spend their time in areas where adult rats have been when they venture from the nest site (Galef & Heiber, in press). The pups also tend to consume their solid food in the area frequented by the adults. This behavior might serve to restrict the exploration and ingestive behaviors of the young to those areas frequented by conspecifics.

Finally, pups appear to consume the anal excreta of the mother rats (Leon, 1974). This behavior might serve to innoculate the weanlings with the enteric flora characteristic of their mother's diet. Since the young favor highly the diet which their mother eats (Galef & Clark, 1971), the acquisition of the flora appropriate to the specific maternal diet may be important for the optimal utilization of the new solid food. It is possible that the cessation of the weaning process occurs when the young have developed their own capacity to produce cecotrophe and are no longer attracted to that of the mother.

References

Alberts, J. R. The role of olfaction and olfactory experience in maternal and sibling interactions of the rat. A.P.A. Proceedings, August, 1974.

Amenomori, Y., Chen, C. L., & Meites, J. Serum prolactin levels in rats during different reproductive states. *Endocrinology*, 1970, **86**, 506–510.

Babicky, A., Parizek, J., Ostadalova, I., & Kolar, J. Initial solid food intake a growth of young rats in nests of different sizes. *Physiologia Bohemoslovenica*, 1973, **22**, 557–566.

Babicky, I., Ostadalova, I., Parizek, J., Kolar, J. & Bibr, B. Use of radioisotope techniques for determining the weaning period in experimental animals. *Physiologia Bohemoslovenica*, 1970, **19**, 457–467.

Cotes, M. P. & Cross, B. A. The influence of suckling on food intake to growth of adult female rats. *Journal of Endocrinology*, 1954, **19**, 363–367.

Galef, B. G. Jr. & Clark, M. M. Mother's milk and adult presence: Two factors determining initial dietary selection by weanling rats. *Journal of Comparative Physiology Psychol.*, 1971, **75**, 341–357.

Galef, B. G. Jr. & Heiber, L. The role of residual olfactory cues in the determination of feeding site selection and exploration patterns of domestic rats. *Journal of Comparative Physiology Psychol.*, in press.

Gregory, E. H. & Pfaff, D. W. Development of olfactory guided behavior in infant rats. *Physiology and Behavior*, 1971, **6**, 573–576.

Grota, L. & Ader, R. Continuous recording of maternal behavior in *Rattus Norvegicus*. *Animal Behavior*, 1969, **17**, 722–729.

Gustafsson, P. Germ-free rearing in the rat. *Acta Pathologica et Microbiologica Scand. Suppl.*, 1948, **72-75**, 1–130.

Hahn, P. J., Krecek, J., & Krechova, J. The development of thermoregulation. I. The development of thermoregulatory mechanisms in young rats. *Physiologia Bohemoslovenica*, 1956, **5**, 283–289.

Harder, W. Zur Morphologie under Physiologie des Blinddarmes der Nagetiere. *Vert. Dtch. Zool Ges.*, 1949, 95–109.

Leon, M. Maternal Pheromone. *Physiology and Behavior*, 1974, **13**, 441–453.

Leon, M. Dietary control of maternal pheromone in the lactating rat. *Physiology and Behavior*, 1975, **14**, 311–319.

Leon, M. Endocrine involvement in the energy balance of mother rats, in preparation.

Leon, M. & Moltz, H. Maternal pheromone: Discrimination by pre-weanling albino rats. *Physiology and Behavior*, 1971, **7**, 265–267.

Leon, M. & Moltz, H. The development of the pheromonal bond in the albino rat. *Physiology and Behavior*, 1972, **8**, 683–868.

Leon, M. & Moltz, H. Endocrine control of the maternal pheromone in the postpartum female rat. *Physiology and Behavior*, 1974, **10**, 65–67.

Marr, J. N. & Gardner, L. E. Early olfactory experience and later social development in the rat: Preference, sexual responsiveness and care of young. *Journal of Genetic Psychology*, 1965, **103**, 167–174.

Marr, J. N. & Lilliston, L. G. Social attachment in rats by odor and age. *Behaviour*, 1969, **33**, 277–282.

Moltz, H. & Leon, M. Stimulus control of the maternal pheromone in the lactating rat. *Physiology and Behavior*, 1973, **19**, 69–71.

Moltz, H. & Robbins, D. Maternal behavior of primiparous and multiparous rats. *J. Comparative Physiology and Psychology*, 1965, **60**, 417–421.

Porter, J. R. & Rettger, L. F. Influence of diet on the distribution of bacteria in the stomach, small intestine and caecum of the white rat. *Journal of Infectious Diseases*, 1940, **66**, 104–110.

Rosenblatt, J. S. The basis of synchrony in the behavioral interaction between the mother and her offspring in the laboratory rat. In B. M. Foss (Ed.), *Determinants of infant behavior*. Vol. 3. London: Methuen, 1965, 3–45.

Shaar, G. J. & Clemens, J. Inhibition of lactation and prolactin secretion in rats by ergot alkaloids. *Endocrinology*, 1972, **90**, 285–288

Singh, P. J. & Tobach, E. Effect of olfactory bulbectomy on nursing behavior in the Wistar (DAB) rat pups. Presented at the Society for Neuroscience, 1972.

Singh, P. J., Hofer, M. A., & Tucker, A. M. Biological, behavioral and neural effects of peripheral anosmia induced by $ZnSO_4$ treatment on rat pups. Presented at the International Society for Developmental Psychobiology, 1973.

Singh, P. J., Tucker, A. M., & Hofer, M. A. Effects of nasal $ZnSO_4$ irrigation and olfactory bulbectomy on rat pups. *Physiology and Behavior*, in press.

Zarrow, M. X., Schlein, P. A., Denenberg, V. H., & Cohen, H. A. Sustained corticosterone release in lactating rats following olfactory stimulation from its pups. *Endocrinology*, 1972, **91**, 191–196.

CHAPTER 8

Development of Attachment and Other Social Behaviors in Rhesus Monkeys

Stephen J. Suomi

Department of Psychology
University of Wisconsin
Madison, Wisconsin

The study of human social development has traditionally encountered formidable ethical, practical, and theoretical obstacles. Researchers striving to collect developmental data from human infants and young children have universally
been faced with probably the most rigorous ethical constraints to be found in all
the behavioral sciences. Parents, teachers, and professional caretakers are quite
properly zealous guardians of their children's welfare. Not surprisingly, their
views regarding what constitutes a harmless experimental manipulation often do
not coincide with those of the child researchers, and in our society there is little
question whose views ultimately prevail. Consequently, investigators of human
social development are limited in what they are able to do to their subjects and in
the nature and duration of data they can collect. Manipulations bordering on the
trite and trivial tend to be the rule, while data collected rarely transcend observational descriptions or scores on some predetermined test, and even more rarely
cover more than a few hours of a given subject's lifetime.

Even if developmental researchers were to have unlimited freedom in experimentation with human infants, they would still face formidable methodological difficulties. Observation in the infant's or young child's natural environment
is often impractical. Not all parents or teachers are willing to let their households
or classrooms be turned into research laboratories; in those environments where
study is permitted it is seldom totally unobtrusive.

Further, certain characteristics of human infant and child subjects themselves make meaningful study difficult. Even neonates are exceptionally respon-

sive to contingencies within their environment; it is thus almost impossible to identify unlearned response patterns because they are so rapidly altered according to the particular characteristics of the subject's immediate environment. On the other hand, the human organism is relatively slow to mature. Longitudinal studies, a potentially powerful tool for the developmental researchers, must almost always be limited in scope and duration. Long-term availability of individual subjects is determined by parents, not researchers—and few researchers have the patience or steady resources necessary to bridge the 20 years or more from birth to maturity, or even a substantial portion of that period.

Probably as a result of these facts, theoretical views of human development are diverse and often conflicting. The lack of definitive data promotes disagreement even in the area of terminology. For many years there have been major arguments concerning the utility of basic concepts such as attachment, dependency, and independence. Furthermore, the scope and importance of individual differences throughout development are seldom clear from available data, and thus considerations of variables which influence and parameters which describe social development are characteristically speculative.

Given this state of affairs, it is not surprising that there is an increasing tendency among some developmental researchers to turn to other species for their data. Prime candidates for such study are the higher nonhuman primates, particularly macaques and apes. The ethical difficulties involved in experimentation with nonhuman primates are less complex than those found in human research. In laboratory situations nonhuman primate subjects can, at least in theory, be observed 24 hours a day in carefully predetermined and controlled social environments. Any emerging response system can thus be identified, and the factors which influence its appearance can be examined systematically. Finally, lifespan longitudinal research is far more practical because few other primates mature as slowly as do humans. For example, rhesus monkeys mature at a rate approximately four times that of human infants. An investigator can follow an infant monkey from birth to sexual maturity in 4 years, not an unreasonable period in today's research climate.

This is, of course, not to say that primate developmental research has or is about to render human study obsolete. Despite the fact that they are closer on the evolutionary scale to humans than any other animals and share many anatomical, physiological, and biochemical characteristics, nonhuman primates are not simply furry little men with tails. They do not possess the cognitive capabilities of their human counterparts, and although they have complex social repertoires and complicated social units, they cannot match the intricacies of human social behavior. These facts tend to influence the subject matter of primate developmental research. For example, study of human speech patterns and development is difficult to perform in organisms that are incapable of comparable communicative capability.

Research investigating the social development of rhesus monkeys has been carried out at the Wisconsin Primate Laboratory for almost two decades. The major thrust of this effort, largely under the direction of Harlow, has been to uncover monkey data which generalize to human development (Harlow, Gluck, & Suomi, 1972). This chapter will describe much of the recent research in social development of rhesus monkeys at Wisconsin. The work has been oriented about three issues: what is the nature of a monkey's social capabilities at various points throughout the course of maturation, in what ways and to what degree can development be influenced by the nature of the social environment, and, finally, what are the specific mechanisms underlying the interaction between response systems and social environment?

Unlearned Response Systems in Monkeys

Considerable research has disclosed that rhesus monkeys possess numerous behavioral capabilities whose initial appearances are relatively independent of environmental contingencies. These phenomena have been described by a number of terms, e.g., prepotent, innate, unlearned, prewired, instinctive, and maturational. Basically they all share two characteristics: each appears initially in an invariant form among monkeys reared and housed in a variety of different social and nonsocial conditions, and each appears at a relatively constant chronological point across all subjects. Hereafter we shall call such phenomena *unlearned response systems*. In rhesus monkeys they are diverse, both in form and in time of appearance.

For example, virtually all rhesus monkey infants exhibit a complex set of reflex behaviors at or shortly after birth. These include a rooting reflex, nutritive and nonnutritive sucking, and strong grasping and clasping reflexes (Mowbray & Cadell, 1962). Such response patterns are not without ethological or adaptive significance: without a rooting and sucking behavior system, an infant would starve, even with its mother's adequate supply of milk. Also, if an infant monkey did not have the capability to support its body weight in clinging to its mother, the mother would either be forced to abandon her infant, separate herself from her social group, or convince the rest of her troop to stop its nomadic movement. None of these events usually occurs in feral environments (Lindburg, 1973). Clearly, at least in the environment from which most generations of rhesus monkeys have evolved, such unlearned capabilities are essential for survival of the infant.

Not all unlearned response systems emerge at birth; several make their initial appearance later in life. For example, as soon as infant monkeys are capable of visually tracking moving objects, they will consistently orient themselves toward novel stimuli; as soon as they are physically able, they will physically approach and manually and orally manipulate those novel objects. Such behavior is readily apparent 6 to 10 days after birth in rhesus monkeys reared in the wild, in group pens, with individual mothers, or in total social isolation.

Harlow (1953) has termed such behavior "curiosity"; it has been given a number of other names, including "exploratory behavior," by other investigators (Berlyne, 1951).

Between 60 and 80 days of age, another unlearned response pattern emerges in the young monkey's repertoire. This behavior, termed the "fear grimace," is illustrated in Figure 1; it is a facial expression which can be loosely described as a monkey smile with teeth exposed. More specifically, it entails retraction of the corners of the mouth, a pulling back of the lips, and full exposure of upper and lower teeth. Another set of behavior patterns, aggression, does not appear as part of the behavioral repertoire of rhesus monkeys until considerably later chronologically, usually at about 6-8 months of age. "Aggression" has tradi-

Fig. 1 Young rhesus monkey exhibiting a fear grimace.

Fig. 2. Aggression among 8-month-old rhesus monkeys. The two subjects on the right are attacking a stranger.

tionally been a rather nebulously defined behavior in both the human and animal literature, and rhesus monkeys provide no exception. In most monkey studies the term is subjectively defined, usually including such behavior patterns as threat, bite, wrestle, and chase with intent to physically injure. An example of what any experienced observer of rhesus monkey behavior would label as aggression is illustrated in Figure 2. Such behavior patterns, with or without intent, simply are not exhibited by monkeys under 6 months of age. After 6 months of age, aggression is exhibited—in one form or another, at one time or another—by every rhesus monkey, independent of social rearing history. It is for this reason that we consider aggression to be a relatively late-emerging but nevertheless unlearned response system.

Both fear and the capability for aggression have intrinsic adaptive values. The organism that fails to feel fear does not alter its behavior in the presence of danger, and hence it is more likely to expose itself to situations which threaten its well-being. Normal fear helps keep animals out of unnecessary trouble. It is

wise, without the ability to aggress, no organism can
and hence is more likely to end in someone else's
clearly adaptive. On the other hand, excessive or
ggression can cause the organism more harm than
ppear to be required.

form or pattern of unlearned response system has been de-
etail by Sackett (1970). This appears to be largely a perceptual
involving unlearned patterns of social preference. For example, Sackett
70) demonstrated that socially naive neonates and infants not only could
identify but actually preferred adults of their own species to adults of closely
related macaque species, despite the fact that the infants had not been exposed to
adults of any of these species. Also, Suomi, Sackett, and Harlow (1970) showed
that infant rhesus monkeys reliably exhibited overwhelming preferences for adult
females over adult male stimulus animals, despite a lack of physical or visual
interactions with adults of either sex prior to testing. However, early in life the
same socially unsophisticated subjects failed to exhibit consistent preferences for
either sex of peer. Peer preferences did eventually emerge in these monkeys, and
when they did they followed predictable chronological changes in social behaviors.

In the above studies it can be argued that the apparently unlearned patterns
of social preference represented ethologically adaptive response systems. It is
reasonable to presume that the ability to recognize and prefer one's own species
to those which are closely related helps insure that it will be raised among
conspecifics. Also, it probably does not hurt the infant's chances for survival to
prefer to remain with adult females, who will care for it diligently, than to stay
with adult males, who most likely will not (Mitchell, 1969). Clearly, such
unlearned preference patterns can be adaptive for a relatively helpless neonatal
macaque.

Interactions Between Maturation and Social Environments

Obviously, a monkey's behavioral repertoire is not determined by genes
and maturation alone. Rhesus monkeys, like all higher primates, are enormously
responsive to their environments. As Harlow (1969) has pointed out, the primates learn so rapidly and develop a behavioral repertoire with such flexibility
that it is difficult to study unlearned response systems because the infants usually
adjust so rapidly to the demands of their particular environment. An unlearned
response system may emerge at the same chronological point in all monkeys, but
its eventual form and the degree to which it will be incorporated into a given
monkey's behavioral repertoire will always be a function of that individual's
particular past and present environment.

The elegance of the interaction between maturation and learning can be readily seen when one charts the social development of infants reared in feral and/or socially adequate laboratory environments. These are situations which at a minimum provide infant monkeys with unlimited access to their mothers and periodic opportunities to interact with peers. Monkeys reared in such environments spend the majority of their first month of life either on or in close proximity to their mothers. The rooting and sucking reflexes present during the first few days of life enable the infant to find and obtain its mother's nipple. Reflexive rooting and sucking have vanished from the developing infant's repertoire by 10–14 days of age (Harlow & Harlow, 1965) but that is a sufficient time for the infant to learn to find its mother's nipple and to suck voluntarily whenever it gets hungry.

More important, at least from the point of view of attachment formation, is the infant's clasping response (Harlow, 1958; & Harlow & Suomi, 1970). Reflexive at birth, the clasping response comes under voluntary control before the end of the second week of life (Mowbray & Cadell, 1962; Milbrath, 1971). By that time it has already become instrumental in allowing the infant to maintain body contact with the mother, even when she is not actively directing her behavior toward it. The infant now deliberately uses clinging to obtain contact comfort (Harlow & Harlow, 1965). It can control its contact with its mother.

At this point, curiosity or exploratory interests emerge in the infant. Whenever possible, the infant will physically approach and manually and orally contact any and all objects, animate or inanimate, within its immediate environment. In a mother–peer rearing situation, be it within a laboratory or out in the field, the infant will usually have plenty of objects to explore. Its exploratory activities become self-reinforcing, and hence it spends an increasing proportion of its time in such endeavor as it enters the second month of life.

In a feral environment (and in some laboratory environments as well) the infant's exploratory activities are not without potential peril to its well-being. At this stage, the infant knows no fear, as that response system has not yet matured, and thus it cannot differentiate the harmless from the deadly. However, two phenomena help to keep the growing infant out of real danger at this time in its life. First, it has not ended its attachment to its mother and continually returns to her after its exploratory forays, as is illustrated in Figure 3. Contact comfort has not lost its appeal. Second, the mother is hardly a passive entity during her infant's explorations. Rather, she watches it like a hawk and is quick to rescue it from any imminent danger or protect it from any predator or threatening conspecific. Thus, the infant is free from any fear, to explore and expose itself to the world beyond its mother, but at the same time is not without adaptive safeguards to minimize any threats to its survival.

By the time that the fear response does mature in the infant monkey, the infant has progressed enough in physical development to be able to separate itself from its mother at distances beyond her immediate reach. In other words, it is

Fig. 3. Young monkey returning to its mother (in this case a surrogate) to gain security.

now capable of getting into real trouble by itself. Hence, the appearance of fear in the infant's repertoire is timely indeed. Moreover, the infant has a place to which to run—its mother. It has had a full 2 months to develop security and trust, in the true Ericksonian sense, and thus does not hesitate to return to its mother when it is frightened.

Nor does the infant hesitate to leave its mother and return to its exploratory activities. The existence of a strong, trusting relationship with its mother enables the infant to overcome its fear rapidly. With a mother available, the infant can develop appropriate cautions without being paralyzed or immobilized by its newly emerged capacity to fear. In an adequate social environment, an infant's maturing fear can be moderated and socialized.

The same principle applies to the emergence of aggression in young monkeys. Strong social attachments are developed prior to its appearance in the monkeys' behavioral repertoires. Between the time of emergence of fear behaviors and the time of emergence of aggressive behaviors, monkeys reared with mothers and peers exhibit enormous development of social behaviors. In particular, interactive play with peers comes to dominate their behavioral repertoires.

Harlow and his associates (Harlow & Harlow, 1965; Harlow, 1969; Suomi & Harlow, 1971, 1975) have consistently argued that social play with age mates provides the primary vehicle for development of social capabilities which will characterize the monkeys' repertoires as adults. Through play activities the infants develop, perfect, and integrate basic patterns of interaction into a complex set of dynamic modes of interchange. During this period they develop attachments to the particular peers with whom they spend their time in play.

When aggression does mature in these monkeys, usually by 7 or 8 months of age, it is gradually integrated into the infants' existing patterns of interactive play. In particular, rough-and-tumble play becomes progressively rougher, involving more vigorous physical contact, more scrapping, and more biting. However, the participants rarely suffer physical injury. In contrast, if a strange monkey is introduced to a group of well-socialized peers, it is likely to be repeatedly and viciously attacked, as illustrated in Figure 2. Clearly, the capability for aggression has matured in 8-month-old monkeys, but it appears only in ethologically appropriate situations.

We believe it is no accident that development of peer attachments precedes development of aggressive capabilities, or that when aggression does emerge, it is exhibited predominantly in the presence of strangers and is almost completely masked in the company of friends. There is no question that in a feral environment the capacity for aggressive action can well serve adaptive functions, as the environment is not without both predators and other potentially competitive troops of conspecifics. However, uncontrolled or indiscriminate aggression within an established social group could readily destroy its integrity. If monkeys within a social unit repeatedly attacked each other, either the group would disperse or its members would kill each other. Therefore, aggression must be socialized—it must be minimized in within-group interactions, but it also must remain a viable response to counter external threat. This goal is accomplished, we believe, by the development of within-group friendships prior to the maturation of aggression. In this way, when aggression does emerge, each monkey knows whom not to attack and how to moderate aggressive impulses through vigorous but basically harmless play activity.

Thus, among monkeys reared in socially adequate environments, maturation and learning interact to maximize the development of a socially competent, socially contributing organism. Some response systems appear and can be modified well before other response systems mature—and in good time for the young monkey to be ready to integrate the new response system into its existing and expanding behavioral repertoire.

The degree to which development of attachment and other social behavior patterns is dependent upon this timing of potential and experience can be readily observed among monkeys who are not provided with socially adequate rearing environments. Consider, for example, the case of infants reared with their mothers in single cages from birth, but denied the opportunity to interact with peers or other conspecifics until near the end of the first year of life (Alexander & Harlow, 1965). Monkeys so reared apparently develop relatively normal relationships with their mothers. Throughout the first month of life they spend most of their time in close contact with their mothers, clinging and sucking in much the same fashion as do infants reared in more socially complex environments. However, these monkeys fail to leave their mothers to explore as early chronologically or as frequently as do infants reared with mothers and peers (Jensen, Bobbitt, & Gordon, 1973; Suomi, DeLizio, & Rush, 1977). This is not surprising, in view of the fact that mother-only-reared infants do not have as interesting an environment to explore as do mother-peer-reared monkeys.

The emergence of fear poses no developmental difficulties for infants reared with only their mothers. However, the emergence of aggression in these animals has clearly adverse consequences. Mother-only-reared monkeys have had no opportunity to develop affectional relationships with any peers, nor have they been able to develop complex social play behaviors, prior to the maturation of aggressive capability. When aggression does appear and these monkeys are first exposed to peers (at 8 months of age in the Alexander & Harlow study), they are hardly capable of socializing the behavior. Consequently, mother-only-reared monkeys are hyperaggressive. They are not good playmates.

Another form of rearing environment studied in detail has been the *together–together* situation. Here, infant monkeys are separated at birth from their mothers and reared in groups of like-aged peers (Chamove, 1966; Harlow & Harlow, 1969; Chamove, Rosenblum & Harlow, 1973; Suomi & Harlow, 1975). In this situation, as was the case for the mother-only situation, the consequences of a less than adequate social environment soon become readily apparent.

First, monkeys reared without mothers possess an innate predisposition to suck, even though there are no maternal nipples available. Consequently, they suck their own digits, as can be seen in Figures 4 and 5. High levels of self-orality are exhibited from the first days of life, and they are maintained for at least the first year. Freud would have described such behavior as oral fixation. Second, infants reared with peers but without mothers are born with predispositions to clasp. With no maternal ventrum available, they soon develop patterns of mutual clinging, as can be seen in Figure 6. Such clinging is not only as intense as any observed between mother–infant pairs, but also it persists far longer chronologically than does clinging to the mother. Together–together-reared monkeys do not begin to show significant declines in levels of mutual clinging until 6 months of age; mother–infant clinging has all but disappeared by 4 months of age in mother-reared infants (Harlow, Harlow, & Hansen, 1963; Suomi & Harlow, 1975).

Prior to emergence of fear responses peer-reared monkeys appear to be as curious as any infants, readily exploring any and all aspects of their environ-

Fig. 4. Self-orality in monkey reared without its mother.

ments. However, when fear appears, these monkeys have no mothers from whom to seek security; they have only each other. Other monkey infants are not nearly as effective in reducing fear as are monkey mothers (Novak, 1973; Meyer, Novak, Bowman, & Harlow, 1975), and consequently the infants stop or severely reduce their exploratory excursions. This situation gradually improves with age, but together–together-reared monkeys remain somewhat timid through adolescence and adulthood, their ongoing activities easily disrupted by environmental stresses (Suomi & Harlow, 1975).

In contrast to mother-only-reared monkeys, together–together-reared infants have little difficulty integrating aggressive behaviors into their existing repertoire when the capability emerges. By that time these monkeys have both

Fig. 5. Toe-sucking in monkey reared without its mother.

well-established play patterns and well-established play partners. Aggressive capabilities are detectable among friends only in the form of ever-rougher play bouts. However, a stranger introduced to a group of together-together monkeys will be readily and repeatedly attacked (Suomi & Dill, 1977). We believe that aggression is socialized in together–together-reared monkeys in the same manner that it is socialized in ferally reared monkeys—through playful peer interactions.

Thus, one can detect meaningful differences in social development among monkeys reared with mothers only, with peers only, or with both mothers and peers. In every case these differences can be attributed to maturation–environment interactions. Sucking, clinging, exploration, fear, and aggression mature in all these monkeys during the same chronological periods. However, the subsequent behavioral repertoires exhibited by the monkeys are very dependent upon the social parameters of their respective environments.

This point is illustrated with considerably greater force when one examines the behavioral development of monkeys reared from birth under conditions of social isolation, in which they are denied the opportunity for physical interaction with all conspecifics. Isolate-reared monkeys are born with the responses of sucking and clinging, and the patterns of exploratory behavior, fear, and aggression mature in isolates at the same chronological points that they mature in socially-reared monkeys. This fact should not be surprising if one views these behavioral patterns as phenomena whose form and time of appearance have been determined by millions of years of evolution. However, an isolate monkey has no maternal nipple to suck, and so it, like together–together-reared monkeys, develops patterns of self-orality. An isolate monkey has no partner, be it mother or peer, with whom to cling, and thus it develops patterns of self-clasping behavior, as is illustrated in Figure 7.

Fig. 6. Mutual clinging among peer-reared infants.

Fig. 7. Self-clasping behavior in isolate-reared monkey.

Curiosity emerges early in an isolate's life, as it does in all infant monkeys, and in its first months the isolate infant readily explores the whole of its limited environment. This trend is arrested with the emergence of the fear response at 60–80 days of age (Sackett, 1966). When fear appears, an isolate monkey has developed no secure attachments, and hence has nowhere to run and nowhere to hide—no mother, no peers, not even an inanimate surrogate. The infant virtually ceases its exploratory activities; instead, it develops idiosyncratic stereotypies and uses these behaviors to shut out novel stimuli (Harlow & Novak, 1973).

Finally, aggression appears in the isolate monkey's repertoire at 7–8 months of age. But the isolate has no history of social interaction and no basis for perceiving friendship, and hence its aggression cannot be socialized. As a result, when an isolate is finally placed in a social setting, it typically exhibits excessive and misdirected aggressive activity. For example, it may try to attack a dominant adult male, an act few normal monkeys are foolish enough to attempt. If left alone, an isolate will often turn against its own body. Typical self-aggression is illustrated in Figure 8.

It is very clear that a young monkey's past and current social environment can greatly influence the form and manner in which emerging response systems are integrated into existing behavioral repertoires. In most feral and socially adequate laboratory environments the resulting behavior patterns appear to be "normal" and adaptive. We believe this is true because the specific prepotent systems have evolved over millions of years to appear at the "right" time in the "right" environment in order for optimal integration of the system to occur. The

Fig. 8. Self-aggression in isolate-reared monkey.

importance of the social environment is most readily apparent when it is inadequate. When prepotent response systems mature in socially sterile environments the resulting behavior repertoires appear to be bizarre.

Mechanisms Underlying the Development of Specific Social Attachment Behaviors

The above studies of monkeys reared in different situations clearly demonstrated that the nature of an infant's social environment can enormously influence its developing behavioral repertoire. What these studies did *not* disclose was the specific mechanisms involved in the acquisition, maintenance, and modification of specific patterns of behavior. One can now predict with fair confidence that a monkey reared in total social isolation is likely to develop idiosyncratic stereotypies while an infant reared with mothers and peers is likely to develop patterns of social play. However, these data do not permit identification of the factors which determine when and why a particular stereotypy will appear in the isolate's repertoire. Nor do they allow the specification of the precise stimuli that serve to initiate and maintain individual play bouts. In other words, the rearing condition studies of monkey development fail to provide the data necessary to identify underlying mechanisms.

One possible solution to this problem is to study the development of organisms in a tightly controlled environment in which levels of only one variable are manipulated across a group of subjects and the resulting behavioral tendencies are monitored over a period of time. This has been the approach of Harlow and his associates in their studies of surrogate mothers (Harlow & Zimmermann, 1959; Harlow & Suomi, 1970). Here, infants were reared on sets of surrogate mothers differing with respect to a single variable, e.g., body surface (cloth versus wire), feeding capability, temperature, or stability. The problem with this approach is that in order to keep all other factors constant, infants must be reared in relatively sterile environments that do not promote normal social development.

An alternative approach is to study in great detail the development of individuals in socially complex environments, and to correlate sequences of behavior with environmental antecedents and consequences. Although the data remain descriptive in nature and no direct causal relationships can be established, strong inferences can be made regarding relationships between the behavior of the organism and its immediate environment. Such inferences, once identified, can then be subjected to direct experimental tests in a more tightly controlled situation. This has been our primary approach over the past few years, and it has involved study of the development of monkeys reared in socially complex *nuclear families*.

The nuclear family environment, created at Wisconsin by the late M. K. Harlow, consists of units with four family cages surrounding a central play area. A family unit is illustrated in Figure 9, and a full description can be found in Harlow (1971). Infants are born and reared with their biological mothers and fathers in each of the four family cages. The play area is connected to each of the family cages by mesh tunnels which are large enough to allow the infants free access to the play area and to other family cages, but which are small enough to confine adult male–female pairs to their respective family cages. As a result, nuclear-family-reared offspring have continual access to both parents and siblings, and considerable access to other adults of both sexes, as well as to peers of varying ages.

These nuclear family setups are admittedly artificial social environments for rhesus monkeys; there exist no exact feral counterparts. In particular, the social activities of adult pairs can be directed only toward each other, their own offspring, and occasionally toward other infants. They cannot interact with other adults of either sex, a limitation which, of course, does not exist in any feral environment. Adult male–female pairs are physically isolated from one another for at least two reasons. First, on the basis of previous findings we were afraid that there would be excessive aggression among the adult males if they were permitted physical interaction with one another. Such aggression, it was feared, might

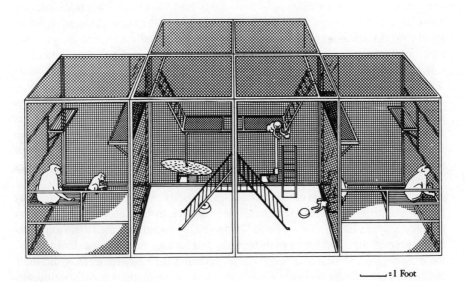

`————— = 1 Foot`

Fig. 9. The nuclear family apparatus. Adult male–female pairs are confined to the four outer living cages (on both sides and in rear of apparatus), while offspring are free to enter the central play area and/or visit adults other than their parents.

result not only in physical injury but also in total disruption of ongoing social activities of the other subjects in the family units. Second, by confining adult male–female pairs to single cages, sexual promiscuity was prohibited and fidelity maintained, thus insuring that the biological fathers of each offspring would be known to the investigators. In this respect, our monkey nuclear families have achieved a state of propriety not matched by Victorian society itself, and thus it is truly an artificial social environment for monkey and man alike. Nevertheless, the nuclear family setups have enabled us to monitor with heretofore unmatched precision the development of infants reared in very complex social environments. Although the data collected to date are largely descriptive in nature, careful examination has yielded information which is highly suggestive with respect to specific mechanisms involved in social development of rhesus monkeys.

For example, even a cursory glance at these developmental data make it clear that adult male monkeys do not take a particularly active role in raising their infants. This hardly represents a novel discovery; Mitchell (1969), in an extensive review of nonhuman primate paternalistic behavior in feral environments, concluded that rhesus monkey adult males are among the least, if not the least, paternalistic of all macaque species.

At any rate, within the nuclear families at the Wisconsin Primate Laboratory, adult males do interact with their offspring and other infants, and even play with them occasionally. However, interactions with infants constitute only a very minor part of their daily activities. Less than 5% of the adult male interactions are directed toward infants under 2 years of age. Moreover, the adult males do not exhibit meaningful levels of behaviors traditionally assigned the paternal role—defense and protection of their offspring. Mothers direct more than five times as many of these behaviors toward their offspring as do fathers, as is illustrated in Figure 10.

However, there exists some degree of selectivity with respect to the participants of play bouts involving adult males and infants. As can be seen in Figure 11, male infants are equally as likely to play with other adult males as with their own fathers. Female infants, in contrast, are far more selective. Virtually all of their play bouts involving an adult male are directed toward their father. Such findings are not inconsistent with existing field data.

Despite the low levels of actual interactions with adult males, nuclear family offspring clearly differentiate their fathers from the other adult males. Indeed, Suomi, Eisele, Grady, and Tripp (1973) found that the offspring actually preferred their fathers to both familiar and strange adult males. In addition, the offspring spent almost as much time watching their fathers as they did their mothers, even though their physical interactions with mothers were six times as frequent as their interactions with fathers, at least during the first 3 years of life. Males watched their fathers more than did females, and the difference became greater as the infants matured. Basically, however, physical interactions with

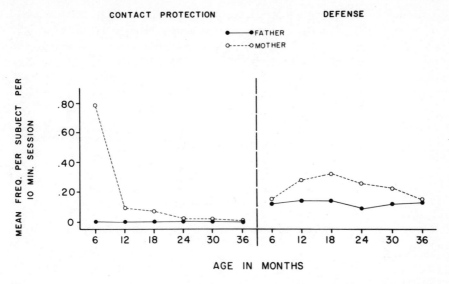

Fig. 10. Infant protection and defense behaviors shown by mothers and fathers toward nuclear family offspring.

fathers constituted a trivial component of the infants' overall behavioral repertoires.

Examination of the more extensive interactions between offspring and their mothers yielded novel findings with respect to mechanisms underlying mother–infant attachment. Most of our data analyses are still preliminary in nature, but some general findings can be offered: variation among mothers was far less than variation among infants, and infants were far more active in loosening the mother–infant ties than has been reported for other environments. More specifically, there was little variation across the scores of mothers, or within the scores of mothers having more than one offspring, in the chronology or levels of behaviors directed toward infants. Contact-achieving or maintaining behaviors by mothers showed an initial rise, then a steady decline throughout the first year of life, while maternal rejection remained at very low and very stable levels during the whole of the first year. These data are illustrated in Figure 12; they are at direct variance with most previous maternal data collected not only at Wisconsin (Hansen, 1966) but at other laboratories as well (Hinde & White, 1974).

We believe the key to the underlying mechanisms can be found in the nature of the infants' behaviors. Most of the variation among mother–infant pairs was attributed to variation among infants, both in the chronology and in the levels of behaviors directed toward the mother. Of particular interest was the infants' development of mother-rejecting behaviors. First, their incidence followed the pattern of rejecting activity shown by the mother in previous studies, as can be

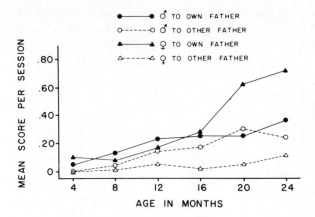

Fig. 11. Infant–adult male play initiates in the nuclear family environment.

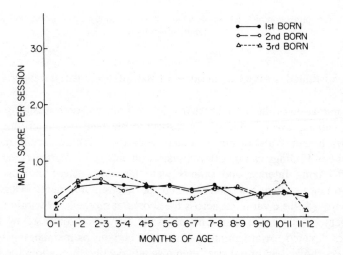

Fig. 12. Levels of rejection of infant shown by nuclear-family mothers.

seen in Figure 13. Second, individual variation was considerable, particularly within families, where clear-cut birth order effects were exhibited. Third, those infants who actively rejected their mothers the most vigorously were also those that sought out contact most persistently. Freud would point to these data as a classic case of ambivalence toward the mother.

Much of the individual variation across groups of infants, particularly the birth-order effects for mother-directed behaviors, seemed to be directly correlated with the social complexity of the environment surrounding mother and infant. Later-born infants left their mothers earlier chronologically and with considerably less hassle. The logical explanation is that they had more potential playmates to visit than first-borns, and they simply followed their exploratory tendencies. First-born infants in the nuclear family units had an average of less than three available playmates during their first year of life while later-borns had two to three times as many available, most of them older than themselves.

Among all nuclear-family-reared infants, play was the predominant social activity from the third month throughout the third year of life. This is a longer period chronologically than has been reported for young rhesus monkeys reared in any other laboratory environment (Ruppenthal, Harlow, Eisele, Harlow, and Suomi, 1974). We believe the prolonged maintenance of peer play in these subjects was a result of the wide diversity in age of available playmates in the nuclear families, a situation not present in most social rearing studies, where offspring are all within weeks of each other in date of birth (e.g., Rosenblum, 1961; Hansen, 1966). Clear sex differences were found among nuclear family infants' levels of behaviors by Ruppenthal *et al.* (1974). Throughout the first 3 years of life males had higher frequencies of total behaviors, total social behaviors, and, most importantly, total play initiates and reciprocations. Females had higher levels of passive social affiliative behaviors. These findings are illustrated in Figures 14 and 15 and are generally consistent with the findings of previous studies of rhesus monkey peer interaction (Harlow & Lauersdorf, 1974).

Prior to this time, however, the mechanisms underlying these sex differences were largely passed off as genetic or biological in nature, explanations which in actuality explain nothing at the behavioral level. The present data are somewhat

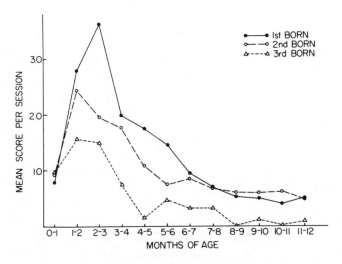

Fig. 13. Levels of rejection of mother shown by nuclear-family-reared infants.

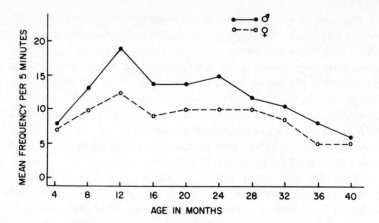

Fig. 14. Sex differences in levels of play behaviors among nuclear-family-reared subjects.

more enlightening. It was found that males initiated higher levels of play toward other males than toward females, while females initiated equal frequencies of play toward both male and female peers, as can be seen in Figure 16. When the nature of responses to those play initiates was examined, significant sex differences were also disclosed. They are illustrated in Figures 17 and 18. A plausible explanation to the high levels of male-male play bouts is that male initiates were reciprocated more often and ignored less often by males; females responded similarly to like initiations from either sex. If reciprocation of play was viewed as

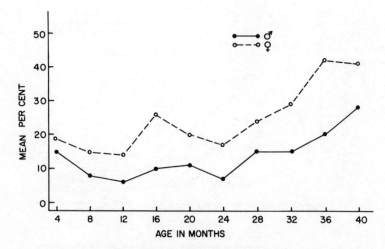

Fig. 15. Sex differences in proportion of social interactions for affiliative behaviors.

a reinforcer for play, then the enhanced level of male–male play is a straightforward S–R prediction. One need not invoke genetic explanations for these behavioral phenomena.

Of course, it must be pointed out that these nuclear family data are only descriptive, and causal relationships can only be inferred, not in any sense deduced. But the inferences can be rather compelling. The complexity of the social environment, the detail of the observational data, and the opportunity for virtually continuous longitudinal study from birth to adulthood permits some rather interesting views of the development of social behavior in monkeys.

At the very least, these data cast doubt on the utility of the "attachment"

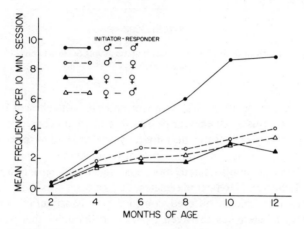

Fig. 16. Initiations of play among nuclear-family-reared monkeys.

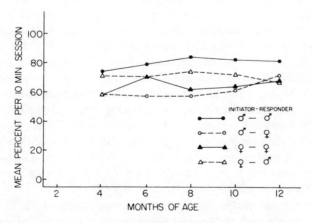

Fig. 17. Reciprocation of play initiates among nuclear-family-reared monkeys.

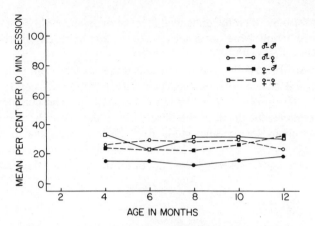

Fig. 18. Levels of ignored play initiates among nuclear-family-
reared monkeys.

concept as a predictor of specific behavior patterns. Attachment is traditionally defined in such terms as "behavior designed to maintain contact or proximity to a specific social object." If this definition is to be applied to the nuclear-family-reared monkeys, then an enormous amount of attachment behavior was indeed exhibited. Nuclear-family-reared monkeys developed strong attachments to mothers, to fathers, and to peer playmates, but the behaviors which characterized these various attachments differed considerably. Most infant attachment behavior toward adult males involved passive observation; that directed toward mothers involved ventral surface and nipple contact; while peer-directed attachment behaviors characteristically could be scored as play. All these behaviors are proximity seeking and/or maintaining activities. Further, within individual attachment relationships, e.g., mother and infant, the quality and quantity of such behaviors changed considerably over a period of time. Indeed, in some cases behaviors seemingly incompatible with a unitary concept of attachment appeared side by side. Infants who showed the highest frequencies of clinging initiates toward mother also exhibited the greatest number of attempts to reject their mothers. At best, one can say that across studies of individuals and relationships one set of attachment behaviors, e.g., clinging, may be empirically as well as functionally unrelated to another set of attachment behaviors, e.g., playing. At worst, such a situation may exist within individuals and specific relationships as well. Thus, at least among nuclear-family-reared monkeys, a unitary concept of attachment turns out to be relatively useless as an index of specific behavior patterns. This is possibly true for humans as well.

Second, these nuclear family studies strongly suggest that the influence of the social environment upon social development is more varied and widespread than was previously suspected. In the past, considerable attention was directed toward specific relationships, such as that embodied by the mother-infant dyad. In other cases, peer relationships were studied, but the composition of the group was somewhat artificial; in order to keep extraneous variables constant, monkeys were exposed to peers within a few days of themselves in age, a situation which seldom occurs outside of the laboratory. Our nuclear family data suggest that these extraneous variables are hardly inconsequential. The composition of the social environment outside of the family unit can have a major effect in not only the development but also the adult exhibition of specific modes of social behavior.

The nuclear family data examined thus far have been descriptive and rather gross. We are currently examining other nuclear family data which are still descriptive but considerably more refined. These are specific sequences of behavior among nuclear family individuals. They include all participants in interactive bouts as well as their behaviors in order of exhibition. Close examination of these sequences can, in theory, identify recurring patterns of interactions, as has been shown on a small scale by Bobbitt, Gourebitch, Miller, and Jensen (1969). More importantly, such data analyses can, in theory, identify antecedents and consequences of particular behaviors for specific individuals. We are most interested in what way, if any, the antecedents and consequences of a behavior such as play initiation, social threat, or sexual present, change throughout the infant's development. Because we possess full maturational data on many of these subjects, it will be possible to compare antecedents and consequences of adult behaviors with those seen during infant and adolescent social development. The data have already been collected, and the appropriate analyses are currently underway.

Of course, such data are only descriptive in nature, and causal mechanisms can only be suggested, not verified, from any observed antecedent-behavior–consequence sequence of activity. However, this approach may readily yield precise hypotheses regarding causality which can then be tested empirically in carefully controlled environments. A case in point is the effect of maternal rejecting behavior upon mother–infant affectional relationships. Recent data collected both at Wisconsin and at other laboratories have suggested that it may serve the purpose of increasing an infant's tendency to seek physical contact with its mother. We are now investigating this question directly by rearing monkeys on surrogate mothers which can physically reject the infant on a schedule controlled by the experimenter. Under these conditions causality can be determined, but it is unlikely that the study would have been performed if the preceding descriptive data had not been available. We are currently developing a family of surrogate peers; with them we hope to be able to test possible mechanisms of the factors which influence peer-directed behavior in monkeys.

Summary and Perspectives

This chapter has concerned itself primarily with study of the social development of monkeys reared under various laboratory conditions. It was pointed out that much of monkey behavior arises initially from basically unlearned response systems. Such systems mature at different points in a monkey's early life and appear in a fashion independent of the immediate environment. However, monkeys rapidly integrate these response systems into their existing behavioral repertoire, which in point of fact is highly dependent upon the individual's present and past social environments. Thus, monkeys reared in total isolation and monkeys reared in nuclear families both develop capabilities for fear and aggression, at approximately 2½–3 months and 6–7 months of age, respectively. However, the form in which these behavior patterns are exhibited by isolates and by nuclear-family-reared monkeys are as different as night and day.

Subsequent research has addressed itself to elucidation of mechanisms underlying the development of specific social behaviors by individual monkeys. This work at present is still in its infancy. Complete descriptive data regarding antecedents and consequences of various social behaviors throughout development do not now exist, but are in the process of being collected. When they have been obtained it is likely that direct empirical tests of hypothesized mechanisms underlying social development can then be achieved.

Such is the current state of research involving the development of social behavior in the rhesus monkey. At the beginning of the chapter it was pointed out that studies of nonhuman primates can serve to augment the data collected in studies of human social development. In many ways, nonhuman primate research has provided precedents for theory and experimentation in human inquiry. A human infant's attachment to its mother was almost universally thought to result from feeding activity until Harlow's surrogate studies with rhesus monkey infants (Harlow, 1958). Quantification of observational scoring techniques were first developed for study of nonhuman primates; only recently have they been applied to the study of human infants, e.g., Patterson (1974). The importance of monkey peer relationships for social development has been stressed for years (e.g., Harlow, 1969); only after many years of disinterest have human developmental researches directed more than passing attention toward the development of infant and childhood friendships (Hartup, 1975). The most recent findings in this area tend to confirm the view that humans and monkeys are remarkably similar in terms of peer attachment development (Lewis, Young, Brooks, & Michalson, 1975; Ross, 1975; Eckerman, Whatley, & Kutz, 1975). It is our prediction that this trend of monkey findings advancing human findings in the area of social development will continue in force.

References

Alexander, B. K., & Harlow, H. F. Social behavior of juvenile rhesus monkeys subjected to different rearing conditions during the first six months of life. *Zool. Jb. Physiol.*, 1965, **71**, 489–508.

Berlyne, D. E. Attention, perception, and behavior therapy. *Psychological Review*, 1951, **58**, 137–146.

Bobbitt, R. A., Gourebitch, V. P., Miller, L. E., & Jensen, G. D. The dynamics of social interactive behavior: A computerized procedure for analyzing trends, patterns, and sequences. *Psychological Bulletin*, 1969, **71**, 110–121.

Chamove, A. S. The effects of varying infant peer experience on social behavior in the rhesus monkey. Unpublished M.A. thesis, University of Wisconsin, 1966.

Chamove, A. S., Rosenblum, L. A., & Harlow, H. F. Monkeys (*Macaca mulatta*) raised only with peers. A pilot study. *Animal Behaviour*, 1973, **21**, 316–325.

Eckerman, C. O., Whatley, J. L., & Kutz, S. L. Growth of social play with peers during the second year of life. *Developmental Psychology*, 1975, **11**, 42–49.

Hansen, E. W. The development of maternal and infant behavior in the rhesus monkey. *Behaviour*, 1966, **27**, 107–149.

Harlow, H. F. Mice, monkeys, men, and motives. *Psychological Review*, 1953, **60**, 23–32.

Harlow, H. F. The nature of love. *American Psychologist*, 1958, **13**, 673–685.

Harlow, H. F. Age-mate or peer affectional system. In D. S. Lehrman, R. A. Hinde, & E. Shaw (Eds.), *Advances in the study of behavior* (Vol. 2). New York: Academic Press, 1969, 333–383.

Harlow, H. F., Gluck, J. P., & Suomi, S. J. Generalization of behavioral data between nonhuman and human animals. *American Psychologist*, 1972, **27**, 709–716.

Harlow, H. F., & Harlow, M. K. The affectional systems. In A. M. Schrier, H. F. Harlow, & F. Stollnitz (Eds.), *Behavior of nonhuman primates* (Vol. 2). New York: Academic Press, 1965, 257–334.

Harlow, H. F., & Harlow, M. K. Effects of various mother-infant relationships on rhesus monkey behaviors. In B. M. Foss (Ed.), *Determinants of infant behavior* (Vol. 4). London: Methuen, 1969, 15–36.

Harlow, H. F., Harlow, M. K., & Hansen, E. W. The maternal affectional system of rhesus monkeys. In H. L. Rheingold (Ed.), *Maternal behavior in mammals*. New York: Wiley, 1963, 254–281.

Harlow, H. F., & Lauersdorf, H. E. Sex differences in passion and play. *Perspectives in Biology and Medicine*, 1974, **17**, 348–360.

Harlow, H. F., & Novak, M. A. Psychopathological perspectives. *Perspectives in Biology and Medicine*, 1973, **16**, 461–478.

Harlow, H. F., & Suomi, S. J. The nature of love—simplified. *American Psychologist*, 1970, **25**, 161–168.

Harlow, H. F., & Zimmermann, R. R. Affectional responses in the infant monkey. *Science*, 1959, **130**, 421–432.

Harlow, M. K. Nuclear family apparatus. *Behavior Research Methods and Instrumentation*, 1971, **3**, 301–304.

Hartup, W. W. The origins of friendship. In M. Lewis & L. A. Rosenblum (Eds.), *The origins of behavior:* ETS Symposium on friendship and peer relations. New York: Wiley, 1975, 11–26.

Hinde, R. A., & White, L. The dynamics of a relationship—rhesus monkey ventroventral contact. *Journal of Comparative and Physiological Psychology*, 1974, **86**, 8–23.

Jensen, G. D., Bobbitt, R. A., & Gordon, B. N. Mothers' and infants' roles in the development of independence of *Macaca nemestrina*. *Primates*, 1973, **14**, 79–88.

Lewis, M., Young, G., Brooks, J., & Michalson, L. The beginning of friendship. In M. Lewis & L. A. Rosenblum (Eds.), *The origins of behavior:* ETS symposium on friendship and peer relations. New York: Wiley, 1975, 27–66.

Lindburg, D. G. The rhesus monkey in North India: An ecological and behavioral study. In L. A. Rosenblum (Ed.), *Primate behavior* (Vol. 2). New York: Academic Press, 1973, 1–106.

Meyer, J. S., Novak, M. A., Bowman, R. E., & Harlow, H. F. Behavioral and hormonal effects of attachment object separation in surrogate-peer-reared and mother-reared infant rhesus monkeys. *Developmental Psychobiology*, 1975, **8**, 425–436.

Milbrath, C. P. The consequences of self-paced environment on perceptual development. Unpublished doctoral dissertation. University of Wisconsin, 1971.

Mitchell, G. D. Paternalistic behavior in primates. *Psychological Bulletin*, 1969, **71**, 399–417.

Mowbray, J. B., & Cadell, T. E. Early behavior patterns in rhesus monkeys. *Journal of Comparative and Physiological Psychology*, 1962, **55**, 350–357.

Novak, M. A. Fear-attachment relationships in infant and juvenile rhesus monkeys. Unpublished doctoral dissertation, University of Wisconsin, 1973.

Patterson, G. R. A basis for identifying stimuli which control behaviors in natural settings. *Child Development*, 1974, **45**, 900–911.

Rosenblum, L. A. The development of social behavior in the rhesus monkey. Unpublished doctoral dissertation, University of Wisconsin, 1961.

Ross, H., & Goldman, B. D. Establishing new social relations in infancy. In T. Alloway, L. Krames, & P. Pliner (Eds.), *Advances in the study of communication and affect* (Vol. 3). New York: Plenum Press, 1976, 61–79.

Ruppenthal, G. C., Harlow, M. K., Eisele, C. D., Harlow, H. F., & Suomi, S. J. Development of peer interactions of monkeys reared in a nuclear-family environment. *Child Development*, 1974, **45**, 670–682.

Sackett, G. P. Monkeys reared in visual isolation with pictures as visual input: Evidence for an innate releasing mechanism. *Science*, 1966, **154**, 1468–1472.

Sackett, G. P. Unlearned response, differential rearing experiences, and the development of social attachments by rhesus monkeys. In L. A. Rosenblum (Ed.), *Primate behavior* (Vol. 1). New York: Academic Press, 1970, 112–140.

Suomi, S. J., Delizio, R., & Rush, D. Effect of different social environments on mother–infant interactions. In preparation, 1977.

Suomi, S. J., & Dill, D. Adolescent behavior among mother-reared and peer-reared rhesus monkeys. In preparation, 1977.

Suomi, S. J., Eisele, C. D., Grady, S. A., & Tripp, R. L. Social preferences of monkeys reared in an enriched laboratory social environment. *Child Development*, 1973, **44**, 451–460.

Suomi, S. J., & Harlow, H. F. Monkeys at play. *Natural History*, 1971, **80**, 72–76.

Suomi, S. J., & Harlow, H. F. The role and reason of peer relationships in rhesus monkeys. In M. Lewis & L. A. Rosenblum (Eds.), *The origins of behavior:* ETS symposium on friendship and peer relations. New York: Wiley, 1975, 153–185.

Suomi, S. J., Sackett, G. P., & Harlow, H. F. Development of sex preferences in rhesus monkeys. *Developmental Psychology*, 1970, **3**, 326–336.

Index

Acquisition, patterns of 212
Acts 52
Adaptation
  social 11
  to strangers 19
Adoption 10
Affective state 89
  of infant 95
  positive 71, 106
Africa 171
Aggregation 169
Aggression 28, 149, 200, 201, 202, 204,
    206, 208, 209, 210
  among adult males, 205
Anal excreta 185, 191, 193, 194
Analysis, functional 116
Ano-genital area 177
Anthropology 26, 145
Antibiotic 188
Anxiety 6, 82
Apes 198
Apparatus, description of 178
Appearance 7
Arousal 6, 9
  level of 147, 152
Attachment 30, 50, 56, 57, 58, 61, 76, 81,
    151, 164, 165, 167, 170, 172, 174
  among males 160, 174
  as an entity 113
  as metaphor 111-113
  as process 111-113
  attenuation 25, 40
  changes 42
  conditioning model of 112
  definition 86

Attachment (cont'd)
  development of 148, 158, 197-225
  effects of infant on mother 109-143
  goal directed 36, 50
  of infant to mother 111
  of mother to infant 111
Attitudes 39, 40, 41, 55
Attractant 3, 179
Awareness,
  of reinforcement contingency 125, 134
  social 117

Baboons, 158, 159-166
  Forest 164
  Hamadryas 162-164, 172
  Savannah 160-162
Bacteria, cecal 188, 189
Begging 45
Behavior 29, 30
  baseline 128
  causal mechanisms 222
  control 48, 121
  exploratory 105, 200
  inhibition of 51
  measures of 88
  modification 212
  reciprocal 48
  reciprocal control 29
  rejecting 34
  repertoire 25, 202
  sequences 221, 222
  sociable 34
  species-specific 110
  transmission of 145
Behavioral—biological synchronization 2

Birds 12
Birth order, effects of 103, 216
Birthday Game 41, 42
Biting 201, 205
Bonds
  mother–infant 2, 148
  parent–child 3
  reaffirmation of 154
  social 147, 149, 168, 169, 172
  tactile 153
Bonnet macaques 146, 159
Breast-feeding 87

Carbohydrates 188
Carrying 163
Cecotrophe 186, 188, 189, 191, 193, 194
Cecum 185, 187, 188
Chasing 152, 201
Children 38
  social development in 14-20
Chimpanzees 28, 165
Clasping 203, 206
Clinging 208, 209, 221
Coat color 27, 146
Cognition 30, 36, 37
  development of 54
Communication 29, 30, 31, 37, 39, 49, 50,
    52, 105, 145, 169
  between infant and mother 81-107
  in social interaction 147
  tactile 148, 150, 152
Comparisons, interspecific 158, 159
Concepts, development of 85
Conciliation 152
Conditioning 112, 113, 121, 128, 135,
    137, 139
  criterion 121
  instrumental 109
  mutual 111, 138
  of mother's behaviors by her infant 116
  procedure 120
Contact 37, 39, 51, 203
  nipple 220
  tactile 147, 148, 150, 151, 153, 157,
    158, 159, 162, 163
  ventral surface 220
  visual 150
Control, physical 33
Cookie Test 32, 33, 50, 51
Cooperation 48, 56, 172
Copulation 169

Criterion, of performance 121
Crying 38, 45, 101, 111, 112, 114
  angry 44
  genetic programming of 83
  operant 85
Culture, transmission of 145
Curiosity 200, 203, 209, 210

Danger 27, 28
Data, descriptive 222
Defecation 185, 191, 193, 194
Dentition 27
Departure, anticipation of 82
Dependence 3, 198
Depression 7
Desert 160
Development 110
  human 199
  mechanisms underlying 212, 222
  social 61
Differences
  individual 85, 87
  situational 85, 87
Distress 15, 82, 83
  infant 101
  lack of 95
  manipulation of 104
  separation 90, 105
  vocal 84, 88, 89, 98, 100, 102
Dog 5, 6, 7, 8, 10, 13, 14, 148
Dominance 154, 156, 172

Eating 7, 179, 190
Ecology 26, 96
Egocentrism 38
Elimination 177, 185, 191, 193, 194
Embracing 169
Emotion 85, 112
Environment
  complexity 90
  social 202-212
Ergocornine 191
Evolution 2
Experimental design
  group 131-134
  single-subject 129-131
Experimental procedures 136
  description of 117-121, 125-127
Exploration 95, 208

Fatigue 9

Fear 6, 61, 82, 200, 201, 202, 203, 206, 207, 208, 209
  of strangers 16, 17, 61, 62
Feedback 13
Fermentation 185
Fertilization 169
Fighting 13
Fixed action pattern 169
Following 88
Forest 166
Friendship 62, 210
Frustation 37
Functional relationships, between the behaviors of mother and infant 138
Fussing 44, 114

Galactofores 191
Games 41, 42, 66, 70, 72, 76, 77
Gibbon 172
Gnawing 7
Goals 31, 35, 36, 37, 38, 39, 42, 51, 53, 55, 56
Grasping 199
Greeting 148, 150, 151, 154, 156, 157, 158, 161, 169
Grooming 7, 146, 147, 148, 149, 150, 151, 158, 159, 162, 163, 169

Habituation 9, 13
Hanuman langurs 146, 158, 159, 166
Harem 148, 149, 160, 162, 164, 165, 172, 173
  as economic unit 163
Head turns, of infant 116, 117-125
Heart rate 6
Homeostasis 9
Hormonal balance 150, 170
Hunger 9, 146
Hyperventilation 6

Ideas 39
Imprinting 12, 148, 149, 170
Independence 198
India 166, 171
Infanticide 166, 167
Infants
  as object of exploration 103
  individual differences among 75, 114
  newborn 150
  retrieval of 102
  social relations between 61-79

Innate releasing mechanism 110, 169
Instinct 82, 199
Institutionalization 81
Interactional development
  dynamics 1-24
  principles 18-20
Interactions
  between offspring and their mothers 215
  mother–infant 109-143
Interference 69
Interrupting 32
Interviews 113, 135
Intestine 185
Invasions 166, 167
IQ scores 114
Isolation
  adaptation to 4-10
  in adults 8
  long-term 11
  physical conditions of 8
Instruction 136

Joy 37

Kidnapping 164

Lactating female, cue emitted by 179
Lactating mother, temperature of breasts 114
Lactation 171, 191
Language 31, 145
Langurs 166-168, 172
Laughing 70, 71
Learning 82, 86, 109, 136, 173, 203
Licking 2
Light 169
Lip-smacking 161, 169
Locomotion 27, 98, 151

Macaques
  bonnet 149-158
  Japanese 171
  pig-tailed 149, 150
  rhesus 171
Maintenance, patterns 212
Masturbation 146
Maternal attractant, onset and offset 181
Maternal pheromone 193
  emission 182, 183
  mechanism of emission 189, 190
  properties of 178

Maternal pheromone (*cont'd*)
  pup stimulation in the control of 182-184
  pups reaction to 193-195
  site of emission 185
  synthesis 188, 189, 193
Maturation 198, 202
Maturity, neurological 51
Microorganisms 188
Mind 38
Monkeys
  adult male role in raising infants 214
  bonnet macaque 8, 11
  java 8, 14
  patas 8, 172
  pigtail 11
  rhesus 5, 13, 14, 68
Mother
  as a base of exploration 104, 105
  as a secure base 95
  as object of exploration 96
  effects of absence 92-97
  effects of departure 92-97
  interactions with litter 177, 178
  nipple 203
  pheromonal mediation of behavior 177-
    196
  predictions of infants behavior 96
  presence of 76
  reactions to stranger 76
  response to 91
  response to separation 99
  role of visibility 93
  surrogate 148, 212
Mounting 148, 159, 161, 162, 163, 167
  as a bond-reinforcing phenomenon 152
  as a gesture of threat 152
  as a greeting gesture 164
  as a nonsexual communicative act 151-158
Mouse 10
Mutilation 10

Nest 177, 178
Netword analysis 146-149
New relationships, formation,10, 11
Nonsocial stimuli 88, 89
Nuclear family environment 213
Nursery schools 38, 83
Nursing 163, 170, 177, 178, 191

Observation
  natural 113

Observation (*cont'd*)
  passive 220
  unit 29
Observational studies 109, 113, 114
Offspring, protection of 170
Olfaction 177-196
One-male unit 162
Ontogeny 25
Orangutans 158, 159, 168, 169

Pair bond 172
Partnership 55, 56
  theory of 38
Peers 58, 62, 161, 165
  infant's interest in 61
  play with 204, 205
  relationship 221
  separation from 68
  social interaction with 68-74
Penis 150
Perspectives
  balance of 55
  communication of 56
  integration of 53
  internal 39, 42, 48
  shared 54
  taking 40, 52
Pheromonal bond
  developmental course of 180-182
  function of 194, 195
  time course of 180
Pheromone, *see* Maternal pheromone
Phylogeny 25
Placentophagia 2
Plans 31, 33, 36, 37, 38, 39, 41, 51, 52, 55,
    56
Play 13, 62, 83, 99, 105, 146, 148, 149,
    150, 151, 152, 158, 159, 161, 208,
    214, 217, 220, 221, 222
  cessation of 85
  rough and tumble 205
  with peers 162, 163
Playmates 217
  selection of 165
Playpen 104
Predation 147, 160, 164, 166, 169, 205
Prolactin 185, 191, 193
Protest 85, 86
Proximity 37, 51, 85, 112
  attenuation of 51
  demands for 39

Proximity (*cont'd*)
  physical 39, 55, 56, 57, 58
  seeking 34, 35, 51
  social 31
Psychologist 145
Psychopathology 6

Race 114
Rats 6, 177-196
Reaching 32
Reciprocity 19, 29
Rehabilitation 13
Reinforcement 37, 85, 116, 119, 134, 136,
    137, 139, 146
Rejection 10, 11, 45, 112, 215
Reproduction 169
Responses
  species-specific 111
  verbal 120
Retrieving 163, 177, 178
Reunion 89
Rodent 5
Rooting 199, 203

Savannah 164
Scrotum 150
Security 206
Selection, biological 147
Separation 4, 5, 15, 37, 89, 112
  brief 81-107
  initiated by infant 94
  initiated by mother 94
  protest 84
  responses to 85-88
Sex differences
  in development of social behavior 217
  in play 218
  in response to separation 97-99
Sexual behavior 146, 148, 152, 163
Sheep 5, 7, 10
Sitting 151, 158
Situations
  separation 105
  strange 33-37
Skills, 40, 114
Sleep 7, 159, 160, 161, 163
Smile 62, 70, 71, 88, 89, 102, 111, 113,
    120, 121, 122, 135, 137
Social attachment 1-24, 212, 222
Social network 167

Social preference 202
Socialization 146, 147, 148, 149, 157, 163,
    165, 169, 174, 175, 204
  bidirectional model of 110
  unidirectional model of 110
Society, structure of 147
Socioeconomic status 114
Sociologist 145
Speech 102, 113, 114
Sri Lanka 166
Status, expression 153
Stimuli, unconditioned 111
Strangers
  approach toward 63, 64, 67
  looking at 63, 64
  physical contact with 64, 67
  playing games with 66
  response to 90
Subordination, gesture 152
Sucking 86, 199, 203, 206, 208, 209

Talking 102, 113, 114
Temperament 86
Temperature 169
Territoriality 173
Thought 38, 40, 41, 42, 51
Threat 28, 147, 164, 201, 222
Touching 62, 85, 88, 102
Toys 63, 67, 88, 99, 100, 102, 104,
  giving of 70
Traditions 146, 148
Troop structure 149, 166, 172

Unlearned response systems 199-202

Values 39, 40
Vegetation 166
Videotape 32
Vigilance 102, 103
Viviparity 170
Vocalizations 62, 70, 122, 135
  maternal 114
  of infants 116, 119, 125, 134
  social consequences of 125
Volatility, chemical 185

Watching 214
Weaning 178
Whining 44
Wrestling 149, 151, 152, 201